SPOKESMEN for the SELF

SPOKESMEN for the SELF

Emerson, Thoreau, Whitman

William E. Bridges
Mills College, Oakland, California

CHANDLER PUBLISHING COMPANY
An Intext Publisher · Scranton / London / Toronto

COPYRIGHT © 1971 BY CHANDLER PUBLISHING COMPANY
ALL RIGHTS RESERVED
LIBRARY OF CONGRESS CATALOG CARD NUMBER: 73-140218
INTERNATIONAL STANDARD BOOK NUMBER: 0-8102-0416-9
PRINTED IN THE UNITED STATES OF AMERICA

Material identified in this book by the source symbol *EL* is reprinted by permission of the publishers from Stephen E. Whicher, Robert E. Spiller, and Wallace E. Williams, eds., *The Early Lectures of Ralph Waldo Emerson,* volume II, Cambridge, Mass.: The Belknap Press of Harvard University Press, Copyright, 1964 by the President and Fellows of Harvard College.

Material identified in this book by the source symbol *JMN* is reprinted by permission of the publishers from William Gilman *et al., The Journals and Miscellaneous Notebooks of Ralph Waldo Emerson,* volumes III, IV, V, and VII, Cambridge, Mass.: The Belknap Press of Harvard University Press, Copyright, III–1963, IV–1964, V–1965, VII–1969, by the President and Fellows of Harvard College.

Book designed by R. Keith Richardson

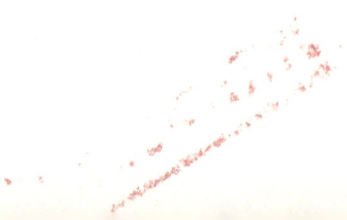

CONTENTS

Sources	vii
Acknowledgments	viii
Introduction: Alienation and Authenticity	1
1. Ralph Waldo Emerson (1803–1882)	25

Society and the Age	25
Self-Recovery and Personal Values	31
Nature as Context and Model	41
The Eternal Moment: Art and Religion	48
Two Addresses	
"Being and Seeming"	59
"Works and Days"	70

2. Henry David Thoreau (1817–1862)	82

Living Authentically	
Emerson on Thoreau	82
Society and Alienation	88
The Business at Hand: Living	103
Nature as Setting and Symbol	118
Two Selections	
"Life at Walden Pond"	125
"A Plea for Captain John Brown"	133

3. Walt Whitman (1819–1892)	151

The Extravagance of the Unsayable	
Thoreau on Whitman	151
Literature as Personal Encounter	154
Standing at the Center, Everything in Its Place	160
The Style of Being	168
The Poem as Utterance	
Several Short Poems	173
"There Was a Child Went Forth"	175
"Song for Occupations"	176
"The Sleepers"	184

"Scented Herbage of My Breast"	192
"Of the Terrible Doubt of Appearances"	193
"The Base of All Metaphysics"	194
"The Wound-Dresser"	194
"When Lilacs Last in the Dooryard Bloom'd"	197
"I Saw in Louisiana a Live-Oak Growing"	203
"When I Heard the Learn'd Astronomer"	204
"Chanting the Square Deific"	204
"So Long"	206
Afterword: Knowing and Knowing About	209

SOURCES

The sources of excerpted passages from the writings of each of our three spokesmen for the self are identified by a coding system, as follows:

EMERSON

W   *The Complete Works of Ralph Waldo Emerson* (Centenary Edition), ed. E. W. Emerson (Boston: Houghton Mifflin Company, 1903–1904)

JMN   *The Journals and Miscellaneous Notebooks of Ralph Waldo Emerson*, ed. William Gilman *et al.* (Cambridge, Mass.: Harvard University Press, 1961–1969)
       Vol. III, 1826–1832, ed. William Gilman and Alfred Ferguson (1963)
       Vol. IV, 1832–1834, ed. Alfred Ferguson (1964)
       Vol. V, 1835–1838, ed. Merton M. Sealts, Jr. (1965)
       Vol. VII, 1838–1842, ed. A. W. Plumstead and Harrison Hayford (1969)

Jour   *The Journals of Ralph Waldo Emerson*, ed. E. W. Emerson and W. E. Forbes (Boston: Houghton Mifflin Company, 1909–1914)

EL   *The Early Lectures of Ralph Waldo Emerson*, Vol. II, 1836–1838, ed. Stephen E. Whicher, Robert E. Spiller, and Wallace E. Williams (Cambridge, Mass.: Harvard University Press, 1964)

Let   *The Letters of Ralph Waldo Emerson*, Vols. I–VI, ed. Ralph L. Rusk (New York: Columbia University Press, 1939)

THOREAU

W   *The Writings of Henry David Thoreau*, 20 vols. (Boston: Houghton Mifflin Company, 1906)
       Vol. II, *Walden*
       Vol. IV, *Cape Cod and Miscellanies* (for "Civil Disobedience" and "A Plea for Captain John Brown")
       Vol. V, *Excursions and Poems* (for "Walking")
       Vols. VII–XX, *Journals*, ed. Bradford Torrey

Corr   *The Correspondence of Henry David Thoreau*, ed. Walter Harding and Carl Bode (New York University Press, 1958)

WHITMAN

Almost all the passages from Whitman's writing can be found in whatever full-scale anthology is most readily at hand. In some cases, however, there will be slight textual variations, since passages from those poems that originally made up the first edition of *Leaves of Grass* (cited "*1855*") have been quoted as they appeared in that edition. Two reprints of that edition are available and useful, one published by Chandler Publishing Company (Scranton) and the other by the Viking Press (New York); both are paperbacks. Poems and passages that were either removed from the final edition of *Leaves* or were never included may be found in Emory Holloway's "Inclusive Edition" of *Leaves* (Garden City, N.Y.: Doubleday, 1926) or in Harold W. Blodgett and Sculley Bradley's "Comprehensive Reader's Edition" (New York University Press, 1965), the latter of which has recently appeared in paperback (New York: W. W. Norton and Company, 1968). Because titles and, where pertinent, section numbers will locate a poem or a passage quickly in whatever edition the reader is using, no attempt has been made to refer the reader to particular pages in particular editions.

ACKNOWLEDGMENTS

To many, many students in my classes, who have shared my excitement and sharpened my insight into these writers.

And to those whose understanding and encouragement undergirded my own self-trust—to Hyatt, Larry, Louis, and Mondi.

SPOKESMEN for the SELF

INTRODUCTION

Alienation and Authenticity

Taken by any standard, Emerson, Thoreau, and Whitman are writers of the first rank. They are, moreover, without parallel in our literature—three major writers, whose work embodies a common vision. No small part of Emerson's importance is the way he served to stimulate and channel the thought and feeling that Thoreau shaped into prose and Whitman into poetry. And yet the result in each case is unique: Thoreau could no more have written "Song of Myself" than Whitman could have written *Walden*. And Emerson could not have written either.

For all that their importance is unquestioned, to come to terms with these three writers has always been difficult. The difficulty is seldom the kind of obscurity that we know so well from our own contemporary writers; by *contemporary* standards Emerson, Thoreau, and Whitman are so simple that we cannot help wondering whether they really saw life whole—or whether life today may not be so much more complex than it was then that their message is outdated. The problem is the simplicity itself. Sentence follows sentence, and the pieces seem to make sense; but the whole—what are they really saying?

That was the question put to Thoreau by his friend Daniel Ricketson. Thoreau summarized the question and his reply in a letter written the year after *Walden* was published:

> He says that he sympathizes with much in my books, but much in them is naught to him,—"namby-pamby,"—"stuff,"—"mystical." Why will not I, having common sense, write in plain English always; *teach* men in detail how to live a simpler life, etc., not go off into ——? But I say that I have no scheme about it,—no designs on men at all; and, if I had, my mode would be to tempt them with the fruit, and not with the manure. To what end do I lead a simple life at all, pray? That I may teach others to simplify their lives?—and so all our lives be *simplified* merely, like an algebraic formula? Or not, rather, that I may make use of the ground I have cleared, to live more worthily and profitably? I would fain lay the most stress forever on that which is the most important,—imports the most to me,—though it were only (what it is likely to be) a vibration in the air. As a preacher, I should be prompted to tell men, not so much how to get their wheat-bread cheaper, as of the bread of life compared with which *that* is bran. Let a man only taste these loaves, and he becomes a skillful economist at once. He'll not waste much time in earning

those. Don't spend your time in drilling soldiers, who may turn out hirelings after all, but give to the undrilled peasantry a *country* to fight for.¹

Beneath the shifting surface of this argument there is a good deal worth noting. At every key point the statement hangs supported on a metaphor: the fruit of the scheme, not the manure; clearing the ground for living; the bread of life, next to which bread itself is bran; man's need for a cause rather than military drill. Behind this style is a poet, a man who uses language as an instrument of liberation, a way of revealing another and a more profound level on which living may take place. Thoreau resists calling this function either *teaching* or *preaching*, though the way in which he makes the denial suggests that the poet's calling is not unlike these others. And finally he focuses his whole thrust on the metaphorical contrast between the well-trained soldier who fights for what is not his and the ordinary person who fights for what is his.

This final metaphor is a good place to begin with Thoreau and Emerson and Whitman, for each of the writers came to believe that most of what passed in their day for mental and moral improvement was simply drilling. What each writer proposed was not to equip the reader with anything extrinsic and new but rather to bring the person back into the center of his own existential world and to help him to recover his ability to respond to it. Whitman's promise in "Song of Myself" says it well:

Stop this day and night with me and you shall possess the origin of all poems,
You shall possess the good of the earth and sun . . . . there are millions of suns left,
You shall no longer take things at second or third hand . . . . nor look through the eyes of the dead . . . . nor feed on the spectres in books,
You shall not look through my eyes either, nor take things from me,
You shall listen to all sides and filter them from yourself.²

It is just at this point that what we imagine these writers to have been saying gets in our way and prevents our really listening to them: "Ah, yes," we say, finishing the passage from Whitman, "he is saying that everyone must see for himself—self-reliance, individualism, democracy, and all that."

¹ Letter to H. G. O. Blake (September 26, 1855) in *The Correspondence of Henry David Thoreau*, ed. Walter Harding and Carl Bode (New York, 1958), p. 384.

² This passage appears in what subsequently became Section 2 of the poem, although in the first edition of *Leaves of Grass* there are no numbered sections. For a facsimile of that edition (and a useful essay on *Leaves* by Richard Bridgman) see the edition issued in 1968 by Chandler Publishing Company. Since most of Whitman's work that I shall be referring to can be located readily by title (and, if the poem is long, the section number) in any of the many editions of *Leaves*, only those passages that would be difficult to find are located by page numbers. Those poems that appeared in the original edition of *Leaves of Grass* are quoted from that source, although the reader is warned that Whitman kept revising many of his poems for subsequent editions, so it is possible to find textual variations between successive versions of the same passage or poem.

Let us straighten out this confusion at the outset, for it is at the heart of misunderstanding that so often renders these writers "interesting" but ultimately not very relevant today. What Whitman is saying has less to do with democracy or individualism than it has to do with psychology. And the concept of Self-Reliance is not so much a program of depending on yourself as it is a program of depending on your Self—for what the whole Emersonian plan ultimately is, is a way of identifying and dealing with that psychological state that we know today as self-estrangement or alienation.

For the full data supporting these generalizations, the reader will have to turn to the selections themselves, but the following excerpt will show that the modern psychologist's terms are congenial to Emerson's way of thinking. "I see plainly the charm which belongs to Alienation or Otherism," he wrote in his *Journal*. " 'What wine do you like best, O Diogenes?' 'Another's,' replied the sage. What fact, thought, word, like we best? Another's. The very sentiment I expressed yesterday without heed, shall sound memorable to me tomorrow if I hear it from another."[3] This, to Emerson, was the central existential problem: man's inability to experience himself in all the fullness of his being. The way in which most people reacted to this threatening expanse of possibility was to deny in themselves some (or in many cases, almost all) of their positive qualities and to project them onto others, where they could be admired and cherished as they could not be before. "The youth, intoxicated with his admiration of a hero, fails to see that it is only a projection of his own soul which he admires."[4]

What Emerson is trying to do is not to deny that there *are* heroic men but only to remind the reader how much of what he "sees" is really not "out there" at all. A basic article of Emerson's faith was that the truly important elements in experience were both objective parts of the environment and real entities in the inner world of response. Until the person can experience his own response to the outer world, he cannot *know* that world—he can only know *about* it. "We are always coming up with the emphatic facts of history in our private experience and verifying them here," Emerson wrote, adding in words that are often misunderstood: "All history becomes subjective; in other words there is properly no history, only biography. Every mind must know the whole lesson for itself—must go over the whole ground. What it does not see, what it does not live, it will not know."[5] To read this as a claim that history is made by

---

[3] *The Journals and Miscellaneous Notebooks of Ralph Waldo Emerson*, Vol. V, ed. Merton M. Sealts, Jr. (Cambridge, 1965), p. 254. (Hereafter referred to as *JMN*.)

[4] *The Complete Works of Ralph Waldo Emerson* (Centenary Edition), ed. E. W. Emerson (Boston, 1903–1904), I, 162. (In footnotes hereafter referred to as Emerson, *Works*.)

[5] Emerson, *Works*, II, 9–10.

men and that it is therefore ultimately little more than the biography of the actors—this is to miss the point.⁶ Emerson's intention could just as easily be embodied in the statement that ultimately there is really no biology or economics or theology—only biography. Only when the inner discovery is made does the outer phenomenon (the "other") become realized.

The attempt to short-circuit this process by knowing about things as externals in a neutral field not only distorts those things but also shrinks the person by invalidating all but his cognitive faculties. When that is done, the person becomes little more than a dependency on the field of his own knowledge. In his famous Divinity School Address, that so offended the religious establishment of his day, Emerson said, "That is always best which gives me to myself. The sublime is excited in me by the great stoical doctrine, Obey thyself. That which shows God in me, fortifies me. That which shows God out of me, makes me a wart and a wen."⁷

To most of his hearers, a statement like that one meant just one thing: pantheism, the heretical doctrine that God is not a supernatural being but rather a universal indwelling spirit. But Emerson's pantheism is metaphorical and not literal, for it is simply his way of driving home to the person that even God must be responded to by the individual if He is to be made real, for the ultimate reality to Emerson is experiential. It is also his way of reminding the reader how diminished the person becomes when he cannot discover and validate within himself those powers that correspond to the powers at work around him. In "Self-Reliance" he writes that the average person finds "no worth in himself which corresponds to the force which built a tower or sculptured a marble god" and so such a person feels "poor when he looks on these. To him a palace, a statue, or a costly book have an alien and forbidding air, much like a gay equipage, and seem to say like that, 'Who are you, Sir?' "⁸

The psychic state that Emerson is here condemning is rather like the Old Testament concept of idolatry. As Erich Fromm has pointed out,

> The prophets of monotheism did not denounce heathen religions as idolatrous primarily because they worshipped several gods instead of one. The essential difference between monotheism and polytheism is not one of the *number* of gods, but lies in the fact of self-alienation. Man spends his energy, his artistic capacities on building an idol, and then he worships this idol, which

---

⁶ This assumption was obviously made by the editors of Bartlett's *Familiar Quotations,* who cross-reference Emerson's statement (or rather, "There is properly no history, only biography") and Carlyle's statement that "The history of the world is but the biography of great men." For further confirmation of Emerson's intent, see *The Journals of Ralph Waldo Emerson,* ed. E. W. Emerson and W. E. Forbes (Boston, 1909–1914), V, 208. (That source will hereafter be referred to as Emerson, *Journals.*)

⁷ Emerson, *Works,* I, 131–132.

⁸ Emerson, *Works,* II, 62.

is nothing but the result of his own human effort. His life forces have flown into a "thing," and this thing, having become an idol, is not experienced as a result of his own productive effort, but as something apart from himself, over and against him, which he worships and to which he submits. . . . [Such a] man does not experience himself as the active bearer of his own powers and richness, but as an impoverished "thing," dependent on powers outside of himself, unto whom he has projected his living substance.⁹

Emerson's own description of the situation was very similar. In the introductory lecture to his Boston series on Human Culture, he said,

Men do not imagine that they are anything more than fringes and tassels to the institutions into which they are born. They take the law from things; they serve their property; their trade or profession; books; other men; some religious dogma; some political party or school of opinion that has been palmed upon them; and bow the neck and the knee and the soul to their own creation. . . . ¹⁰

The extent to which Emerson's thought can be illuminated by being considered as a psychological analysis is suggested by the notable parallels between his statement and Fromm's, and anyone who goes further into Fromm's writing with Emerson in mind will find many other parallels. Emerson's early lecture, "The Present Age," for example, foreshadows many of Fromm's ideas on the impact of modern life upon the individual.¹¹

Emerson's prescription for man's idolatry or alienation was a continual effort at repossession of himself. In *Nature* he calls for "a continual self-recovery" and in "Experience" he speaks of the "vigorous self-recoveries" that are necessary to "possess our axis more fully."¹² In "Circles" he wrote that "the power of self-recovery" puts man in a position where he "cannot have his flank turned, cannot be out-generaled, but put him where you will, he stands."¹³ Although it is difficult not to speak of it in such terms, self-recovery is not the recovery of a thing—a self. It is, rather, the reopening of the lines of inner communication so that the person can once again respond authentically and openly to life around him.

Emerson wrote of the individual's difficulties in knowing and saying what he really felt and called them signs of a tragic loss of human power; in so doing, he foreshadowed in many ways the modern-day Gestalt therapists who have shown so clearly modern man's inability to respond to experience as a natural and total organism. To Emerson, it was only the *poets* (who were only true and complete persons, not specially tal-

⁹ *The Sane Society* (Greenwich, Conn., 1965), pp. 112–114.
¹⁰ *The Early Lectures of Ralph Waldo Emerson,* Vol. II, ed. Stephen E. Whicher, Robert E. Spiller, and Wallace E. Williams (Cambridge, 1964), p. 218.
¹¹ *Ibid.,* 157–172.
¹² Emerson, *Works,* I, 66, and II, 81.
¹³ Emerson, *Works,* II, 309.

ented writers) who retained what should be the universal power of responsiveness. "Too feeble fall the impressions of nature on us to make us artists," he wrote in "The Poet."

> Every touch should thrill. Every man should be so much an artist that he could report in conversation what had befallen him. Yet, in our experience, the rays or appulses have sufficient force to arrive at the senses, but not enough to reach the quick and compel the reproduction of them in speech.[14]

This state of heightened awareness that the poet enjoyed and that all men could recover was one of complete presence, a state in which the whole person is present and responsive; it is a state in which the intellectualizing capacity to conceptualize and pattern experience is submerged in the larger response of the total organism. In prescribing such a state to himself, he wrote in his *Journal*,

> Keep your eye & ear open to all impressions, but deepen no impression by effort, but take the opinion of the Genius within, what ought to be retained by you & what rejected by you. Keep, that is, the upright position. Resign yourself to your thoughts, & then every object will make that mark, that modification on your character which it ought.[15]

This state is one of "present-ness" in another sense as well, for not only is the *whole person* there; the whole person is *there*, too, in that none of him is oriented toward a past full of causes or an effect-laden future. To Emerson, the tendency to view the present as the intersection of time-past and time-future robbed it of its whole meaning by making memory and anticipation the only real states of mind. Man ought, he urged, to consider the present as a state of awareness and of being, and to regard past and future as mental constructs—logical patterns created to enhance man's ability to calculate and control. Emerson readily admitted that man could not live without the power of calculation that he called the Understanding, but he argued that this power tended to feed on itself and to destroy the person's ability to respond fully to the here-and-now. Speaking of the resulting habit of displacing the highest potentialities of the present into past and future, he wrote, "We say Paradise was; Adam fell; the Golden Age; & the like. We mean man is not as he ought to be; but our way of painting this is on Time, and we say *Was*."[16]

A person could escape from this world of sequence, where the present was lost between tomorrow's purposes and yesterday's regrets, by going out into the woods and fields. Describing nature as a setting conducive to a state of presence in which the person could flourish in all his fullness, Emerson wrote that there the person's attention is "absorbed by new pictures and by thoughts fast succeeding each other, until by degrees the

---

[14] Emerson, *Works*, III, 6.
[15] *JMN*, V, pp. 6–7.
[16] *Ibid.*, p. 371.

recollection of home was crowded out of the mind, all memory obliterated by the tyranny of the present."[17] The process that he was describing was obviously what we should call therapeutic, for in his journals he describes the woods as the place where "the mind integrates itself again. The attention, which had been distracted into parts, is reunited, reinsphered. The whole of nature addresses itself to the whole man. We are reassured. It is more than a medicine. It is health."[18]

"Our health," Emerson wrote on another occasion, "is our sound relation to external objects."[19] The concept of *relation* seemed so important to him, in fact, that he announced "that a man is a bundle of relations, that his entire strength consists not in his properties but in his innumerable relations."[20] The relations between most people and their environments were those produced by the projection and alienation discussed above, and those relations had to be destroyed before anything constructive could take their place. This necessity of undermining the relation between the individual and his environment led Emerson to make some apparently paradoxical attacks on the merely personal or individual relation to things: witness his advice in *Nature* to be "resolute to detach every object from personal relations" and his description of the artist's power (in "The Poet") as that of bringing us out of "that jail-yard of individual relations in which [we are] enclosed."[21] It is admittedly a bit confusing to find the prophet of Individualism writing in his *Journal* that "that which is individual and remains individual in my experience is of no value,"[22] but the confusion is simply verbal. He is using *individual* here to refer to those relations that exist between a self-estranged individual and his environment. Those relations were not those of a whole man but only of a "biographical Ego" to a particular time and place, and a trust in *that* ego was the very opposite of what Emerson was prescribing.[23]

Emerson once wrote that "Subjective . . . is made to cover two things, a good and a bad,"[24] but he never acknowledged that the same ambiguity burdened *individual, personal,* and all the words derived from *self*. Each could mean either the old destructive relations between the person and his experience or the new liberating ones. When he uses the terms negatively he is exhorting his hearers to abandon "their" worlds, which are really only projected patterns of "identities" that are not out there at all, but in the hearers themselves. When he uses the terms positively, he is calling on his hearers to confront a world that is "theirs"

---

[17] "Nature," *Works*, III, 170.
[18] *JMN*, V, 19.
[19] *Journal*, V, 63.
[20] *JMN*, V, 266.
[21] Emerson, *Works*, I, 74, and III, 28.
[22] *Journal*, V, 36.
[23] *Journal*, VIII, 79.
[24] *Journal*, V, 347.

in a much more radical sense than they have suspected—a world which can be actualized only when the person himself is totally present in a state of full awareness. And this presence can be achieved only by the repossession of those alienated portions of oneself that most people never dream are theirs.

Emerson reduced this complex problem to a single image in his most famous address, "The American Scholar." Referring to the ancient fable that the gods originally turned Man into men to divide up more conveniently the labors necessary to sustain life, Emerson said,

> The old fable covers a doctrine ever new and sublime; that there is One Man,—present to all particular men only partially, or through one faculty; and that you must take the whole society to find the whole man. Man is not a farmer, or a professor, or an engineer, but he is all. . . . In the *divided* or social state these functions are parcelled out to individuals, each of whom aims to do his stint of the joint work, whilst each other performs his. The fable implies that the individual, to possess himself, must sometimes return from his own labor to embrace all the other laborers. But, unfortunately, this original unit, this fountain of power, has been so distributed to multitudes, has been so minutely subdivided and peddled out, that it is spilled into drops, and cannot be gathered. The state of society is one in which the members have suffered amputation from the trunk, and strut about so many walking monsters,—a good finger, a neck, a stomach, an elbow, but never a man.[25]

The audience that Emerson was addressing was the Commencement Day audience at Harvard College, and the class that was graduating included a young man from Concord named Henry Thoreau. Emerson knew him, though not so well at this time as he would later, and it may be that Thoreau himself did not even go to hear Emerson speak on the day in question. But whether he heard the speech or not, the passage quoted above provides a useful bridge between Emerson and Thoreau, for in many ways Thoreau's career was an investigation of the possibilities of regaining the status of Man as Emerson sketched them in "The American Scholar."

Thoreau lived and thought through those aspects of self-recovery that Emerson himself was least clear on, for there is no denying that Emerson offered precious little guidance when it came to realizing his program in the day-to-day world. His own life was buoyed up by the presence of a modest income from stock that he inherited from his first wife, and he supplemented this with money earned as a writer and lecturer. Surely these were conditions that not all men could enjoy, for even discounting the unearned income, it was still obvious that not everyone could make his living through literature. Moreover, there was something ironical—perhaps even self-contradictory—about such a radical prophet as Emerson making a living out of a prophecy that seldom concerned itself with such mundane matters as making a living.

[25] Emerson, *Works*, I, 82–83.

Emerson himself had acknowledged that the person "was no whole man until he knew how to earn a blameless livelihood. Society is barbarous until every industrious man can get his living without dishonest customs."[26] But Emerson's own example offered his audience little guidance in how this might be done. Thoreau's example did, though his life must be seen as a whole rather than as a prelude and sequel to *Walden* for the nature of the example to be clear.

Emerson viewed Thoreau's life with some ambivalence, for if he was the younger writer's earliest and most faithful advocate, he remained disappointed that Thoreau was content to do so little in the public world. "Had his genius been only contemplative, he had been fitted to his life," wrote Emerson in his eulogy of Thoreau, "but with his energy and practical ability he seemed born for great enterprise and for command." Putting down this failure to a lack of ambition, Emerson wrote that "wanting this, instead of engineering for all America, he was the captain of a huckleberry party. Pounding beans is good to the end of pounding empires one of these days; but if, at the end of years, it is still only beans!"[27]

One can sympathize with Emerson to a certain extent, for there is a sense of unrealized potential surrounding the career of Thoreau, a career cut short by his death at the age of forty-four. During his twenty-odd years of adulthood, he supported himself with odd jobs, preferring to trim his expenditures rather than to expand his income. His only full-time work came in the four years after his graduation from Harvard, when he ran a private school in Concord with his brother, John. From time to time, and particularly toward the end of his life, he did a good deal of surveying. He also earned occasional small fees as a lecturer and writer. To those who found such minimal labor little more than vagrancy, Thoreau had a characteristically straight-faced reply:

> For many years I was self-appointed inspector of snow-storms and rain-storms, and did my duty faithfully; surveyor, if not of highways, then of forest paths and all across-lot routes, keeping them open, and ravines bridged and passable at all seasons, where the public heel had testified to their utility.
> I have looked after the wild stock of the town, which give a faithful herdsman a good deal of trouble by leaping fences; and I have had an eye to the unfrequented nooks and corners of the farm. . . . I have watered the red huckleberry, the sand cherry and the nettle tree, the red pine and the black ash, the white grape and the yellow violet, which might have withered else in dry seasons.[28]

And, as Emerson noted despairingly, he pounded beans.

Emerson had complained that bean-culture was a valid enough means

---

[26] *Journal,* IV, 299.
[27] Emerson, *Works,* X, 480.
[28] *Walden,* vol. II of *The Writings of Henry David Thoreau* (Boston, 1906), pp. 19–20.

to some higher end, but that it was no sort of an end itself. Emerson's own life had fairly complex machinery of means—stocks and bonds, lecture series and speaking tours here and abroad, family and community responsibilities, and the like. The freedom that he enjoyed and cultivated was in fact built on a foundation of security, and the foundation cost him no small amount of labor to achieve and maintain.

Thoreau thought otherwise. Looking about him at the means available to secure comfort and security, he decided that the end became lost in the workings of the apparatus designed to secure it. This was true even of the farmer's supposedly simple life:

> The farmer is endeavoring to solve the problem of a livelihood by a formula more complicated than the problem itself. To get his shoestrings, he speculates in herds of cattle. With consummate skill he has set his trap with a hair spring to catch comfort and independence, and then, as he turned away, got his own leg into it.[29]

What startled Thoreau was how much of man's activity was not the means to an end, but simply the means to a further means—a support for a support for a support. To those, for example, who argued that he wasted his time walking on long trips, he argued that they failed to count the time that they spent working to earn the money to go on such trips. It took the day laborer, he figured, about a day to earn the fare for a thirty-mile train trip; a person could walk those thirty miles in a day, however.[30] So while he was carrying on the journey (or, more generally, life itself), his fellows were lost in their preparations; while he was living, they were getting ready to live. If that had been only their temporary situation, little harm would have been done. But as he saw them, getting ready to live was their permanent occupation, and most of them died without having ever enjoyed the fruits of their labors.

The first two chapters of *Walden* and his late essay, "Life Without Principle," contain Thoreau's most sustained analyses of and attacks upon the life-style of an acquisitive and competitive society. Calling the division of labor "a principle which should never be followed but with circumspection," he set out to attack the principle in practice. In words that echo the fable Emerson cited in "The American Scholar," Thoreau wrote,

> It is not the tailor alone who is the ninth part of a man; it is as much the preacher, and the merchant, and the farmer. Where is this division of labor to end? and what object does it finally serve? No doubt another *may* also think for me; but it is not therefore desirable that he should do so to the exclusion of my thinking for myself.[31]

And so he built his own house, an activity that seemed to him to serve directly the end of living. It appealed to him to consider that house-

---

[29] *Ibid.*, p. 36.
[30] *Ibid.*, p. 58–59.
[31] *Ibid.*, p. 51.

building was so basic an activity that the animals themselves engaged in it, and he speculated on the regenerative powers of such life-serving work: "Who knows but if men constructed their dwellings with their own hands, and provided food for themselves and families simply and honestly enough, the poetic faculty would be universally developed, as birds universally sing when they are so engaged?"[32]

Seen thus, those labors that fulfilled the basic needs (food, shelter, clothing, and fuel) were not means to some higher end but were themselves an aspect of living. Those who worked for money to buy food raised by others, cooked with wood cut by others, living in a house built by others, wearing clothes made by others—these people were the true spendthrifts, so uneconomically did their lives operate. Thoreau's own life was devoted to as nearly a full-time involvement in living as he could manage, and that commitment required a degree of independence that others found impossible. "It is desirable that a man . . . live in all respects so compactly and preparedly," he wrote, "that, if an enemy take the town, he can, like the old philosopher, walk out the gate empty-handed without anxiety."[33]

It was on this basis that Thoreau built his own life, a life that disappointed Emerson but that also realized Emerson's concept of self-recovery in memorable form. Emerson had, in a sense, envisioned such a career when he wrote, in "The Uses of Great Men,"

> If a wise man should appear in our village he would create, in those who conversed with him, a new consciousness of wealth, by opening their eyes to unobserved advantages; he would establish a sense of immovable equality, calm us with assurances that we could not be cheated; as every one would discern the checks and guarantees of condition. The rich would see their mistakes and poverty, and the poor their escapes and their resources.[34]

The Walden months of his life (two years, with time out for visits and travels) were but the epitome of his career. At the pond he found a setting for living that facilitated his lifelong endeavor to achieve a full state of presence—to be *all there* in every moment of the day. "I went to the woods," he wrote, "because I wished to live deliberately, to front only the essential facts of life, and see if I could not learn what it had to teach, and not, when I came to die, discover that I had not lived."[35] Following the Emersonian principle that the person must abandon conceptualization and instead see his surroundings as things-in-themselves, Thoreau turned often to the image of "fronting the facts":

> If you stand right fronting and face to face to a fact, you will see the sun glimmer on both its surfaces, as if it were a cimeter, and feel its sweet edge dividing you through the heart and marrow, and so you will happily conclude

[32] *Ibid.*, p. 50.
[33] *Ibid.*, pp. 26–27.
[34] Emerson, *Works*, IV, pp. 18–19.
[35] *Walden*, pp. 100–101.

your mortal career. Be it life or death, we crave only reality. If we are really dying, let us hear the rattle in our throats and feel cold in the extremities; if we are alive, let us go about our business.[36]

And go about his business, Thoreau did. Trudging the countryside and hoeing his beans and summoning his fellow townsmen to the Concord Town Hall to hear him speak in behalf of the condemned John Brown; sending new flora and fauna to the great Harvard scientist Louis Agassiz; talking with his woodchopper friend, Alex Therien; spending a night in jail for refusing to pay his taxes in protest of the Mexican War; making the best pencils in America in his father's shop; and writing, writing, writing, writing. A man of extraordinary talents, Thoreau was as well equipped to recover his own alienated powers and enjoy their fruits as he was committed to doing so.

Almost everyone who knew him respected him. The independence of his life was matched by the independence of his judgment, and every encounter with another person was seized as an occasion for and a test of self-realization. "I almost shrink from the arduousness of meeting men erectly day by day," he admitted in his journal. Then, to remind himself of the crucial issue involved, he added,

Be resolutely and faithfully what you are. . . . Man's noblest gift to man is his sincerity, for it embraces his integrity also. Let him not dole out of himself anxiously, to suit their weaker or stronger stomachs, but make a clean gift of himself, and empty his coffers at once. I would be in society as in the landscape; in the presence of nature there is no reserve, nor effrontery.[37]

One gets the impression from both his own accounts and those of others that this resolute honesty tended to slide over into simple opposition sometimes and that he was never quite satisfied that he had been perfectly honest unless he had offended someone slightly in the process. Emerson noted these tendencies in his eulogy, recalling the comment of one of their mutual friends: "I love Henry . . . but I cannot like him; and as for taking his arm, I should as soon think of taking the arm of an elm-tree."[38]

In civic affairs this independence made him, as he said, a bad subject. Subjection of any sort, even the kind that most men accept as part of citizenship, seemed to Thoreau to be dehumanizing. Upon his return to Concord after graduating from Harvard, he tangled with the town authorities over his refusal to contribute to the local church. A few years later he began to withhold his poll-tax as a way of dramatizing his refusal to be an accomplice to a political policy that condoned slavery and led to a war with Mexico. He spent a night in jail on that occasion and would have stayed there much longer if someone (probably his aunt) had not

[36] *Ibid.*, p. 109.
[37] Journal entry, January 24, 1841, Thoreau, *Writings*, VII, 174.
[38] Emerson, *Works*, X, 456.

paid the tax for him without his consent. As the Civil War approached, he became more and more anguished at the failure of the national government to take a strong, moral stand against slavery. Then Captain John Brown made his own violent protest against slavery in the form of the attack on Harpers Ferry, Virginia, an attack that he hoped would set off a widespread slave insurrection. Thoreau had met Brown briefly, and the sincerity of the man and the decisiveness of his act caught Thoreau's imagination. He became immediately Brown's champion, speaking on his behalf before unfriendly audiences.

Out of the poll-tax controversy came "Civil Disobedience," and out of his response to Harpers Ferry came "A Plea for John Brown." In them he worked out the implications of one aspect of the individual's recovery of his own alienated powers—the recovery of the alienated power of government. "Must the citizen ever for a moment, or in the least degree, resign his conscience to the legislator?" he asked.[39] Answering negatively, Thoreau went on to explore the possibilities open to the person who disagreed with the state and came to the conclusion that only the absolute refusal to participate in the administration of injustice would satisfy the demands of conscience. "Under a government which imprisons any unjustly," he wrote, "the true place for a just man is also a prison." Calling for the person's whole presence in the political arena as surely as in nature, he continued,

> Cast your whole vote, not a strip of paper merely, but your whole influence. A minority is powerless while it conforms to the majority; it is not even a minority then; but it is irresistible when it clogs by its whole weight. If the alternative is to keep all just men in prison, or give up war and slavery, the State will not hesitate which to choose.[40]

The logic of this position and the essay, "Civil Disobedience," have probably been more influential abroad than has *Walden* or Thoreau's system of thought as a whole. Mahatma Gandhi found his own thinking crystalized by the essay, and through him it had an enormous influence on the course of Indian history when the idea of civil disobedience became a central part of the struggle for independence from Great Britain. Wherever the defenders of freedom have needed a sanction for the resistance to tyranny, Thoreau's essay has found devoted readers.

Emerson's goal was an inward freedom: the freedom to respond and know what one thinks and feels, the freedom to evaluate and come to terms with experience on one's own. Acknowledging that the social patterns of his day made this difficult, he yet turned within for the way out of the difficulty. He was convinced, he said, that little "was gained by manipular attempts to realize the world of thought,"[41] for the result was

[39] Thoreau, *Writings*, IV, 358.
[40] *Ibid.*, 370–371.
[41] Emerson, *Works*, III, 85.

not the open relation to experience that he sought but simply a new rule or system or form to impede further movement.

Thoreau shared his mentor's distrust of regulation and systematic reform, but he had a far more radical notion of the life-style conducive to the freedom that they both sought. Socially engaged where Emerson was simply the outspoken critic, and a student of nature in a sense that Emerson never was, Thoreau shaped Emersonian insights and convictions to his own purposes. In a verse printed in *A Week on the Concord and Merrimack Rivers,* he argued, "My life has been the poem I would have writ / I could not both live and utter it."[42] This is more than an apology for unwritten poetry. It is essentially the claim that life is itself creative and created and that the person's own world is of his making, whether it be the product of his passive acquiescence or of his active response. In that he was living out and realizing the principle that Emerson first stated in *Nature,* where he wrote,

> Every spirit builds itself a house, and beyond its house a world, and beyond its world a heaven. Know then that the world exists for you. . . . All that Adam had, all that Caesar could, you have and can do. Adam called his house, heaven and earth; Caesar called his house, Rome; you perhaps call yours, a cobbler's trade; a hundred acres of ploughed land; or a scholar's garret. Yet line for line and point for point your dominion is as great as theirs, though without fine names. Build therefore your own world.[43]

What the Emersonian program offered and what Thoreau staked his whole life on was an idea of human freedom and human power that was quite different from that being promulgated from the pulpits and the platforms of the society around them. The mid-nineteenth-century American was being encouraged from all sides to "build his own world," but that world was commonly conceived in terms of the physical and social environment, a wilderness to be cultivated and a social order to be democratized. But the other side of this coin was a kind of implicit fatalism about the person's inner world: *that* world was very much at the mercy of circumstances, a fact that made it all the more necessary to control and to believe in man's power to control those circumstances.

Emerson and Thoreau believed this confidence about external possibilities and discouragement over man's state of mind to be an inversion of man's real situation in the world. Their position is revealed in the letter that Thoreau wrote his friend Isaiah Williams in 1842. Thoreau's brother John, his closest friend, had just died unexpectedly of lockjaw, and barely two weeks later Emerson's young son, of whom Thoreau had been very fond, had died too. Remarking on man's inability to control such events, Thoreau wrote Williams, " 'Tis true, as you say, 'Man's ends are shaped for him' "; but then he added, "but who ever dared confess the extent of

[42] Thoreau, *Writings,* I, 453.
[43] Emerson, *Works,* I, 76.

his free agency?" This freedom was the inner freedom of response, the freedom of choosing how circumstances will be met and, ultimately, of who, amid the world of circumstances, one will *be*. "If God shapes my ends," he wrote Williams, "he shapes me also." Acknowledging that "my destiny is now arrived," he states,

> I believe that what I call my circumstances will be a very true history of myself. . . . I welcome my fate for it is not trivial nor whimsical. Is there not a soul in circumstances?—and the disposition of the soul to circumstances—is that not the crowning circumstance of all? But after all it is *intra*-stances, or how it stands within me that I am concerned about.[44]

Thoreau's exploration of the world of *intra*-stance disclosed to him one state of mind (or, metaphorically, a part of himself) in which he could rise above external circumstance. He recorded this discovery in *Walden*:

> With thinking we may be beside ourselves in a sane sense. By a conscious effort of the mind we can stand aloof from actions and their consequences; and all things, good and bad, go by us like a torrent. We are not wholly involved in Nature. . . . I only know myself as a human entity; the scene, so to speak, of thoughts and affections; and am sensible of a certain doubleness by which I can stand as remote from myself as from another. However intense my experience, I am conscious of the presence and criticism of a part of me, which, as it were, is not a part of me, but spectator, sharing no experience, but taking note of it; and that is no more I than it is you.[45]

Walt Whitman made a very similar discovery, writing in one of his early notebooks, "I cannot understand the mystery, but I am always conscious of myself as two—as my soul and I: and I reckon it is the same with all men and women."[46] In section 4 of "Song of Myself" he inventoried the surrounding world of circumstance ("People I meet, the effect upon me of my early life . . . The sickness of one of my folks or of myself . . . Battles . . .") and distinguished them from the world of intra-stance by writing,

> They come to me days and nights and go from me again,
> But they are not the Me myself.
>
> Apart from the pulling and hauling stands what I am,
> Stands amused, complacent, compassionating, idle, unitary, . . .

He is, as he says a few lines later, "both in and out of the game."

Whitman's poetry explores the relation between the-Me-myself and experience in a manner comparable to Thoreau's and yet quite different. The two men were almost precise contemporaries, some fifteen years younger than Emerson. But whereas Thoreau had shared the older writer's New England background and had known him well from the age of twenty, Whitman came to Emerson much later, after a career as a New

---

[44] Thoreau, *Correspondence*, pp. 67–68.
[45] *Walden*, pp. 149–150.
[46] Roger Asselineau, *The Evolution of Walt Whitman* (Cambridge, 1960), I, 71.

York newspaperman. Thoreau's natural style was very close to Emerson's, and Edward Emerson traced his father's friendship with Thoreau back to a day when a mutual friend remarked on the similarity between a passage that she had read in one of Henry's journals to a statement made by Emerson in a subsequent lecture. Whitman's early manner, on the other hand, was quite unlike anything Emersonian. He had far less education than had Emerson and Thoreau, and for a dozen years he lived and worked amidst the sensationalism and politics and sentimentality of the era's popular press. Although he also loved the Long Island countryside, he felt as much at home in Broadway's crowds as Thoreau did in the woods and fields around Concord.

There was little surprise when Thoreau produced his books and essays, for everyone who knew him sensed in him an unusual and brilliant mind, an extraordinary articulateness, and a profound dedication to thinking and writing. With Whitman, though, it was different. He had, of course, written a great deal in the course of his newspaper career, including a novel and some poetry. But the nonfiction was relatively ordinary, typical of its time and place; and the creative writing was really very poor, the sentimental and sensationalistic stuff that a thousand of his contemporaries could and did produce by the carload. Such was the case, however, only until around 1850 when a profound change began to take place within Whitman. Just what brought it about and what its stages were are things that cannot now be documented except in a very general way. In his notebooks appear sentences, sometimes alone and sometimes in paragraphs or the long lines of free verse he later developed, that sound unlike anything he had written before. These sentences contain ideas and phrases that he would subsequently incorporate into *Leaves of Grass*, and many of them contain echoes of Emerson.

Just what Emerson's role was in the sudden and rather late growth of this poet is somewhat hidden by the obscurity surrounding the growth itself. Five years after the first edition of *Leaves* was published, Whitman explained to a young admirer that he would not have been able to write his poems if he had not "come to himself" in those crucial months during the early fifties and that it was Emerson's writing that helped him to "find himself."[47] In the open letter to Emerson that he included in the second edition of *Leaves*, he addressed the older writer repeatedly as "Master" and closed the letter with this fervent paragraph:

> Receive, dear Master, these statements and assurances through me, for all the young men, and for an earnest that we know none before you, but the best following you; and that we demand to take your name into our keeping, and that we understand what you have indicated, and find the same indicated in ourselves, and that we will stick to it and enlarge upon it through These States.[48]

[47] Gay Wilson Allen, *The Solitary Singer* (New York, 1955), p. 242.
[48] *Leaves of Grass* (Comprehensive Reader's Edition), ed. by Harold W. Blodgett and Sculley Bradley (New York, 1968), p. 739.

It is hard to imagine a style less similar to Thoreau's, and yet it is clear that they are each inheritors of an Emersonian legacy.

When he told his acquaintance that Emerson helped him to find himself, he was saying simply that the purpose of Emerson's work was realized in him. He might have added that this was what he, in his own different way, meant to do for *his* readers. We have already noticed his promise, made early in "Song of Myself," to put the reader in a position where he can view his experience directly instead of through the lenses of someone else's conceptualizations—where the reader can "listen to all sides and filter them from yourself."

If his goal was like Emerson's, his tactic was very different. Whereas Emerson had sought to describe and prescribe—to portray modern man's debilitating Otherism and to encourage him to recover the estranged power that was meant to be his—Whitman set out to do two things: first, he sought to provide his readers with a model of the self-actualized person; and second, he created a new kind of poetry designed not simply to talk about the process of self-recovery but actually to assist in that process.

It was the first of these goals that Whitman referred to in a letter concerning the 1860 (the third) edition of *Leaves*. He wrote that he was "satisfied with Leaves of Grass, (by far the most of it) as expressing what was intended, namely, to express by sharp-cut self assertion, One's Self and also, or may be still more, to map out, to throw together for American use, a gigantic embryo or skeleton of Personality,—fit for the West, for native models."[49] Writing twenty-five years later, Whitman said that he had sought "from first to last, to put a *Person,* a human being (myself, in the latter half of the Nineteenth Century, in America,) freely, fully and truly on record."[50]

In the latter instance he went on to make a startling claim: "No one will get at my verses who insists upon viewing them as a literary performance, or attempt at such performance. . . ." Literature was aimed at an audience, at creatures called "readers"; it was, that is, a product to be admired or learned from or enjoyed by that portion of the person skilled at reading. He had little faith in the usual transaction between author and reader, commenting in one poem that "in libraries I lie as one dumb, a gawk" and that

> . . . it is not for what I have put into it that I have written this book,
> Nor is it by reading it you will acquire it . . .
> For all is useless without that which you may guess at many times and
>   not hit, that which I hinted at. . . .

[49] Quoted in Roy Harvey Pearce's Introduction to a reprinting of the 1860 edition of *Leaves* (Ithaca, New York, 1961), p. xxvii.
[50] *Leaves* (Comprehensive Reader's Edition), pp. 573–574.

It is not through the reader's absorption of the writer's *meaning* that Whitman's goal will be reached but rather in a kind of interaction that he can only describe metaphorically in physical terms:

> . . . back of a rock in the open air, . . .
> . . . just possibly with you on a high hill, first watching lest any person for miles around approach unawares,
> Or possibly with you sailing at sea, or on the beach of the sea or some quiet island,
> Here to put your lips upon mine I permit you,
> With the comrade's long-dwelling kiss or the new husband's kiss,
> For I am the new husband and I am the comrade.[51]

It is tempting to "read" lines like these in the very way that Whitman is asking us not to—that is, as content being transferred from "writer" to "reader." In that sort of (mis)reading, we would puzzle over the exact nature of the hint mentioned in the first set of lines and worry a good deal about the sexual irregularities suggested in the last set of lines. But Whitman's poetry is characteristically meant not to be understood but to be responded to, and its aim is to *evoke from* the reader rather than to bestow something *on* him. Speaking of related arts, Whitman wrote,

> All architecture is what you do to it when you look upon it,
> (Did you think it was in the white or gray stone? or the lines of the arches and cornices?)
>
> All music is what awakes from you when you are reminded by the instruments,
> It is not the violins and the cornets, it is not the oboe nor the beating drums, nor the score of the baritone singer singing his sweet romanza, nor that of the men's chorus, nor that of the women's chorus,
> It is nearer and farther than they.[52]

In a late preface to his work he summarized some of the characteristics of his poetry, and the first was what he called its "suggestiveness." Explaining what he meant by this term, he wrote,

> I round and finish little, if anything; and could not, consistently with my scheme. The reader will always have his or her part to do, just as much as I have had mine. I seek less to state or display any theme or thought, and more to bring you, reader, into the atmosphere of the theme or thought—there to pursue your own flight.[53]

Whitman's poetry is an attempt to meet head-on a problem that Emerson saw clearly enough but was content simply to describe. People characteristically approach books in a way that only intensifies their difficulty in experiencing themselves as creative beings. As Emerson explained it in "The American Scholar,"

---

[51] "Whoever You Are Holding Me Now in Hand."
[52] "Song for Occupations."
[53] *Leaves* (Comprehensive Reader's Edition), p. 570.

The sacredness which attaches to the act of creation, the act of thought, is transferred to the record. The poet chanting was felt to be a divine man: henceforth the chant is divine also. . . . Instantly the book becomes noxious: the guide is a tyrant.[54]

This was a basic Emersonian appeal—to stop mistaking the vehicle for the cargo. In the Divinity School Address he made essentially the same point in talking about the way in which the life of Jesus had been distorted by the human tendency to convert examples of *being* into rules of conduct:

Alone in all history [Christ] estimated the greatness of man. One man was true to what is in you and me. He saw that God incarnates himself in man, and evermore goes forth anew to take possession of his World. He said, in this jubilee of sublime emotion, "I am divine. Through me, God acts; through me, speaks. Would you see God, see me; or see thee, when thou also thinkest as I now think." . . . The understanding [i.e., the cognitive faculty of alienated man] caught this high chant from the poet's lips, and said, in the next age, "This was Jehovah come down out of heaven. I will kill you, if you say he was a man."[55]

Emerson *said* these things—they have never been said better—but he found no way to avoid the pitfall he had located. (It is all too easy to read Emerson for his content and to emerge from having read him as a slightly better informed but otherwise unchanged person.)

It is also possible to read Whitman without being affected by the experience, but Whitman tried hard to make that outcome difficult. Again and again he used images of physical meeting and embrace to joggle the reader's passivity and to dramatize his appeal for the reader's response:

Come closer to me,
Push close my lovers and take the best I possess,
Yield closer and closer and give me the best you possess.

This is unfinished business with me . . . . how is it with you?
I was chilled with the cold types and cylinder and wet paper between
    us.

I pass so poorly with paper and types . . . . I must pass with the contact
    of bodies and souls.[56]

"I have arrived," he wrote in another poem, "To be wrestled with as I pass for the solid prizes of the universe."[57]

The prize to be won from the experience of the poetry was no less than the repossession of oneself and the relocation of oneself in the center of his own world. The way in which this was to take place was through an interpersonal encounter between Walt Whitman and the reader, an encounter that foreshadows in many ways the manner of client-centered

[54] Emerson, *Works*, I, 88–89.
[55] *Ibid.*, 128–129.
[56] "Song for Occupations."
[57] "Starting from Paumanok."

therapy and one that transforms poetry, thereby, into a therapeutic experience. The characteristics of the client-centered therapist, as described by Carl Rogers, have such close parallels to the way in which Whitman addresses his readers that they deserve to be quoted at some length:

> It has been found that personal change is facilitated when the psychotherapist is what he *is*, when in the relationship with his client he is genuine and without "front" or facade, openly being the feelings and attitudes which at that moment are flowing *in* him. We have coined the term "congruence" to try to describe this condition. . . .
>
> Now the second condition. When the therapist is experiencing a warm, positive, and acceptant attitude toward what *is* in the client, this facilitates change. It involves the therapist's genuine willingness for the client to be whatever feeling is going on in him at that moment,—fear, confusion, pain, pride, anger, hatred, love, courage, or awe. It means that the therapist cares for the client, in a non-possessive way. It means that he prizes the client in a total rather than a conditional way. By this I mean that he does not simply accept the client when he is behaving in certain ways, and disapprove of him when he behaves in other ways. It means an outgoing positive feeling without reservations, without evaluations. . . .
>
> The third condition we may call empathic understanding. When the therapist is sensing the feelings and personal meanings which the client is experiencing in each moment, when he can perceive these from "inside," as they seem to the client, and when he can successfully communicate something of that understanding to his client, then this third condition is fulfilled.[58]

The goal of this complex of attitude and behavior is the validation of the client as the-one-that-he-is. That validation makes it far more possible than it would be otherwise for the client to experience himself (which means far more than simply *knowing* himself) as the-person-that-he-is, and thereby to recover contact with those aspects of himself that have been estranged from him.

Turning from these descriptions to Whitman's poetry, certain passages come to mind at once. As examples of empathic understanding, numerous passages from the longest section (number 33) of "Song of Myself" might be offered, passages that materialize in one form or another the claim made there in the lines, "Agonies are one of my changes of garments, / I do not ask the wounded person how he feels, I myself become the wounded person. . . ." For examples of the unconditional and nonpossessive acceptance of the other person, consider these lines:

> I do not ask who you are . . . . that is not important to me,
> You can do nothing and be nothing but what I will infold you.
>
> Souls of men and women! it is not you I call unseen, unheard, untouchable and untouching,
> It is not you I go argue pro and con about, and to settle whether you are alive or no,
> I own publicly who you are, if nobody else owns . . . .

[58] *On Becoming a Person* (Boston, 1961), pp. 61–62.

> [The poet] judges not as the judge judges but as the sun falling round a helpless thing . . .[59]

And as to congruence, the genuineness that the client senses when the therapist can experience his own feelings fully, Whitman's verses everywhere reveal a self-acceptance that is so complete that some readers are put off by it.

This quality of congruence, however, is more than an element in gaining the other's trust, for in living congruently and expressing his own deeply felt responses, the poet-therapist discovers that he says things that speak for and to others as well. Rogers has spoken of discovering that "what is most personal is most general," adding that his experience has led him to "believe that what is most personal and unique in each one of us is probably the very element which would, if it were shared or expressed, speak most deeply to others."[60] In the opening lines of "Self-Reliance" Emerson defined genius as the conviction "that what is true for you in your private heart is true for all men," and he counseled, "Speak your latent conviction, and it shall be the universal sense."[61] Whitman shared this faith, and in what seems to have been an early version of the opening of "Song of Myself" he wrote,

> I am your voice—It was tied in you—In me it begins to talk.
> I celebrate myself to celebrate every man and woman alive;
> I loosen the tongue that was tied in them,
> It begins to talk out of my mouth.[62]

Congruence, thus, serves not only to facilitate the regenerative encounter between poet and reader but also offers the reader a chance to experience self-acceptance vicariously.

To catalogue the ways in which Whitman offered himself as a model of self-recovery and self-reliance would be little less than to anthologize his poetry; but it may be useful to characterize several aspects of the right relation between person and world as it is portrayed in Whitman's poetry. The manner of *relation* is as central to his poetry as it is to Emerson's prose, and in his original preface to *Leaves* Whitman made that clear: "The land and sea, the animals fishes and birds, the sky of heaven and the orbs, the forests mountains and rivers, are not small themes . . . but folks expect of the poet to indicate more than the beauty and dignity which always attaches to dumb real objects . . . . they expect him to indicate the path between reality and their souls."[63]

As with Emerson, there are two orders of relation between the person

---

[59] "Song of Myself" (Sec. 40), "Song of Occupations," and "By Blue Ontario's Shore."
[60] *On Becoming a Person*, p. 26.
[61] Emerson, *Works*, II, 45.
[62] *Leaves* (Comprehensive Reader's Edition), p. 550.
[63] *Ibid.*, p. 714.

and his experiential world: there is the need-dominated relation of the estranged person to a world full of things to be used and guarded against and fitted in to a preconceived pattern; and there is the relation made possible by the state of Being, a relation with things as ends in themselves, a relation wherein simple perception is an act rich with meaning. The latter relation is one in which the degree to which things are themselves, rather than their value in some system of instrumental value, determines their worth: "To be in any form, what is that? / If nothing lay more developed the quahaug [a type of clam] in its callous shell were enough."[64]

Passage after passage from *Leaves* sets forth the way that the world looks to the person who has overcome the state of Otherism which led man to be, in Emerson's words, "the dwarf of himself." To read Whitman's poetry is to experience another way of seeing, and to respond to the poetry is actually an exercise in self-discovery. But beyond these things it is hard to describe what happens, for the description all too readily turns into one more system to be *read* and *learned,* one more way of knowing about the world and of not experiencing it. Whitman shied away from explanations for this very reason, and justified doing so by contrasting the ineffectuality of words with the force of natural objects. "I swear I begin to see little or nothing in audible words," he wrote in "A Song of the Rolling Earth," and in what appears to be an early version of a section of "Song of Myself" he reflected,

> Doctrine gets empty consent or mocking politeness,
> It wriggles through mankind, it is never loved or believed.
> The throat is not safe that speaks it aloud.
> I will take a sprig of parsley and a budding rose and go through the whole earth.
> You shall see I will not find one heretic against them.
> Can you say as much of all the lore of the priesthood?[65]

"If you would understand me go to the heights or water-shore," he wrote in Section 47 of "Song of Myself"; "The nearest gnat is an explanation and a drop or motion of waves a key, / The maul the oar the handsaw second my words." In "Song of the Open Road" he announced, "I and mine do not convince by arguments, similes, rhymes, / We convince by our presence."

It is precisely that—a *presence* as real as the natural object's—that is Whitman's greatest achievement as a writer. Emerson scarcely ever aimed at such an effect, while Thoreau was satisfied to record moments of presence and reflections on them. Only Whitman sought to transform literature into a surrogate for actual personal presence—a presence in

---

[64] "Song of Myself" (Sec. 27).
[65] *Leaves of Grass* (Inclusive Edition), ed. Emory Holloway (Garden City, New York, 1926), p. 568.

which the reader's task of self-discovery and self-recovery was facilitated.

In this respect Whitman is quite unlike most writers. Where they would develop a relation to the reader for the sake of what they have to say to him, Whitman would say things to him mainly for the sake of the relation he is seeking to establish. Nor is there any doubt that that relation is meant to be therapeutic:

Behold I do not give lectures or a little charity,
What I give I give out of myself.

You there, impotent, loose in the knees, open your scarfed chops till I blow grit within you,
Spread your palms and lift the flaps of your pockets,
I am not to be denied . . . . I compel . . . . I have stores plenty and to spare,
And any thing I have I bestow.

I do not ask who you are . . . . that is not important to me,
You can do nothing and be nothing but what I will infold you.

To a drudge of the cottonfields or emptier of privies I lean . . . . on his right cheek I put the family kiss,
And in my soul I swear I never will deny him.

On women fit for conception I start bigger and nimbler babes,
This day I am jetting the stuff of far more arrogant republics.

To any one dying . . . . thither I speed and twist the knob of the door,
Turn the bedclothes toward the foot of the bed,
Let the physician and the priest go home.

I seize the descending man . . . . I raise him with resistless will.

O despairer, here is my neck,
By God! you shall not go down! Hang your whole weight upon me.

I dilate you with tremendous breath . . . . I buoy you up;
Every room of the house do I fill with an armed force . . . . lovers of me, bafflers of graves:
Sleep! I and they keep guard all night;
Not doubt, not decease shall dare to lay finger upon you,
I have embraced you, and henceforth possess you to myself,
And when you rise in the morning you will find what I tell you is so.[66]

That is Whitman's promise; it is surely an extraordinary one, and one that quite justifies his claim that he did not want to be taken simply as a writer of "literature."

In making it (as in describing all his most dramatic actions and memorable stances) he is running a serious risk; that is that the reader will become so entranced with the spectacle of Walt Whitman that he will forget that Whitman is being himself only as an encouragement for the reader to be *himself*. Thoreau, too, ran this danger, and it is impossible to guess how many of his readers have imagined that they were

[66] "Song of Myself" (Sec. 40) = 1855, pp. 44–45.

meant to find Waldens of their own after reading him. That is, of course, the irony of memorable individuality—that it so easily becomes a model to be imitated rather than an example to be followed in one's own terms. Whitman himself went as far as one reasonably could in guarding against this misreading, reminding the reader not only that he must find his own answers but also assuring him, "He that by me spreads a wider breast than my own proves the width of my own, / He most honors my style who learns under it to destroy the teacher."[67]

This concern that each of us find his own style and his own way in responding to the writing could be paralleled in the work of Emerson and Thoreau too. Emerson set the tone for all three by calling imitation suicidal and by calling on men to embark on a venture in Being—on an experiment in making the selves that they were by nature the goal of their endeavors. Thoreau took this goal to heart and constructed for himself a way of life to make Being a daily reality. Whitman moved beyond personal Being into a poetry of relation in which he could bring others back into the center of their own experiential worlds. Each writer sought in his own way to bring the reader to himself.

---

[67] "Song of Myself" (Sec. 47) = 1855, p. 52.

1. Ralph Waldo Emerson
(1803-1882)

SOCIETY AND THE AGE

Emerson's reputation as an idealist and an individualist obscures the fact that he was also a very acute social critic. Hampered by the lack of any systematic theory of social processes or of personality structure, he nonetheless sketched out a surprisingly accurate picture of the mass society and its impact on the individual. He understood the central paradox of the mass society, so far as the individual is concerned: that modern conditions of work, the concentration of large groups in urban areas, and the atomistic tendencies of democracy combined to liberate the individual in some ways, only to enslave him in others. They liberated him from the old tyrannies of the hereditary guilds, the fixed roles in village life, and the given places in an aristocratic social order. But at the same time that they liberated him from these restraints, the new social forces trapped him with new kinds of routinized work, new kinds of anxiety over whether he could find a significant place in his society, and a new social tyranny—that of public opinion. For most of his contemporaries, he believed, the result of these disruptions was a way of life bereft of joy or significance and a psychic state for which he had no name, but which we should call self-estrangement.

The present day is marked, as we have already had occasion to say, by the immense creation of property and so by the increase of the political importance of individuals everywhere, or the steady progress of the democratical element. The first effect of this is everywhere to unlock the chain of caste, of monopoly, of taxation, and of forced residence, which had pinioned men's arms to their sides, and now to enable each to use what cunning lay in his hand or arm for his own profit. . . .

The immense majority of men live chiefly to their senses, and the sensual life is necessarily an important element in the life of all men. Consequently the conspicuous effect of freedom must be the multiplication and improvement of all fruits and instruments that serve the senses, the swarm of inventions in the useful, ornamental, and luxurious arts; houses, gardens, roads, manufactories, furniture, dress, meats, drinks. . . .

2. The congregation of men into large masses and the universal

facility of communication with metropolitan refinement and opinion has had the effect of grinding off the asperities of individual character, introducing the dominion of fashion, putting all the ambition and wealth of the world under the dominion of the leading class in the capital, and so substituting an universal regard to decorum for the sinews of virtue and intellect. . . .

Decorum is a shadow or imitation of virtue and where virtue is not, this pantomime can very well be performed by very ordinary persons. The increased importance of individuals, the disuse of all badges of distinction, the abolition of orders of nobility, all give every man an opportunity to win respect by his behaviour and force every man to respect the opinion of multitudes where once it was sufficient to consult the good will of a few. In the multitudes of modern society and in the domestic life which has taken the place of the camp or the public table of the ancient communities, opportunity of intimate acquaintance with each citizen is not afforded; so that decorum answers to the eye of the public the purpose of virtue and wisdom, and is a mark infinitely easier to hit. . . .

3. Another trait which contrasts the spirit of our age with those that preceded it is the diffusion instead of the concentration of knowledge, and of course what is gained in surface is lost in depth. Men come forward faster into life. We have precocity for erudition. . . .

But the trait which philosophers agree to designate our age withal is its Reflective character. It is alleged that the habit of the cultivated intellect of the present day is reflection, not instinct. Ours is distinguished from the Greek and Roman and Gothic ages and all the periods of childhood and youth by being the age of the second thought. The golden age is gone and the silver is gone—the blessed eras of unconscious life, of intuition, of genius. . . .

But we surrender ourselves never. We take no leaps in the dark. We have intention in action; intention in manners; intention in discourse; intention even in thought. As Saturn, they say, devoured his children, so we, so soon as we have thought, turn short upon ourselves to inquire how the thought arose. We have a morbid growth of eyes. We see with our feet. The ancients were self-united. We have found out the difference of outer and inner. They described. We reason. They acted. We philosophise. They describe what happened. We what is thought and felt. . . .

In other times a man never came out of pupilage. His mother delivered him to the schoolmaster; the schoolmaster to the public institution. When he was adult, he was the thrall of the state or of a feudal lord or of an omnipresent superstition that was to him no superstition but a sincere and awful faith. Always over the man impended something greater than he, to command his reverence and to call out all his faculties.

But we are of age. We have lost all reverence for the state. It is merely our boardinghouse. We have lost all reverence for the Church; it is also republican. We call a spade, a spade. We have great contempt for the superstitions and nonsense which blinded the eyes of all foregoing generations.

But we pay a great price for this freedom. The old faith is gone; the new loiters on the way. The world looks very bare and cold. We have lost our Hope, we have lost our spring. "A man," said Cromwell, "never rises so high as when he knows not whither he is going." Out of this measuring and decorum and prudence what refreshment can ever issue? And behold the consequence on the timid and melancholy forehead of the population. I have heard that after thirty a man wakes up sad every morning. I have heard that no man sees his face in the glass without a melancholy emotion. . . .   "The Present Age" EL 157–172, passim

Wealth.—Conversation, character, were the avowed ends; wealth was good as it appeased the animal cravings, cured the smoky chimney, silenced the creaking door, brought friends together in a warm and quiet room, and kept the children and the dinner-table in a different apartment. Thought, virtue, beauty, were the ends; but it was known that men of thought and virtue sometimes had the headache, or wet feet, or could lose good time whilst the room was getting warm in winter days. Unluckily, in the exertions necessary to remove these inconveniences, the main attention has been diverted to this object; the old aims have been lost sight of, and to remove friction has come to be the end. That is the ridicule of rich men; and Boston, London, Vienna, and now the governments generally of the world, are cities and governments of the rich; and the masses are not men, but *poor men,* that is, men who would be rich; this is the ridicule of the class, that they arrive with pains and sweat and fury nowhere; when all is done, it is for nothing. They are like one who has interrupted the conversation of a company to make his speech, and now has forgotten what he went to say. . . . Hence the appearance which everywhere strikes the eye of an aimless society, an aimless nation, an aimless world. The earth is sick with that sickness. The man was made for activity, and action to any end has some health and pleasure for him.   *Journal entry* Jour VI, 108–109

There was a simple man grew so suddenly rich that, coming one day into his own stately door & hall in a reverie, he felt on his mind the accustomed burden of fear that now he should see a great person, & was making up his mouth to ask, firmly if ——— was at home, when he bethought himself, Who is ———? who is it I should ask for?, & on second thought, he saw it was his own house, & he was ———.
    Journal entry JMN V, 460

But a man must keep an eye on his servants, if he would not have them rule him. Man is a shrewd inventor and is ever taking the hint of a new machine from his own structure, adapting some secret of his own anatomy in iron, wood and leather to some required function in the work of the world. But it is found that the machine unmans the user. What he gains in making cloth, he loses in general power. There should be temperance in making cloth, as well as in eating. A man should not be a silkworm, nor a nation a tent of caterpillars. The robust rural Saxon degenerates in the mills to the Leicester stockinger, to the imbecile Manchester spinner—far on the way to be spiders and needles. The incessant repetition of the same hand-work dwarfs the man, robs him of his strength, wit and versatility, to make a pin-polisher, a buckle-maker, or any other specialty. . . . *"Wealth," English Traits W V, 166–167*

The railroad makes a man a chattel, transports him by the box and the ton; he waits on it. *Journal entry Jour V, 380*

The common experience is that the man fits himself as well as he can to the customary details of that work or trade he falls into, and tends it as a dog turns a spit. Then is he a part of the machine he moves; the man is lost. *"Spiritual Laws," W II, 142*

I see man is not what man should be. He is the treadle of a wheel. He is a tassle at the apron-string of society. He is a money-chest.
Journal entry Jour IV, 242

A question which well deserves examination now is the Dangers of Commerce. This invasion of Nature by Trade with its Money, its Credit, its Steam, its Railroad, threatens to upset the balance of man, and establish a new, universal Monarchy more tyrannical than Babylon or Rome.
Journal entry Jour V, 285

This whole business of trade gives me to pause and think, as it constitutes false relations between men; inasmuch as I am prone to count myself relieved of any responsibility to behave well and nobly to that person whom I pay with money; whereas if I had not that commodity, I should be put on my good behavior in all companies, and man would be a benefactor to man as being himself his only certificate that he had a right to those aids and services which he asked of the other.
"New England Reformers" W III, 256

Nothing is more melancholy than to treat men as pawns & ninepins. If I leave out their heart, they take out mine. *Journal entry JMN V, 199*

> What boots thy zeal,
> O glowing friend,
> That would indignant rend
> The northland from the south?
> Wherefore? to what good end?
> Boston Bay and Bunker Hill
> Would serve things still;
> Things are of the snake.

The horseman serves the horse,
The neatherd serves the neat,
The merchant serves the purse,
The eater serves his meat;
'Tis the day of the chattel,
Web to weave, and corn to grind;
Things are in the saddle,
And ride mankind.

There are two laws discrete,
Not reconciled,
Law for man, and law for thing;
The last builds town and fleet,
But it runs wild,
And doth the man unking.

'Tis fit the forest fall,
The steep be graded,
The mountain tunnelled,
The sand shaded,
The orchard planted,
The glebe tilled,
The prairie granted,
The steamer built.

Let man serve law for man;
Live for friendship, live for love,
For truth's and harmony's behoof;
The state may follow how it can,
As Olympus follows Jove.
  "*Ode*" (*Inscribed to W. H. Channing*) W IX, 77–78

S. gave a sad definition of his friend in saying he resembled a nest of Indian boxes, one after the other, each a new puzzle & when you came to the last there's nothing in it. So with each man, a splendid barricade of circumstances, the renown of his name, the glitter of his coach, then his great professional character, then comes another fine shell of manners & speech but go behind all these & the Man[—]the self—is a poor, shrunken, distorted, imperceptible thing.   *Journal entry* JMN *IV, 51*

Men go through the world each musing on a great fable, dramatically pictured and rehearsed before him. If you speak to the man, he turns his eyes from his own scene, and slower or faster endeavors to comprehend what you say. When you have done speaking, he returns to his private music. Men generally attempt early in life to make their brothers first, afterwards their wives, acquainted with what is going forward in their private theatre, but they soon desist from the attempt, or finding that they also have some farce, or perhaps some ear and heart-rending tragedy forward on their secret boards, on which they are intent, all parties acquiesce at last in a private box with the whole play performed before himself *solus*.   *Journal entry* Jour VII, 75

Is it not pathetic that the action of men on men is so partial? We never touch but at points. The most that I can have or be to my fellow man, is it the reading of his book, or the hearing of his project in conversation? I approach some Carlyle with desire & joy. I am led on from month to month with an expectation of some total embrace & oneness with a noble mind, & learn at last that it is only so feeble & remote & hiant action as reading a Mirabeau or a Diderot paper, & a few the like. This is all that can be looked for. More we shall not be to each other. Baulked soul! It is not that the sea & poverty & pursuit separate us. Here is Alcott by my door,—yet is the union more profound? No, the Sea, vocation, poverty, are seeming fences, but Man is insular, and cannot be touched. Every man is an infinitely repellent orb, & holds his individual being on that condition.   *Journal entry* JMN V, 328

A new disease has fallen on the life of man. Every Age, like every human body, has its own distemper. Other times have had war, or famine, or a barbarism, domestic or bordering, as their antagonism. Our forefathers walked in the world and went to their graves tormented with the fear of Sin and the terror of the day of Judgment. These terrors have lost their force, and our torment is Unbelief, the Uncertainty as to what we ought to do; the distrust of the value of what we do, and the distrust that the Necessity (which we all at last believe in) is fair and beneficent. . . . The genius of the day does not incline to a deed, but to a beholding. It is not that men do not wish to act; they pine to be employed, but are paralyzed by the uncertainty what they should do. . . .

"Lecture on the Times" W I, 281–283

SELF-RECOVERY AND PERSONAL VALUES

Ralph Waldo Emerson wrote and spoke on an amazingly wide range of topics—literature, religion, politics, philosophy, and education, to name only the broadest categories. But beneath the surface, his subject was always the same, for whatever the topical framework of his discourse, his concern was for the person and the quality of the person's life. Whether in the personal accents of his private journals or the generalizations of his essays, he drew on his own experience and his observations of others for evidence that beneath the distortions of acquired behavior and sentiment, the person is essentially trustworthy at the deepest levels of his being; that there is within the person's own experience a pattern that will give his life more meaning than anything external that he could "believe in"; and that much that the person fears or envies or admires in the world around him is really some unacknowledged part of himself that he projects onto that world. The person, in short, makes his own world— and does so whether he means to or not. What he sees about him corresponds to what is going on within him. And so, the process of discovering meaning and value in existence must begin with the inner discovery of a unique wholeness that is the self.

The ruin or the blank that we see when we look at nature, is in our own eye. The axis of vision is not coincident with the axis of things, and so they appear not transparent but opaque. The reason why the world lacks unity, and lies broken and in heaps, is because man is disunited with himself. *Nature* W I, 73

What would it avail me, if I could destroy my enemies? There would be as many tomorrow. That which I hate and fear is really in myself, and no knife is long enough to reach to its heart. *"Character"* W X, 120

It is an important fact that a man carries about with him favor or disgrace. We impute our reception in society to the will of others & forget that we ourselves alone determine what that reception shall be, that a man may always before he enters the door of a house forestal his welcome by consulting his own mind. It will render him a true & faithful reply. Society seems to be severe on faults. It is merely a mirror reflecting back your own sentence on yourself. We wonder what shall befall us one place or at a future time instead of deciding what we will have befal us i.e. what we will do. . . .

Do not you see that every misfortune is misconduct; that every honour is desert; that every affront is an insolence of your own?

Don't you see that you are the Universe to yourself? You carry your fortunes in your own hand. Change of place won't mend the matter. You will weave the same web at Pernambuco as at Boston if you have only learned how to make *one* texture.

A sermon first preached 11/29/28 JMN III, 143–144

Otherism—We overestimate the conscience of our friend. His goodness seems better than our goodness. His nature finer, his temptation less. Everything that was his, his name, his form, his dress, his books, fancy enhances. . . . Our own expressed thought strikes us as new & of some more weight from the mouth of a friend.   *Journal entry* JMN V, 162

Men in history, men in the world of today, are bugs, are spawn, and are called "the mass" and "the herd." In a century, in a millennium, one or two men; that is to say, one or two approximations to the right state of every man. All the rest behold in the hero or the poet their own green and crude being—ripened; yes, and are content to be less, so *that* may attain to its full stature. What a testimony, full of grandeur, full of pity, is borne to the demands of his own nature, by the poor clansman, the poor partisan, who rejoices in the glory of his chief. The poor and the low find some amends to their immense moral capacity, for their acquiescence in a political and social inferiority. They are content to be brushed like flies from the path of a great person, so that justice shall be done by him to that common nature which it is the dearest desire of all to see enlarged and glorified. They sun themselves in the great man's light, and feel it to be their own element. They cast the dignity of man from their downtrod selves upon the shoulders of a hero, and will perish to add one drop of blood to make that great heart beat, those giant sinews combat and conquer. He lives for us, and we live in him.

"The American Scholar" W I, 106–107

Familiar as the voice of the mind is to each, the highest merit we ascribe to Moses, Plato and Milton is that they set at naught books and traditions, and spoke not what men, but what *they* thought. A man should learn to detect and watch that gleam of light which flashes across his mind from within, more than the lustre of the firmament of bards and sages. Yet he dismisses without notice his thought, because it is his. In every work of genius we recognize our own rejected thoughts; they come back to us with certain alienated majesty. Great works of art have no more affecting lesson for us than this. They teach us to abide by our spontaneous impression with good-humored inflexibility then most when the whole cry of voices is on the other side. Else tomorrow a stranger will say with masterly good sense precisely what we have thought and felt all the time, and we shall be forced to take with shame our own opinion from another.   *"Self-Reliance"* W II, 45

Our age is retrospective. It builds the sepulchres of the fathers. It writes biographies, histories, and criticism. The foregoing generations beheld God and nature face to face; we, through their eyes. Why should not we also enjoy an original relation to the universe? Why should not we have a poetry and philosophy of insight and not of tradition, and a religion by revelation to us, and not the history of theirs? Embosomed for a season in nature, whose floods of life stream around and through us, and invite us by the powers they supply, to action proportioned to nature, why should we grope among the dry bones of the past, or put the living generation into masquerade out of its faded wardrobe? The sun shines today also. There is more wool and flax in the fields. There are new lands, new men, new thoughts. Let us demand our own works and laws and worship. *Nature* W I, 3

Is it possible that, in the solitude I seek I shall have the resolution, the force, to work as I ought to work,—as I project in highest, most far-sighted hours? Well, & what do you project? Nothing less than to look at every object in its relation to Myself. *Journal entry* JMN IV, 272

A low self-love in the parent desires that his child should repeat his character and fortune; an expectation which the child, if justice is done him, will nobly disappoint. By working on the theory that this resemblance exists, we shall do what in us lies to defeat his proper promise and produce the ordinary and mediocre. I suffer whenever I see that common sight of a parent or senior imposing his opinion and way of thinking and being on a young soul to which they are totally unfit. Cannot we let people be themselves, and enjoy life in their own way? You are trying to make that man another *you.* One's enough. *"Education"* W X, 137–138

It seems as if the Deity dressed each soul which he sends into nature in certain virtues and powers not communicable to other men, and sending it to perform one more turn through the circle of beings, wrote *"Not transferable"* and *"Good for this trip only,"* on these garments of the soul. There is somewhat deceptive about the intercourse of minds. The boundaries are invisible, but they are never crossed.
"Uses of Great Men" W IV, 28

There is no history. There is only Biography. The attempt to perpetrate, to fix a thought or principle, fails continually. You can only live for yourself; your action is good only whilst it is alive—whilst it is in you. The awkward imitation of it by your child or your disciple is not a repetition of it, is not the same thing, but another thing. The new individual must work out the whole problem of science, letters and theology for himself; can owe his fathers nothing. There is no history; only biography. *Journal entry* Jour V, 208

There is a time in every man's education when he arrives at the conviction that envy is ignorance; that imitation is suicide; that he must take himself for better or worse as his portion; that though the wide universe is full of good, no kernel of nourishing corn can come to him but through his toil bestowed on that plot of ground which is given to him to till. The power which resides in him is new in nature, and none but he knows what that is which he can do, nor does he know until he has tried. Not for nothing one face, one character, one fact, makes much impression on him, and another none. This sculpture in the memory is not without preëstablished harmony. The eye was placed where one ray should fall, that it might testify of that particular ray. We but half express ourselves, and are ashamed of that divine idea which each of us represents. It may be safely trusted as proportionate and of good issues, so it be faithfully imparted, but God will not have his work made manifest by cowards. A man is relieved and gay when he has put his heart into his work and done his best; but what he has said or done otherwise shall give him no peace. It is a deliverance which does not deliver. In the attempt his genius deserts him; no muse befriends; no invention, no hope.

Trust thyself: every heart vibrates to that iron string. Accept the place the divine providence has found for you, the society of your contemporaries, the connection of events. Great men have always done so, and confided themselves childlike to the genius of their age, betraying their perception that the absolutely trustworthy was seated at their heart, working through their hands, predominating in all their being. And we are now men, and must accept in the highest mind the same transcendent destiny; and not minors and invalids in a protected corner, not cowards fleeing before a revolution, but guides, redeemers and benefactors, obeying the Almighty effort and advancing on Chaos and the Dark.

"Self-Reliance" W II, 46–47

There are objections to every course of life and action, and the practical wisdom infers an indifferency, from the omnipresence of objection. The whole frame of things preaches indifferency. Do not craze yourself with thinking, but go about your business anywhere. Life is not intellectual or critical, but sturdy. Its chief good is for well-mixed people who can enjoy what they find, without question. Nature hates peeping, and our mothers speak her very sense when they say, "Children, eat your victuals, and say no more of it." To fill the hour,—that is happiness; to fill the hour and leave no crevice for a repentance or an approval. . . . To finish the moment, to find the journey's end in every step of the road, to live the greatest number of good hours, is wisdom. It is not the part of men, but of fanatics, or of mathematicians if you will, to say that, the shortness of life considered, it is not worth caring whether for so short a duration we were sprawling in want or sitting high. Since our office is with moments, let us husband them. Five minutes of today are worth as much to me as five minutes in the next millennium. Let us be poised, and wise, and our own, today. Let us treat the men and women well; treat them as if they were real; perhaps they are. Men live in their fancy, like drunkards whose hands are too soft and tremulous for successful labor. It is a tempest of fancies, and the only ballast I know is a respect to the present hour. Without any shadow of doubt, amidst this vertigo of shows and politics, I settle myself ever the firmer in the creed that we should not postpone and refer and wish, but do broad justice where we are, by whomsoever we deal with, accepting our actual companions and circumstances, however humble or odious, as the mystic officials to whom the universe has delegated its whole pleasure for us.

"Experience" W III, 59–61

There is guidance for each of us, and by lowly listening we shall hear the right word. Why need you choose so painfully your place and occupation and associates and modes of action and of entertainment? . . . I say, *do not choose;* but that is a figure of speech by which I would distinguish what is commonly called choice among men, and which is a partial act, the choice of the hands, of the eyes, of the appetites, and not a whole act of the man. But that which I call right or goodness, is the choice of my constitution; and that which I call heaven, and inwardly aspire after, is the state or circumstance desirable to my constitution; and the action which I in all my years tend to do, is the work for my faculties.

"Spiritual Laws" W II, 139–140

Our spontaneous action is always the best. You cannot with your best deliberation and heed come so close to any question as your spontaneous glance shall bring you, whilst you rise from your bed, or walk abroad in the morning after meditating the matter before sleep on the previous night. Our thinking is a pious reception. Our truth of thought is therefore vitiated as much by too violent direction given by our will, as by too great negligence. We do not determine what we will think. We only open our senses, clear away as we can all obstruction from the fact, and suffer the intellect to see. We have little control over our thoughts. We are the prisoners of ideas. They catch us up for moments into their heaven and so fully engage us that we take no thought for the morrow, gaze like children, without an effort to make them our own. By and by we fall out of that rapture, bethink us where we have been, what we have seen, and repeat as truly as we can what we have beheld. As far as we can recall these ecstasies we carry away in the ineffaceable memory the result, and all men and all the ages confirm it. It is called truth. But the moment we cease to report and attempt to correct and contrive, it is not truth.

"Intellect" W II, 328–329

It is my habit to assume always as purely as I can, the attitude of an observer, & to record what I see. I am not responsible for the fact; for the truth of the record, I am. All that is out of my field of sight, I neither affirm nor deny; but I believe I am not unrelated to it; in good time, it may, it will come into sight & influence.

Letter to George Bush, 9/2/38 Let II, 156

I suppose no man can violate his nature. All the sallies of his will are rounded in by the law of his being, as the inequalities of Andes and Himmaleh are insignificant in the curve of the sphere. Nor does it matter how you gauge and try him. A character is like an acrostic or Alexandrian stanza—read it forward, backward, or across, it still spells the same thing. In this pleasing contrite wood-life which God allows me, let me record day by day my honest thought without prospect or retrospect, and, I cannot doubt, it will be found symmetrical, though I mean it not and see it not. My book should smell of pines and resound with the hum of insects. The swallow over my window should interweave that thread or straw he carries in his bill into my web also. We pass for what we are. Character teaches above our wills. Men imagine that they communicate their virtue or vice only by overt actions, and do not see that virtue or vice emit a breath every moment. *"Self-Reliance" W II, 58*

There is no privacy that cannot be penetrated. No secret can be kept in the civilized world. Society is a masked ball, where everyone hides his real character, and reveals it by hiding. If a man wish to conceal anything he carries, those whom he meets know that he conceals somewhat, and usually know what he conceals. Is it otherwise if there be some belief or some purpose he would bury in his breast? 'Tis as hard to hide as fire. He is a strong man who can hold down his opinion. A man cannot utter two or three sentences without disclosing to intelligent ears precisely where he stands in life and thought. *"Worship" W VI, 223-224*

Some great decorum, some fetish of a government, some ephemeral trade, or war, or man, is cried up by half mankind and cried down by the other half, as if all depended on this particular up or down. The odds are that the whole question is not worth the poorest thought which the scholar has lost in listening to the controversy. Let him not quit his belief that a popgun is a popgun, though the ancient and honorable of the earth affirm it to be the crack of doom. In silence, in steadiness, in severe abstraction, let him hold by himself; add observation to observation, patient of neglect, patient of reproach, and bide his own time—happy enough if he can satisfy himself alone that this day he has seen something truly. Success treads on every right step. For the instinct is sure, that prompts him to tell his brother what he thinks. He then learns that in going down into the secrets of his own mind he has descended into the secrets of all minds. He learns that he who has mastered any law in his private thoughts, is master to that extent of all men whose language he speaks, and of all into whose language his own can be translated. The poet, in utter solitude remembering his spontaneous thoughts and recording them, is found to have recorded that which men in crowded cities find true for them also. The orator distrusts at first the fitness of his frank confessions, his want of knowledge of the persons he addresses, until he finds that he is the complement of his hearers—that they drink his words because he fulfils for them their own nature; the deeper he dives into his privatest, secretest presentiment, to his wonder he finds this is the most acceptable, most public, and universally true. The people delight in it; the better part of every man feels, This is my music; this is myself.

In self-trust all the virtues are comprehended. Free should the scholar be—free and brave. Free even to the definition of freedom, "without any hindrance that does not arise out of his own constitution." Brave; for fear is a thing which a scholar by his very function puts behind him. Fear always springs from ignorance. . . . The world is his who can see through its pretension. What deafness, what stone-blind custom, what overgrown error you behold is there only by sufferance—by your sufferance. See it to be a lie, and you have already dealt it its mortal blow.

"The American Scholar" W I, 102–105

Every spirit builds itself a house, and beyond its house a world, and beyond its world a heaven. Know then that the world exists for you. For you is the phenomenon perfect. What we are, that only can we see. All that Adam had, all that Caesar could, you have and can do. Adam called his house, heaven and earth; Caesar called his house, Rome; you perhaps call yours, a cobbler's trade; a hundred acres of ploughed land; or a scholar's garret. Yet line for line and point for point your dominion is as great as theirs, though without fine names. Build therefore your own world. As fast as you conform your life to the pure idea in your mind, that will unfold its great proportions. *Nature* W I, 76

People hold to you as long as you please yourself with the Ideal life only as a pretty dream & concede a resistless force to the limitations of the same, to structure, or organization, & to society. But as quickly as you profess your unlimited allegiance to the first so far as to be no longer contented with doing the best you can in the circumstances but demand that these mountain circumstances should skip like rams and the little hills like lambs before the presence of the Soul, then they distrust your wisdom & defy your resolutions. And yet Nature is in earnest. . . . The prayer of the soul predicts its own answer in facts. The moral nature is not a patch of light here, whilst the social world is a lump of darkness there, but tends incessantly to rectify and ennoble the whole circumference of facts. *Journal entry* JMN VII, 289–290

Virtue is the adherence in action to the nature of things. . . . It consists in a perpetual substitution of being for seeming, and with sublime propriety God is described as saying, I AM. *"Spiritual Laws"* W II, 160

The objection to conforming to usages that have become dead to you is that it scatters your force. It loses your time and blurs the impression of your character. If you maintain a dead church, contribute to a dead Bible-society, vote with a great party either for the government or against it, spread your table like base housekeepers,—under all these screens I have difficulty to detect the precise man you are: and of course so much force is withdrawn from your proper life. But do your work, and I shall know you. Do your work, and you shall reinforce yourself. . . . Well, most men have bound their eyes with one or another handkerchief, and attached themselves to some one of these communities of opinion. This conformity makes them not false in a few particulars, authors of a few lies, but false in all particulars. Their every truth is not quite true. Their two is not the real two, their four not the real four; so that every word they say chagrins us and we know not where to begin to set them right.
"Self-Reliance" W II, 54–55

But why should you keep your head over your shoulder? Why drag about this corpse of your memory, lest you contradict somewhat you have stated in this or that public place? Suppose you should contradict yourself; what then? . . . A foolish consistency is the hobgoblin of little minds, adored by little statesmen and philosophers and divines. With consistency a great soul has simply nothing to do. He may as well concern himself with his shadow on the wall. Speak what you think now in hard words and tomorrow speak what tomorrow thinks in hard words again, though it contradict everything you said today.—"Ah, so you shall be sure to be misunderstood."—Is it so bad then to be misunderstood? Pythagoras was misunderstood, and Socrates, and Jesus, and Luther, and Copernicus, and Galileo, and Newton, and every pure and wise spirit that ever took flesh. To be great is to be misunderstood.
"Self-Reliance" W II, 57–58

There are two confessionals, in one or the other of which we must be shriven. You may fulfil your round of duties by clearing yourself in the *direct,* or in the *reflex* way. Consider whether you have satisfied your relations to father, mother, cousin, neighbor, town, cat and dog—whether any of these can upbraid you. But I may also neglect this reflex standard and absolve me to myself. I have my own stern claims and perfect circle. It denies the name of duty to many offices that are called duties. But if I can discharge its debts it enables me to dispense with the popular code. If any one imagines that this law is lax, let him keep its commandment one day. *"Self-Reliance"* W II, 74

Whoso would be a man, must be a nonconformist. He who would gather mortal palms must not be hindered by the name of goodness, but must explore if it be goodness. Nothing is at last sacred but the integrity of your own mind. Absolve you to yourself, and you shall have the suffrage of the world. I remember an answer which when quite young I was prompted to make to a valued adviser who was wont to importune me with the dear old doctrines of the church. On my saying, "What have I to do with the sacredness of traditions, if I live wholly from within?" my friend suggested, "But these impulses may be from below, not from above." I replied, "They do not seem to me to be such; but if I am the Devil's child, I will live then from the Devil." No law can be sacred to me but that of my nature. Good and bad are but names very readily transferable to that or this; the only right is what is after my constitution; the only wrong what is against it. A man is to carry himself in the presence of all opposition as if everything were titular and ephemeral but he. I am ashamed to think how easily we capitulate to badges and names, to large societies and dead institutions. Every decent and well-spoken individual affects and sways me more than is right. I ought to go upright and vital, and speak the rude truth in all ways. *"Self-Reliance"* W II, 50–51

Every man's condition is a solution in hieroglyphic to those inquiries he would put. He acts it as life, before he apprehends it as truth.
Nature W I, 4

The world—this shadow of the soul, or *other me*—lies wide around. Its attractions are the keys which unlock my thoughts and make me acquainted with myself. I run eagerly into this resounding tumult. I grasp the hands of those next me, and take my place in the ring to suffer and to work, taught by an instinct that so shall the dumb abyss be vocal with speech. I pierce its order; I dissipate its fear; I dispose of it within the circuit of my expanding life. So much only of life as I know by experience, so much of the wilderness have I vanquished and planted, or so far have I extended my being, my dominion. I do not see how any man can afford, for the sake of his nerves and his nap, to spare any action in which he can partake. It is pearls and rubies to his discourse. Drudgery, calamity, exasperation, want, are instructors in eloquence and wisdom. The true scholar grudges every opportunity of action past by, as a loss of power. It is the raw material out of which the intellect moulds her splendid products. A strange process too, this by which experience is converted into thought, as a mulberry leaf is converted into satin. The manufacture goes forward at all hours.
"The American Scholar" W I, 95–96

But the best read naturalist who lends an entire and devout attention to truth, will see that there remains much to learn of his relation to the world, and that it is not to be learned by any addition or subtraction or other comparison of known quantities, but is arrived at by untaught sallies of the spirit, by a continual self-recovery, and by entire humility.
Nature W I, 66

I will not live out of me
I will not see with others' eyes
My good is good, my evil ill
I would be free—I cannot be
While I take things as others please to rate them
I dare attempt to lay out my own road
That which myself delights in shall be Good,
That which I do not want—indifferent,
That which I hate is Bad. That's flat.

Journal entry JMN *IV, 47*

NATURE AS CONTEXT AND MODEL

Both because Emerson's first publication was Nature *and because he so often wrote about the natural landscape, he is remembered as a "nature writer." But just what that phrase means is not so obvious. Unlike Thoreau, his knowledge of plants, animals, and minerals was rather superficial and he seldom tried to write about that world in any detailed way. Nor was he particularly interested, as eighteenth-century writers had been, in the natural order as the evidence of a divine plan and a hierarchical system of places proper to each creature. Rather he was interested in nature as the most suitable setting for the person's self-recovery; away from the pull of social forces, the person could better hear the inner voice which called him back to the center of his own being. But that was not all. Looking about him, the person could see in natural objects an analogy to what he might do in his own life: the natural object existed purely in the present; it was all there at every moment of its existence.*

At the gates of the forest, the surprised man of the world is forced to leave his city estimates of great and small, wise and foolish. . . . The incommunicable trees begin to persuade us to live with them, and quit our life of solemn trifles. Here no history, or church, or state, is interpolated on the divine sky and immortal year. How easily we might walk onward into the opening landscape, absorbed by new pictures and by thoughts fast succeeding each other, until by degrees the recollection of home was crowded out of the mind, all memory obliterated by the tyranny of the present, and we were led in triumph by nature. These enchantments are medicinal, they sober and heal us.

Nature W III, 170–171

Nature will not have us fret and fume. She does not like our benevolence or our learning much better than she likes our frauds and wars. When we come out of the caucus, or the bank, or the Abolition-convention, or the Temperance-meeting, or the Transcendental club into the fields and woods, she says to us, 'So hot? my little Sir.'

"Spiritual Laws" W II, 135

To go into solitude, a man needs to retire as much from his chamber as from society. I am not solitary whilst I read and write, though nobody is with me. But if a man would be alone, let him look at the stars. The rays that come from those heavenly worlds will separate between him and what he touches. *Nature* W I, 7

[You have] two worlds, your solitude & your society; one, heaven; the other, earth; one, real, the other apparent. . . . And then will our true heaven be entered, when we have learned to be the same manner of person to others that we are alone, say the same things to them, we think alone, & to pass out of solitude into society without any change or effort. . . . The only remedy must be from the growth of his true self, & its mastering predominance over him so that the men . . . & things which looked so great shall shrink to their true dimensions. . . .

Journal entry JMN IV, 66

If he pines in a lonely place, hankering for the crowd, for display, he is not in the lonely place. . . . Not insulation of place, but independence of spirit is essential, and it is only as the garden, the cottage, the forest, and the rock, are a sort of mechanical aids to this, that they are of value. Think alone, and all places are friendly and sacred.

"*Literary Ethics*" W I, 173–174

. . . Nature is no sentimentalist—does not cosset or pamper us. We must see that the world is rough and surly, and will not mind drowning a man or a woman, but swallows your ship like a grain of dust. The cold, inconsiderate of persons, tingles your blood, benumbs your feet, freezes a man like an apple. The diseases, the elements, fortune, gravity, lightning, respect no persons. The way of Providence is a little rude. The habit of snake and spider, the snap of the tiger and other leapers and bloody jumpers, the crackle of the bones of his prey in the coil of the anaconda— these are in the system, and our habits are like theirs. You have just dined, and however scrupulously the slaughter-house is concealed in the graceful distance of miles, there is complicity, expensive races—race living at the expense of race. The planet is liable to shocks from comets, perturbations from planets, rendings from earthquake and volcano, alterations of climate, precessions of equinoxes. Rivers dry up by opening of the forest. The sea changes its bed. Towns and counties fall into it. At Lisbon an earthquake killed men like flies. At Naples three years ago ten thousand persons were crushed in a few minutes. The scurvy at sea, the sword of the climate in the west of Africa, at Cayenne, at Panama, at New Orleans, cut off men like a massacre. Our western prairie shakes with fever and ague. The cholera, the smallpox, have proved as mortal to some tribes as a frost to the crickets, which, having filled the summer with noise, are silenced by a fall of the temperature of one night. Without uncovering what does not concern us, or counting how many species of parasites hang on a bombyx, or groping after intestinal parasites or infusory biters, or the obscurities of alternate generation—the forms of the shark, the *labrus*, the jaw of the sea-wolf paved with crushing teeth, the weapons of the grampus, and other warriors hidden in the sea, are hints of ferocity in the interiors of nature. Let us not deny it up and down. Providence has a wild, rough, incalculable road to its end, and it is of no use to try to whitewash its huge, mixed instrumentalities, or to dress up that terrific benefactor in a clean shirt and white neckcloth of a student in divinity. *"Fate"* W VI, 6–8

There must be the Abyss, Nox [night, darkness] and Chaos, out of which all come, and they must never be far off. Cut off the connection between any of our works and this dread origin, and the work is shallow and unsatisfying. *Journal entry* Jour VII, 131

There may be two or three or four steps, according to the genius of each, but for every seeing soul there are two absorbing facts,—*I and the Abyss.* *Journal entry* Jour X, 171

The man who stands on the seashore, or who rambles in the woods, seems to be the first man that ever stood on the shore, or entered a grove, his sensations and his world are so novel and strange. Whilst I read the poets, I think that nothing new can be said about morning and evening. But when I see the daybreak I am not reminded of these Homeric, or Shakespearean, or Miltonic, or Chaucerian pictures. No, but I feel perhaps the pain of an alien world; a world not yet subdued by the thought; or I am cheered by the moist, warm, glittering, budding, melodious hour, that takes down the narrow walls of my soul, and extends its life and pulsation to the very horizon. *That* is morning, to cease for a bright hour to be a prisoner of this sickly body, and to become as large as nature.
"Literary Ethics" W I, 168

Nature, as we know her, is no saint. The lights of the church, the ascetics, Gentoos and corn-eaters, she does not distinguish by any favor. She comes eating and drinking and sinning. Her darlings, the great, the strong, the beautiful, are not children of our law; do not come out of the Sunday School, nor weigh their food, nor punctually keep the commandments. If we will be strong with her strength we must not harbor such disconsolate consciences, borrowed too from the consciences of other nations. We must set up the strong present tense against all the rumors of wrath, past or to come. *"Experience"* W III, 64

Man is timid and apologetic; he is no longer upright; he dares not say "I think," "I am," but quotes some saint or sage. He is ashamed before the blade of grass or the blowing rose. These roses under my window make no reference to former roses or to better ones; they are for what they are; they exist with God today. There is no time to them. There is simply the rose; it is perfect in every moment of its existence. Before a leaf-bud has burst, its whole life acts; in the full-blown flower there is no more; in the leafless root there is no less. Its nature is satisfied and it satisfies nature in all moments alike. But man postpones or remembers; he does not live in the present, but with reverted eye laments the past, or, heedless of the riches that surround him, stands on tiptoe to foresee the future. He cannot be happy and strong until he too lives with nature in the present, above time.   *"Self-Reliance"* W II, 67

Every man beholds his human condition with a degree of melancholy. As a ship aground is battered by the waves, so man, imprisoned in mortal life, lies open to the mercy of coming events. But a truth, separated by the intellect, is no longer a subject of destiny. We behold it as a god upraised above care and fear. And so any fact in our life, or any record of our fancies or reflections, disentangled from the web of our unconsciousness, becomes an object impersonal and immortal. It is the past restored, but embalmed. A better art than that of Egypt has taken fear and corruption out of it. It is eviscerated of care. It is offered for science. What is addressed to us for contemplation does not threaten us but makes us intellectual beings.   *"Intellect"* W II, 327

Intellect separates the fact considered, from *you*, from all local and personal reference, and discerns it as if it existed for its own sake. . . . The intellect goes out of the individual, floats over its own personality, and regards it as a fact, and not as *I* and *mine*.   *"Intellect"* W II, 326

There is a great parallax in human nature ascertained by observing it from different states of mind. If I look at an action from the low ground of the effect upon the immediate actors & neighbors, it appears important. If I look at it from the high ground of the relation of the actors to the Universe & to the Eternal generation of Beings it is too insignificant for thought. Yet each of those views is perfectly just.

Journal entry JMN IV, 22

The constant warfare in each heart is betwixt Reason & Commodity [utility]. The victory is won as soon as any soul has learned always to take sides with Reason against himself; to transfer his *Me* from his person, his name, his interests, back upon Truth & Justice, so that when he is disgraced & defeated & fretted and disheartened & wasted by nothing, he bears it well, never one instant relaxing his watchfulness, & as soon as he can get a respite from the insults or the sadness, records all these phenomena, pierces their beauty as phenomena, and, like a God, oversees himself. Thus he harvests his losses, & turns the dust of his shoes to gems.

Keep the habit of the observer & as fast as you can, break off your association with your personality and identify yourself with the Universe. Be a football to time & chance the more kicks, the better, so that you inspect the whole game & know its uttermost law.

Journal entry JMN V, 391

      The rounded world is fair to see,
      Nine times folded in mystery:
      Though baffled seers cannot impart

> The secret of its laboring heart,
> Throb thine with Nature's throbbing breast,
> And all is clear from east to west.
> Spirit that lurks each form within
> Beckons to spirit of its kin;
> Self-kindled every atom glows
> And hints the future which it owes.
>
> *Nature* W III, 167

It has already been illustrated, that every natural process is a version of a moral sentence. The moral law lies at the center of nature and radiates to the circumference. It is the pith and marrow of every substance, every relation, and every process. All things with which we deal, preach to us. What is a farm but a mute gospel? The chaff and the wheat, weeds and plants, blight, rain, insects, sun,—it is a sacred emblem from the first furrow of spring to the last stack which the snow of winter overtakes in the fields. But the sailor, the shepherd, the miner, the merchant, in their several resorts, have each an experience precisely parallel, and leading to the same conclusion: because all organizations are radically alike. Nor can it be doubted that this moral sentiment which thus scents the air, grows in the grain, and impregnates the waters of the world, is caught by man and sinks into his soul. The moral influence of nature upon every individual is that amount of truth which it illustrates to him. Who can estimate this? Who can guess how much firmness the sea-beaten rock has taught the fisherman? how much tranquility has been reflected to man from the azure sky, over whose unspotted deeps the winds forevermore drive flocks of stormy clouds, and leave no wrinkle or stain? how much industry and providence and affection we have caught from the pantomime of brutes? What a searching preacher of self-command is the varying phenomenon of Health!

Herein is especially apprehended the unity of Nature,—the unity in variety,—which meets us everywhere. All the endless variety of things make an identical impression. Xenophanes complained in his old age, that, look where he would, all things hastened back to Unity. He was weary of seeing the same entity in the tedious variety of forms. The fable of Proteus has a cordial truth. A leaf, a drop, a crystal, a moment of time, is related to the whole, and partakes of the perfection of the whole. Each particle is a microcosm, and faithfully renders the likeness of the world.

Nature W I, 41–43

> Teach me your mood, O patient stars!
>   Who climb each night the ancient sky,
> Leaving on space no shade, no scars,
>   No trace of age, no fear to die.
>
> [*Untitled verse*] W IX, 340

In the presence of nature a wild delight runs through the man, in spite of real sorrows. Nature says,—he is my creature, and maugre all his impertinent griefs, he shall be glad with me. Not the sun or the summer alone, but every hour and season yields its tribute of delight; for every hour and change corresponds to and authorizes a different state of the mind, from breathless noon to grimmest midnight. Nature is a setting that fits equally well a comic or a mourning piece. In good health, the air is a cordial of incredible virtue. Crossing a bare common, in snow puddles, at twilight, under a clouded sky, without having in my thoughts any occurrence of special good fortune, I have enjoyed a perfect exhilaration. I am glad to the brink of fear. In the woods, too, a man casts off his years, as the snake his slough, and at what period soever of life is always a child. In the woods is perpetual youth. Within these plantations of God, a decorum and sanctity reign, a perennial festival is dressed, and the guest sees not how he should tire of them in a thousand years. In the woods, we return to reason and faith. There I feel that nothing can befall me in life,—no disgrace, no calamity (leaving me my eyes), which nature cannot repair. Standing on the bare ground,—my head bathed by the blithe air and uplifted into infinite space,—all mean egotism vanishes. I become a transparent eyeball; I am nothing; I see all; the currents of the Universal Being circulate through me; I am part or parcel of God. The name of the nearest friend sounds then foreign and accidental: to be brothers, to be acquaintances, master or servant, is then a trifle and a disturbance. I am the lover of uncontained and immortal beauty. In the wilderness, I find something more dear and connate than in streets or villages. In the tranquil landscape, and especially in the distant line of the horizon, man beholds somewhat as beautiful as his own nature.

The greatest delight which the fields and woods minister is the suggestion of an occult relation between man and the vegetable. I am not alone and unacknowledged. They nod to me, and I to them. The waving of the boughs in the storm is new to me and old. It takes me by surprise, and yet is not unknown. Its effect is like that of a higher thought or a better emotion coming over me, when I deemed I was thinking justly or doing right. *Nature* W I, 9–11

I shall therefore conclude this essay with some traditions of man and nature, which a certain poet sang to me; and which, as they have always been in the world, and perhaps reappear to every bard, may be both history and prophecy.

"The foundations of man are not in matter, but in spirit. But the element of spirit is eternity. To it, therefore, the longest series of events, the oldest chronologies are young and recent. In the cycle of the universal man, from whom the known individuals proceed, centuries are points, and all history is but the epoch of one degradation.

"We distrust and deny inwardly our sympathy with nature. We own and disown our relation to it, by turns. We are like Nebuchadnezzar, dethroned, bereft of reason, and eating grass like an ox. But who can set limits to the remedial force of spirit?

"A man is a god in ruins. When men are innocent, life shall be longer, and shall pass into the immortal as gently as we awake from dreams. Now, the world would be insane and rabid, if these disorganizations should last for hundreds of years. It is kept in check by death and infancy. Infancy is the perpetual Messiah, which comes into the arms of fallen men, and pleads with them to return to paradise.

"Man is the dwarf of himself. Once he was permeated and dissolved by spirit. He filled nature with his overflowing currents. Out from him sprang the sun and moon; from man the sun, from woman the moon. The laws of his mind, the periods of his actions externized themselves into day and night, into the year and the seasons. But, having made for himself this huge shell, his waters retired; he no longer fills the veins and veinlets; he is shrunk to a drop. He sees that the structure still fits him, but fits him colossally. Say, rather, once it fitted him, now it corresponds to him from far and on high. He adores timidly his own work. Now is man the follower of the sun, and woman the follower of the moon. Yet sometimes he starts in his slumber, and wonders at himself and his house, and muses strangely at the resemblance betwixt him and it. He perceives that if his law is still paramount, if still he have elemental power, if his word is sterling yet in nature, it is not conscious power, it is not inferior but superior to his will. It is instinct." Thus my Orphic poet sang.

At present, man applies to nature but half his force. He works on the world with his understanding alone. He lives in it and masters it by a penny-wisdom; and he that works most in it is but a half-man, and whilst his arms are strong and his digestion good, his mind is imbruted, and he is a selfish savage. His relation to nature, his power over it, is through the understanding, as by manure; the economic use of fire, wind, water, and the mariner's needle; steam, coal, chemical agriculture; the repairs of the human body by the dentist and the surgeon. This is such a resumption of power as if a banished king should buy his territories inch by inch, instead of vaulting at once into his throne. *Nature* W I, 70–72

It seems as if the day was not wholly profane in which we have given heed to some natural object. *Nature* W IV, 172

THE ETERNAL MOMENT: ART AND RELIGION

The power regained by the person in the process of self-recovery was the power to be—to respond fully and authentically to the reality of the present. In such a state of consciousness, time was transformed from being a past-and-future (with an almost invisibly thin present sandwiched in between) to a continuous state of present-ness. In that state the process of perception and response crowded out remorse over the past and anxiety over the future, the two emotional orientations that keep most persons from living in the here-and-now.

It is in this context that Emerson's discussions about religion and about art must be read, for each of these two great human activities was to him simply the scene of an aspect of being. Art, he argued, is simply the utterance of the self-recovered person, so naturally real and vital that it takes on a unique form and coloring of its own that sets it above ordinary discourse. Religion, on the other hand, was simply the character of the life and knowledge that the person found natural to him when he recovered his rightful place in the center of his experiential world. The artist and the prophet, therefore, spoke and lived out of their own experience, not so that we might model ourselves after them but that we might, like them, find ourselves. Shakespeare's legacy, thus, is not a form and a style; it is a trust in one's own creativity, comparable to his. Christ's message was not for us to be Christ-like; it was for us to be us-like.

Jesus Christ belonged to the true race of prophets. He saw with open eye the mystery of the soul. Drawn by its severe harmony, ravished with its beauty, he lived in it, and had his being there. Alone in all history he estimated the greatness of man. One man was true to what is in you and me. He saw that God incarnates himself in man, and evermore goes forth anew to take possession of his World. He said, in this jubilee of sublime emotion, "I am divine. Through me, God acts; through me, speaks. Would you see God, see me; or see thee, when thou also thinkest as I now think." But what a distortion did his doctrine and memory suffer in the same, in the next, and the following ages! There is no doctrine of the Reason which will bear to be taught by the Understanding. The understanding caught this high chant from the poet's lips, and said, in the next age, "This was Jehovah come down out of heaven. I will kill you, if you say he was a man." The idioms of his language and the figures of his rhetoric have usurped the place of his truth; and churches are not built on his principles, but on his tropes. Christianity became a Mythus, as the poetic teaching of Greece and of Egypt, before. He spoke of miracles; for he felt that man's life was a miracle, and all that man doth, and he knew that this daily miracle shines as the character ascends. But the word Miracle, as pronounced by Christian churches, gives a false impression; it is Monster. It is not one with the blowing clover and the falling rain.

He felt respect for Moses and the prophets, but no unfit tenderness at postponing their initial revelations to the hour and the man that now is; to the eternal revelation in the heart. Thus was he a true man.
"Divinity School Address" W I, 128–130

Each age, it is found, must write its own books; or rather, each generation for the next succeeding. The books of an older period will not fit this.
Yet hence arises a grave mischief. The sacredness which attaches to the act of creation, the act of thought, is transferred to the record. The poet chanting was felt to be a divine man: henceforth the chant is divine also. The writer was a just and wise spirit: henceforward it is settled the book is perfect; as love of the hero corrupts into worship of his statue. Instantly the book becomes noxious; the guide is a tyrant. The sluggish and perverted mind of the multitude, slow to open to the incursions of Reason, having once so opened, having once received this book, stands upon it, and makes an outcry if it is disparaged. Colleges are built on it. Books are written on it by thinkers, not by Man Thinking; by men of talent, that is, who start wrong, who set out from accepted dogmas, not from their own sight of principles. Meek young men grow up in libraries, believing it their duty to accept the views which Cicero, which Locke, which Bacon, have given; forgetful that Cicero, Locke, and Bacon were only young men in libraries when they wrote these books.
"The American Scholar" W I, 88–89

The poet has a new thought; he has a whole new experience to unfold; he will tell us how it was with him, and all men will be the richer in his fortune. For the experience of each new age requires a new confession, and the world seems always waiting for its poet. *"The Poet"* W III, 10

I hate quotations. Tell me what you know. *Journal entry* Jour VIII, 20

People forget that it is the eye which makes the horizon, and the rounding mind's eye which makes this or that man a type or representative of humanity, with the name of hero or saint. Jesus, the "providential man," is a good man on whom many people are agreed that these optical laws shall take effect. By love on one part and by forbearance to press objection on the other part, it is for a time settled that we will look at him in the center of the horizon, and ascribe to him the properties that will attach to any man so seen. *"Experience"* W III, 76–77

I do not see in [Christ] cheerfulness: I do not see in him the love of Natural Science: I see in him no kindness for Art; I see in him nothing of Socrates, of Laplace, of Shakespeare. The perfect man should remind us of all great men. Do you ask me if I would rather resemble Jesus than any other man? If I should say Yes, I should suspect myself of superstition. *Journal entry* JMN V, 71–72

For it is not metres, but a metre-making argument that makes a poem—a thought so passionate and alive that like the spirit of a plant or an animal it has an architecture of its own, and adorns nature with a new thing. The thought and the form are equal in the order of time, but in the order of genesis the thought is prior to the form. *"The Poet"* W III, 9–10

The difference between poetry and stock poetry is this, that in the latter the rhythm is given and the sense adapted to it; while in the former the sense dictates the rhythm. I might even say that the rhyme is there in the theme, thought and image themselves. Ask the fact for the form. For a verse is not a vehicle to carry a sentence as a jewel is carried in a case: the verse must be alive, and inseparable from its contents, as the soul of man inspires and directs the body, and we measure the inspiration by the music. *"Poetry and Imagination"* W VIII, 54

I value men as they can complete their creation. One man can hurl from him a sentence which is spheral, and at once and forever disengaged from the author. Another can say excellent things, if the sayer and the circumstances are known and considered; but the sentences need a running commentary, and are not yet independent individuals that can go alone. *Journal entry* Jour VII, 518

Write, that I may know you. Style betrays you, as your eyes do. We detect at once by it whether the writer has a firm grasp on his fact or thought—exists at the moment for that alone, or whether he has one eye apologizing, deprecatory, turned on his reader. In proportion always to his possession of this thought is his defiance of his readers. There is no choice of words for him who clearly sees the truth. That provides him with the best word. . . .

If your subject do not appear to you the flower of the world at this moment, you have not rightly chosen it. No matter what it is, grand or gay, national or private, if it has a natural prominence to you, work away until you come to the heart of it: then it will, though it were a sparrow or a spider-web, as fully represent the central law and draw all tragic or joyful illustration, as if it were the book of Genesis or the book of Doom. The subject—we must so often say it—is indifferent. Any word, every word in language, every circumstance, becomes poetic in the hands of a higher thought. *"Poetry and Imagination"* W VIII, 33–34

The poet is the Namer or Language-maker, naming things sometimes after their appearance, sometimes after their essence, and giving to every one its own name and not another's, thereby rejoicing the intellect, which delights in detachment or boundary. The poets made all the words, and therefore language is the archives of history, and, if we must say it, a sort of tomb of the muses. For though the origin of most of our words is forgotten, each word was at first a stroke of genius, and obtained currency because for the moment it symbolized the world to the first speaker and to the hearer. The etymologist finds the deadest word to have been once a brilliant picture. Language is fossil poetry. As the limestone of the continent consists of infinite masses of the shells of animalcules, so language is made up of images or tropes, which now, in their secondary use, have long ceased to remind us of their poetic origin. But the poet names the thing because he sees it, or comes one step nearer to it than any other. This expression or naming is not art, but a second nature, grown out of the first, as a leaf out of a tree. *"The Poet"* W III, 21–22

The language of the street is always strong. What can describe the folly & emptiness of scolding like the word *jawing*? I feel too the force of the double negative, though clean contrary to our grammar rules. And I confess to some pleasure from the stinging rhetoric of a rattling oath in the mouth of truckmen & teamsters. How laconic & brisk it is by the side of a page of the *North American Review*. Cut these words & they would bleed; they are vascular & alive; they walk & run. Moreover they who speak them have this elegancy, that they do not trip in their speech. It is a shower of bullets, whilst Cambridge men & Yale men correct themselves & begin again at every half sentence.

Journal entry Jour V, 419–420

. . . the same movement which effected the elevation of what was called the lowest class in the state, assumed in literature a very marked and as benign an aspect. Instead of the sublime and beautiful, the near, the low, the common, was explored and poetized. That which had been negligently trodden under foot by those who were harnessing and provisioning themselves for long journeys into far countries, is suddenly found to be richer than all foreign parts. The literature of the poor, the feelings of the child, the philosophy of the street, the meaning of the household life, are the topics of the time. It is a great stride. It is a sign—is it not?—of new vigor when the extremities are made active, when currents of warm life run into the hands and the feet. I ask not for the great, the remote, the romantic; what is doing in Italy or Arabia; what is Greek art, or Provençal minstrelsy; I embrace the common, I explore and sit at the feet of the familiar, the low. Give me insight into today, and you may have the antique and future worlds. What would we really know the meaning of? The meal in the firkin; the milk in the pan; the ballad in the street; the news of the boat; the glance of the eye; the form and the gait of the body—show me the ultimate reason of these matters; show me the sublime presence of the highest spiritual cause lurking, as always it does lurk, in these suburbs and extremities of nature; let me see every trifle bristling with the polarity that ranges it instantly on an eternal law; and the shop, the plough, and the ledger referred to the like cause by which light undulates and poets sing—and the world lies no longer a dull miscellany and lumber-room, but has form and order; there is no trifle, there is no puzzle, but one design unites and animates the farthest pinnacle and the lowest trench.   "The American Scholar" W I, 110–112

> Daughters of Time, the hypocritic Days,
> Muffled and dumb like barefoot dervishes,
> And marching single in an endless file,
> Bring diadems and fagots in their hands.
> To each they offer gifts after his will,
> Bread, kingdoms, stars, and sky that holds them all.
> I, in my pleachéd garden, watched the pomp,
> Forgot my morning wishes, hastily
> Took a few herbs and apples, and the Day
> Turned and departed silent. I, too late,
> Under her solemn fillet saw the scorn.
>
>   "Days" W IX, 228

If the imagination intoxicates the poet, it is not inactive in other men. The metamorphosis excites in the beholder an emotion of joy. The use of symbols has a certain power of emancipation and exhilaration for all men. We seem to be touched by a wand which makes us dance and run about happily, like children. We are like persons who come out of a cave or cellar into the open air. This is the effect on us of tropes, fables, oracles and all poetic forms. Poets are thus liberating gods. Men have really got a new sense, and found within their world another world, or nest of worlds; for, the metamorphosis once seen, we divine that it does not stop.   "The Poet" W III, 30

It is a secret which every intellectual man quickly learns, that beyond the energy of his possessed and conscious intellect he is capable of a new energy (as of an intellect doubled on itself), by abandonment to the nature of things; that beside his privacy of power as an individual man, there is a great public power on which he can draw, by unlocking, at all risks, his human doors, and suffering the ethereal tides to roll and circulate through him; then he is caught up into the life of the Universe, his speech is thunder, his thought is law, and his words are universally intelligible as the plants and animals. The poet knows that he speaks adequately then only when he speaks somewhat wildly, or "with the flower of the mind"; not with the intellect used as an organ, but with the intellect released from all service and suffered to take its direction from its celestial life; or as the ancients were wont to express themselves, not with intellect alone but with the intellect inebriated by nectar. As the traveler who has lost his way throws his reins on his horse's neck and trusts to the instinct of the animal to find his road, so must we do with the divine animal who carries us through this world. For if in any manner we can stimulate this instinct, new passages are opened for us into nature; the mind flows into and through things hardest and highest, and the metamorphosis is possible. *"The Poet"* W III, 26–27

Valor consists in the power of self-recovery, so that a man cannot have his flank turned, cannot be out-generaled, but put him where you will, he stands. This can only be by his preferring truth to his past apprehension of truth, and his alert acceptance of it from whatever quarter; the intrepid conviction that his laws, his relations to society, his Christianity, his world, may at any time be superseded and decease.
"Circles" W II, 309

I would write on the lintels of the door-post, *Whim.* I hope it is somewhat better than whim at last, but we cannot spend the day in explanation. *"Self-Reliance"* W II, 51–52

Nature ever flows, stands never still. Motion or change is her mode of existence. The poetic eye sees in Man the Brother of the River, & in Woman the Sister of the River. Their life is always transition. Hard blockheads only drive nails all the time; forever remember; which is fixing. Heroes do not fix, but flow, bend forward ever & invent a resource for every moment. *Journal entry* JMN VII, 539–540

Reason is the highest faculty of the soul—what we mean often by the soul itself; it never *reasons,* never proves, it simply perceives; it is vision. The Understanding toils all the time, compares, contrives, adds, argues, near sighted but strong sighted, dwelling in the present the expedient the customary. *Letter to Edward Emerson, 1834* Let I, 412–413

The Understanding possesses the world. It fortifies itself in History, in Laws, in Institutions, in Property, in the prejudice of Birth, of Majorities, in Libraries, in Creeds, in Names; Reason, on the other hand, contents himself with animating a clod of clay somewhere for a moment, & through a word withering all these to old dry cobwebs.

Journal entry JMN VII, 45–46

The same law of eternal procession ranges all that we call the virtues, and extinguishes each in the light of a better. The great man will not be prudent in the popular sense; all his prudence will be so much deduction from his grandeur. But it behooves each to see, when he sacrifices prudence, to what god he devotes it; if to ease and pleasure, he had better be prudent still; if to a great trust, he can well spare his mule and panniers who has a winged chariot instead. Geoffrey draws on his boots to go through the woods, that his feet may be safer from the bite of snakes; Aaron never thinks of such a peril. In many years neither is harmed by

such an accident. Yet it seems to me that with every precaution you take against such an evil you put yourself into the power of the evil.
"Circles" W II, 314–315

But the quality of the imagination is to flow, and not to freeze. The poet did not stop at the color or the form, but read their meaning; neither may he rest in this meaning, but he makes the same objects exponents of his new thought. Here is the difference betwixt the poet and the mystic, that the last nails a symbol to one sense, which was a true sense for a moment, but soon becomes old and false. For all symbols are fluxional; all language is vehicular and transitive, and is good, as ferries and horses are, for conveyance, not as farms and houses are, for homestead. Mysticism consists in the mistake of an accidental and individual symbol for an universal one. *"The Poet"* W III, 34

Let Nature bear the expense. The attitude, the tone, is all. Let our eyes not look away, but meet. Let us not look east and west for materials of conversation, but rest in presence and unity. A just feeling will fast enough supply fuel for discourse, if speaking be more grateful than silence. When people come to see us, we foolishly prattle, lest we be inhospitable. But things said for conversation are chalk eggs. Don't *say* things. What you *are* stands over you the while, and thunders so that I cannot hear what you say to the contrary. *"Social Aims"* W VIII, 96

The truest state of mind, rested in, becomes false. Thought is the manna which cannot be stored. It will be sour if kept, & tomorrow must be gathered anew. . . . Not in his goals but in his transition man is great. *Journal entry* JMN V, 38

A classification or nomenclature used by the scholar only as a memorandum of his last lesson in the laws of Nature, and confessedly a makeshift, a bivouac for a night, and implying a march and a conquest tomorrow—becomes through indolence a barrack and a prison, in which the man sits down immovably, and wishes to detain others.
"The Comic" W VIII, 166–167

If a man should consider the nicety of the passage of a piece of bread down his throat, he would starve. *"Experience"* W III, 58

Words are finite organs of the infinite mind. They cannot cover the dimensions of what is in truth. They break, chop, and impoverish it.
Nature W I, 44–45

It seems as if the present age of words should naturally be followed by an age of silence, when men shall speak only through facts, & so regain their health. We die of words. We are hanged, drawn & quartered by dictionaries. We walk in the vale of shadows. It is an age of hobgoblins.

... When shall we attain to be real, and be born into the new heaven & earth of nature & truth? *Journal entry* JMN VII, 240

Men in all ways are better than they seem. They like flattery for the moment, but they know the truth for their own. It is a foolish cowardice which keeps us from trusting them and speaking to them rude truth. They resent your honesty for an instant, they will thank you for it always. What is it we heartily wish of each other? Is it to be pleased and flattered? No, but to be convicted and exposed, to be shamed out of our nonsense of all kinds, and made men of, instead of ghosts and phantoms. We are weary of gliding ghostlike through the world, which is itself so slight and unreal. We crave a sense of reality, though it comes in strokes of pain. *"New England Reformers"* W III, 273–274

Too feeble fall the impressions of nature on us to make us artists. Every touch should thrill. Every man should be so much an artist that he could report in conversation what had befallen him. Yet, in our experience, the rays or appulses have sufficient force to arrive at the senses, but not enough to reach the quick and compel the reproduction of themselves in speech. *"The Poet"* W III, 6

... the poet is representative. He stands among partial men for the complete man, and apprises us not of his wealth, but of the common wealth. The young man reveres men of genius, because, to speak truly, they are more himself than he is. They receive of the soul as he also receives, but they more. Nature enhances her beauty, to the eye of loving men, from their belief that the poet is beholding her shows at the same time. He is isolated among his contemporaries by truth and by his art, but with this consolation in his pursuits, that they will draw all men sooner or later. For all men live by truth and stand in need of expression. In love, in art, in avarice, in politics, in labor, in games, we study to utter our painful secret. The man is only half himself, the other half is his expression.
"The Poet" W III, 5

I believe the man & the writer should be one, & not diverse, as they say Bancroft, as we know Bulwer is. Wordsworth gives us the image of the true-hearted man, as Milton, Chaucer, Herbert do; not ruffled fine gentlemen who condescend to write like Shaftesbury, Congreve, &, greater far, Walter Scott. Let not the author eat up the man, so that he shall be a balcony & no house. Let him not be turned into a dapper, clerical anatomy, to be assisted like a lady over a gutter or a stone wall. In meeting Milton, I feel that I should encounter a real man but Coleridge is a writer, & Pope, Waller, Addison and Swift and Gibbon, though with attributes, are too modish. It is not Man, but the fashionable wit they would be. Yet Swift has properties. Allston is respectable to me. Novalis, Schiller are only voices, no men. Dr. Johnson was a man though he lived in unfavorable solitude & society of one sort, so that he was an unleavened lump at last on which a genial unfolding had only begun. Humanity cannot be the attribute of these people's writing; humanity, which smiles in Homer, in Chaucer, in Shakespeare, in Milton, in Wordsworth. Montaigne is a man. *Journal entry* JMN V, 425

The intuition of the moral sentiment is an insight of the perfection of the laws of the soul. These laws execute themselves. They are out of time, out of space, and not subject to circumstance. Thus in the soul of man there is a justice whose retributions are instant and entire. He who does a good deed is instantly ennobled. He who does a mean deed is by the action itself contracted. He who puts off impurity, thereby puts on purity. If a man is at heart just, then in so far is he God; the safety of God, the immortality of God, the majesty of God do enter into that man with justice. If a man dissemble, deceive, he deceives himself, and goes out of acquaintance with his own being. A man in the view of absolute goodness, adores, with total humility. Every step so downward, is a step upward. The man who renounces himself, comes to himself.
"Divinity School Address" W I, 122

The gods deal very strictly with us, make out quarterbills, an exact specie payment, allow no partnerships, no stock companies, no arrangements, but hold us personally liable to the last cent. Ah, say I, I cannot do this and that, my cranberry field, my burned woodlot, the rubbish lumber about the summer house, my grass, my crop, my trees—can I not have some partner; can't we organize our new Society of poets and lovers, and have somebody with talent for business to look after these things, some deacons of trees and grass and cranberries, and leave me to letters and philosophy?

But the nettled gods say, No, go to the devil with your arrangements. You, you, you personally, you alone, are to answer body and soul for your things. Leases and covenants are to be punctually signed and sealed.
Journal entry Jour VII, 496

How strongly it came to mind the other eve. at the Teachers' Meeting (as oft before) that nothing needs so much to be preached as the law of Compensation out of the nature of things, that the good exalts & the evil degrades us not hereafter but in the moment of the deed.
Journal entry JMN V, 192

We say Paradise was; Adam fell; the Golden Age; & the like. We mean man is not as he ought to be; but our way of painting this is on Time, and we say *Was*. *Journal entry* JMN V, 371

Culture, the height of culture, highest behavior consist in the identification of the Ego with the universe, so that when a man says I think, I hope, I find,—he might properly say, the human race thinks, hopes, finds, he states a fact which commands the understandings and affections of all the company, and yet, at the same time, he shall be able continually to keep sight of his biographical Ego,—I had an ague, I had a fortune; my father had black hair, etc., as rhetoric, fun, or footman, to his grand and public Ego, without impertinence or ever confounding them.

Journal entry Jour VIII, 79

One key, one solution to the mysteries of human condition, one solution to the old knots of fate, freedom, and foreknowledge, exists; the propounding, namely, of the double consciousness. A man must ride alternately on the horses of his private and his public nature, as the equestrians in the circus throw themselves nimbly from horse to horse, or plant one foot on the back of one and the other foot on the back of the other. *"Fate"* W VI, 49

Our philosophy is to *wait*. We have retreated on Patience, transferring our oft-shattered hope now to larger and eternal good. We meant well, but our uncle was crazy and must be restrained from waking the house. The roof leaked, we were out of wood, our sisters were unmarried and must be maintained; there were taxes to pay, and notes, and, alas, a tomb to build: we were obliged continually to postpone our best action, and that which was life to do could only be smuggled in to odd moments of the month and year. Then we say, Dear God, but the life of man is not by man, it is consentaneous and far-related, it came with the sun and Nature, it is crescive and vegetative, and it is with it as with the sun and the grass. *Journal entry* Jour VII, 520–521

The terrible aristocracy that is in Nature. Real people dwelling with the real, face to face, undaunted: then, far down, people of taste, people dwelling in a relation, or rumor, or influence of good and fair, entertained by it, superficially touched, yet charmed by these shadows—and, far below these, gross and thoughtless, the animal man, billows of chaos, down to the dancing and menial organizations.   *"Aristocracy"* W X, 33

Succession, division, parts, particles—this is the condition, this the tragedy of man. All things cohere & unite. Man studies the parts, strives to tear the part from its connexion, to magnify it, & make it a whole. He sides with the part against other parts; & fights for parts, fights for lies, & his whole mind becomes an *inflamed part*, an amputated member, a wound, an offence. Meantime within him is the soul of the whole, the wise silence, the Universal Beauty to which every part & particle is equally related, the eternal one. Speech is the sign of partiality, difference, ignorance, and the more perfect the understanding between men, the less need of words. And when I know all, I shall cease to commend any part. An ignorant man thinks the divine wisdom is conspicuously shown in some fact or creature: a wise man sees that every fact contains the same. I should think Water the best invention, if I were not acquainted with Fire & Earth & Air. But as we advance, every proposition, every action, every feeling, runs out into the infinite. If we go to affirm anything we are checked in our speech by the need of recognizing all other things, until speech presently becomes rambling, general, indefinite, & merely tautology. The only speech will at last be action, such as Confucius describes the speech of God. *Journal entry* Jour V, *83–84*

It is strange, how simple a thing it is to be a man; so simple that almost all fail by overdoing it. *Journal entry* Jour IV, *55*

TWO ADDRESSES

Many of the foregoing selections are taken from Emerson's best-known essays and addresses—pieces like "Self-Reliance," Nature, *and "The American Scholar." That situation, together with the fact that such pieces are available wherever Emerson's writing is anthologized and is, therefore, easily accessible to the interested student, made it seem useful to turn to less well-known works for this anthology. The first of these, "Being and Seeming," is an address he gave first in January, 1838, in a lecture series that he was presenting in Boston. Its emphasis on personal authenticity catches the spirit of Emerson's earlier work, the product of his thirties and the material that first brought him wide recognition as an exciting speaker and writer. The second selection was delivered as a lecture to audiences in the Middle West when Emerson was in his midfifties, a world-famous man whose most notable literary accomplishments lay behind him. Again he works with a contrast, but this time it is between the outer world of accomplishment (works) and the inner world of experience (days). This polarity complements that on which the earlier lecture was based, for the outward and performance orientation of works was the corollary to seeming, while the solid grounding of the person in the reality of his days was the source of being.*

As both of the selections are essentially oral compositions, they are typical productions in manner as well as in content. Emerson was basically a speaker first and a writer second. His earliest audience was the congregation that he served for several years before his doubts about formal Christianity led to his resignation, and the pulpit manner and the sermon format remained natural throughout his life. Such a background might have led another man into a career of essays and speeches on morality and dogma, but for Emerson it served only as a model for the person who presumes to speak to his fellow men on profound issues of common concern. For him, religion comprehended whatever made the person's life meaningful, whatever gave it depth and height and rescued it from triviality. Both of the following addresses are religious in this sense, and both of them show him at his characteristic best.

BEING AND SEEMING

In my last lecture I considered the powers of affection or the Heart. There is still another sense in which we use the same word the Heart,—a sense scarcely less weighty than that of affection. I mean that of intellectual integrity. The right state of man is (is it not?) Earnestness. What he does, he should do, we say, with the heart. It is the character of all great and good action, speech, and thinking, that it proceeds from Necessity;

that the doer feels it must be. It is done by such relinquishment of caprice and self-will, such abandonment to the promptings of nature and instinct, that the individual agent holds himself no wise accountable. He followed a thread of divine leading and the world is guarantee for his deed.

Do they not make a bridge somewhere of such construction that the strength of the whole is made to bear the strain on any one plank? Do they not sometimes charter banks on the provision that the entire property of all the stockholders is accountable for every dollar note of their issue? Such a bridge, such a bank is a man. In the present discourse I shall confine myself to the illustration of the nature and benefit of this total action, this action from and with the First Cause, as compared with the half action of common life.

I adverted to a fact of much interest in our constitution, namely, the excess of social tendency in us, a certain otherism or overregard to the virtues and opinions of society. These social relations which in their health are called the Heart do certainly exercise their pernicious effect also. If a man lived alone it is plain he could never act foolishly, never with affection, but always he would be in earnest. It is with Society that Seeming comes in. The child is sincere, and the man when he is alone; but on the entrance of the second person hypocrisy begins. When the eyes of men behold him, he breaks his being into shows. Society is full of pretension. Augur keeps augur in countenance. One vocation another. All the professions are timid, tentative, and traditional. The youthful practitioners who enter them are overawed by the authority and the extent of the routine nor venture for a long time to break its magical circle. Afterwards when they might from experience and matured judgment be supposed competent to rate forms at their worth, they still find routine so much easier than creation, routine so inoffensive and so commodious that they cry also, Great is Diana.

Hence the tedium of life; hence the ennui. Hence the million drunk with the opium of time and custom. See to what paltry uses it is put. I find it the worst thing in life that I can put it to no better use. As we drive the matter it wants worthy objects sadly. But which way shall I turn? Where get a mode of occupation that is fit? It is not that not I, it is that nobody employs it well. A young man of real greatness of soul must condescend very far to make the dignity of either of the professions or the chairs of the state or any accepted mode of practical ability altogether satisfactory to his ambition. Who does not find his vocation some obstacle to the exhibition of majestic traits, to the flow of his being into adequate action? Who does not find his profession cripple his imagination, his affection, his invention? Who remembers in its exercise the dreams of his youth? Who ascends steadily to purer heights of the Ideal?

The redemption from this ruin must come from a reliance on the instincts. We want a greater faith in human nature. We do not sufficiently discriminate between what appears and what is. Indeed Culture has got on so little way that men are hardly agreed often, which is the real and which the apparent. Bread and flesh men think are real; and thought and will they think are less real. A man esteems himself as a mere circumstance and not as the container of the central mundane nature. He thinks his spiritual parts vanishing opaline colors which will not bear scrutiny or description. Let him try them and come again after twenty years. Let him compare them with things called durable. He will find they outshine the sun; and will grind to powder, the iron and the diamond of outward permanence. You see two men of opposite tendency, one boasting himself a practical man and so wedded to that which can be touched, smelled, and tasted that he seems like steel bars and granite ledges: and the other so entirely wrapt in his meditations on the Absolute Cause of all things, that he has become ridiculous by his inattention to sensible objects, and, as we say, can hardly keep himself out of fire and water. It should moderate our mirth to reflect that this eternal superiority belongs to the contemplative man over his more forcible and honored neighbor; that the former moves in a real world, the latter in a phenomenal; that though the seasons of the former's activity may be rare and with intermissions of gloom and pain, yet when he works, it is life, properly so called; whilst the latter's endless activity and boundless pretension reminds us too often of the poor laborer whom a mistaken charity employed all winter in shovelling one ton of coal from the yard to the cellar and back again from the cellar to the yard.

Yet grave, inquiring moments come to every man amid the heedless hurry and din of living, in which he asks himself the question, Is not all that I behold a fleeting apparition? And what is it that in this running sea endures?

He feels that Something Is. Amid a world of shows he is very conscious of an underlying substance. The oath that is heard in the street and the jargon profanity of boys points not less distinctly than a church at the conviction in man of absolute being as distinct from apparent and derivative nature. Oaths invoke the sun, the moon, St. Paul, Jesus, and God as witness that the speaker speaks truth. I suppose they refer to that conviction suggested by every object that something *Is*, and signify, *If anything is*, then I did so and so. They import something separate from and superior to the will of the individual. By Day and Night, By Jupiter, By St. Nicholas, etc. that is, My will which interferes to color and change all objects, interferes not here. This is. Every man is very conscious of the presence of this reality to his own existence. It is the ground of his being. Let him lean upon it and he is immensely strong. Now to the end of Culture why might not a little minority of men leave others to Seem, and themselves trust Being? Why may you not say—"I abjure pretension. I will doom myself if need be to endless lowness, but I at least will be true. I will not move my hand,—I will not wag my tongue, beyond what the need is, though I should sit still a month. I bear society no ill will. I am willing the powers that be, and the shows that show, should last as long as time, so they do not insist on my cooperation and good word. If they do, I draw myself into the shell of a deaf and dumb contumacy." — Studiously, morosely, let him fall back upon nature, and empty himself of all seeming. If he can do nothing else, let him abstain from doing; let him sit still; let him sleep. Sleeping is as expressive as waking. So dear to us is nature that whatever resolves and destroys individual will, and shows us instead the overpowering force of nature, is always commanding.

Such is sickness; such is silence; such [is] sleep; such is death. Everybody is respectable when he is silent. It is said, there is somewhat awful in sleep. And so death instantly elevates with a certain sublimity the corpse of a vagabond or a felon.

It may be stated as the end of Culture to teach us to Be. I cheerfully trust so far the goodness of the First Cause as to believe that if I adhere to nature, nor go one hairsbreadth beyond my card, I shall not be worse. In this low-levelled aim, simply *to be,* there will not be competition, and need not be failure. To shine, to dazzle, to shake the world, demands rare talents. Few have Beauty or Manners or Command; but Nature holds out an universal invitation to Be.

The invitation is resisted by a compunction. The young man relying on his instincts who has only a good intention is apt to feel ashamed of his inaction and the slightness of his virtue when in the presence of the active and zealous leaders of the philanthropic enterprizes, of Universal Temperance, Peace, and Freedom. He only loves like Cordelia after his duty. Trust it nevertheless. A man's income is not sufficient for all things. If he spend here he must save there. If he choose to build a solid hearth he must postpone painting or raising a cupola. Let each follow his own taste but let not him who loves fine porticoes and avenues reprove him that chooses to have all weathertight and solid within. It is a grandeur of character which must have unity, and reviews and pries ever into its domestic truth and justice, loving quiet probity better than a proclaiming zeal. But this good intention which seems so cheap beside this other brave zeal, is the backbone of the world: when the trumpeters and heralds have been scattered, it is this which must bear the brunt of the fight. This is the martyrable stuff. Let it for God's sake, grow free and wild under wind, under sun, to be solid heart of oak, and last forever.

Let a man empty himself of all display even if thereto he need to stop all action. Inaction will not last long. Action is as natural and inevitable as rest and presently he will be impelled to do somewhat which he can do in as great a mind as his repose. He that waits for this rising of the general tide in his particular creek or bay, he that does nothing until he can act wholly and earnestly has the immense advantage of not being a part but of merging his private nature in the world and he makes on you the same refreshing impression that stars and waters do. His action, his word gives to vulgar actions and words an impertinent and mean appearance whilst the air gladly bears his accents and the sun and moon shine friendly on his form.

Such action has the inexhaustible strength of nature. A man will presently weary in acting a part. The fatigue of violent exertions soon stops them. But the man of instinct is equally able after he has dealt his stroke, for a new blow. And, indeed, his power is cumulative, and his present moment is always reinforced by the entire mass of foregone natural actions. I have heard a man speak on false information and very limited views to such disadvantage, that it was very easy for the next speaker to discredit all his statements and quite dislodge him from all his positions. I pitied the first speaker and felt pain for him, until in some casual intercourse I presently found that he was as glad as any to be set right, that he was not in the least disheartened, nor had so much as looked at the effect of his speech, but was in perfect spirits, and eager to speak again on a new matter which he had much at heart. Then I pity him no more. I see him to be destined to move society.

I have heard an experienced counsellor say that he feared never for the effect upon a jury of a lawyer who does not believe in his heart that his client ought to have a verdict. If he does not believe it, his unbelief will appear to the jury, despite all his protestations, and become their unbelief. This is that law, (is it not?) whereby a work of art, of whatever kind, sets us in the same state of mind as the artist was when he made it. That which we do not believe, we cannot adequately say, though we may repeat the words never so often. It was this conviction which Swedenborg expressed when he described a group of persons in the spiritual world endeavoring in vain to articulate a proposition which they did not believe, but they could not, though they twisted and folded their lips even to indignation. But say what you believe and feel, and the voluble air will become music and all surrounding things will dance attendance and coin themselves into words for your sense. Every word shall be sovereign, noble, and new, and full of matchless felicities. The way to avoid mannerism, the way to speak or to write what shall not go out of fashion, is to speak or write sincerely, to transcribe your doubt, or regret, or whatever state of mind, without the airs of a fine gentleman or great philosopher, without timidity or display, casting on God the responsibility of the facts. This is to dare.

Truth always overpowers the poor nature of a deceiver and shines through the very fables in which it was attempted to be hidden. In literary history, Moore's life of Sheridan is a flagrant example of a book which damns itself. The writer aims to secure our sympathies for Sheridan, our tears for his misfortune and poverty, our admiration for his genius, and our indignation against the king and grandees who befriended that butterfly in his prosperity, and forsook him in his jail. He details the life of a mean, fraudulent, vain, quarrelsome player, whose wit lay in cheating tradesmen, whose genius was used in studying jokes and bonmots at home for a dinner or a club; who laid traps for the admiration of coxcombs; who never did anything good and never said anything wise. He came, as he deserved, to a bad end. In short, the whole life is the life of a seemer, with its just retribution and, contrasting as it does all along with the life of Burke, a man of heart and a man in earnest who spoke what he thought, redounds to the infamy of one and to the other's renown.

Trust *being* and let us seem no longer. Perhaps we shall find the mild satisfactions of merely constituting a part of nature, and witnessing in obscurity the ongoing of the world, and of being as far as we go, solid, some compensation for ceasing to glitter. Presently a greater insight into the law of the world, will dissipate all our fears. We may feel how idle is all curiosity concerning other people's estimate of us: how idle is the discontent at remaining unknown. If a man know that he can do any thing: that he can do it better than any one else: he has a perfect assurance before him of an acknowledgment of that fact by all persons, as surely as his shadow follows his body. The world is full of Judgment Days and into every assembly that a man enters, in every action he attempts, he is gauged and stamped. In every troop of boys that whoop and run in each yard and square, a newcomer is as well and accurately weighed in the balance in the course of a few days, stamped, (so to speak,) with his right number, as if he had undergone a formal trial of his strength, speed, and temper. A stranger comes from a distant school with better dress, with trinkets in his pockets, with airs and pretension: an old boy sniffs thereat and says to himself, It's of no use, we shall find him out tomorrow.

In the education of women most unhappily society seem to have lost sight of so much confidence in truth as they elsewhere manifest, and aim not at Being but primarily at Appearance. Especially does this doctrine address itself to women in whom the tendency of example, of precept, of constitution, I might almost say, and of their first experience is almost irresistible in favor of preferring appearances. Let them know that whatever they think they have seen to the contrary it is not the form or the face, much less the skill of dress that conquers opinion and hearts, but that faces are urns into which they may infuse an inexpressible loveliness, and that everything they do, every noble choice they make, every forbearance, every virtue, beautifies them with a charm to all beholders. Let them know that as God liveth they that be shall have, and not they that seem. One class win now, glitter, and disappear; the other class begins and grows and becomes for ever. Already I see an early old age creeping over faces that were yesterday rosebuds—because they aimed to seem: I see again the divinity of hope and power beaming out of eyes that never sparkled with gratified vanity.

It is not to be denied that extreme difficulties will attend any man's effort to make himself thoroughly genuine. But let him trust to Being and let him fortify himself on all sides by habitual reflection on the true position of man in nature.

Do not profess anything. Why need you take it upon you at every turn to answer for the Universe? Why need we be so wise? The first questions are still to be asked, after we have studied and reasoned fifty years: and a philosopher who has run the round of the sciences, may be gravelled by a child at his supper table. A question is asked of the understanding which lies in the province of the Reason; and the understanding foolishly tries to make an answer. Our constructiveness overpowers our love of truth. How noble is it, when the mourner looks for comfort in your face, to give only sympathy and confession; confession that it is great grief and the greater because we are not yet arrived at the apprehension of its nature. But thus you baulk expectation. Be it so. Who set you up for professor, omniscience, and showman to the Universe? Why teach? Learn rather. Learn and Wait. "They also serve who only stand and wait."

In a true and ingenuous mind the appeal is always being made to the future. The boy we know is allowed to be ignorant and helpless because of the tacit appeal to what he shall be and do. Then comes the young man, the young woman; they have studied much Latin and German, but do not know the meaning of this sentence and are ashamed to use the dictionary, or to say,—I do not know. In like manner, to the adult come the great questions that always besiege the human reason, and he is tempted in his turn to dogmatize. Consent to be despised as ignorant now, and boldly appeal to the future still. You are old if you reckon the short human life but if you compare your years with the eternity into which you advance, to your extreme youth this unskilfulness will appear very reasonable. And this I think is the reason why genius is said to retain the feelings and freshness of childhood, because to it the horizon does not shut down a short way before the eye, but opens indefinitely. Be a spectator with all others of the great agencies of the world nor purse up your mouth as if behind the curtain in the secret of God. Be for once a guest in nature. Do not speak but hear. For once bask in beauty and do not always govern the nation, manage commerce, or carry on a farm. Need we be such stone-blind bats that the whole beauty of heaven and earth and sea and man cannot entertain us unless we too must hold a candle and bedabble God's world with a smutch of our own insignificance?

This patience and trust—patience with obscurity, nay sometimes with a painful sense of imbecility; and this trust that if a man will but stand by the truth, it will stand by him and advance him infinitely—this patience and trust shall not lose their reward. Indeed it almost seems superfluous to repeat these saws, but that life all around us forgets and denies them.

There is very little life in a lifetime. Who can point to an individual who acts, who does anything more than accept the decorum, the standards of value, the vocations, and the vices of society? So much of our time is preparation, so much is routine, and so much is retrospect that the real pith of each man's genius seems to contract itself to a very few hours. There is very little life in a lifetime.

As the history of literature—get the net result of Tiraboschi, Warton, or Schlegel—is a story of very few ideas and of very few original tales;—the rest is imitation and variation of these: So in this great society wide lying around us a critical analysis would find very few spontaneous actions. Almost all is custom or mere obedience to the senses. A new action is one which flows from character; it is a new hearkening to the divine oracle and instantly strikes us as a creation. A new action commands us and is the Napoleon or Luther of the hour. So with Manners. They are sometimes the unequivocal expression of the mind, a perpetual creation, and so do charm and govern us. So with opinions. An opinion is seldom given. Everyone we have heard weighs with us. Let an opinion be given upon a book or a public transaction; the indolence of the general mind is proved by the circulation this sentence has. It runs through a round of newspapers and social circles and finds mere acquiescence in thousands. If the subject is one which has a political or commercial bearing it commonly happens that another individual protests against the opinion and affirms his own to be just the reverse. In that case still I should think is there but one opinion affirmed or denied; there is yet no new quality shown.

And yet whilst we and all Society go floating thus down stream, shrinking from the declaration of individual independence and a man's subjugation of his practices and allowances to his Reason and so the deliberate originating of his deed, yet do all the facts of life preach to us that we should aim to Be. For only so much as truth and reality come in, does life rise to any civility and power. And the plausibilities and appearances of the world owe all their permanence to what fraction of sincere virtue and truth lies beneath them. The forms of Government, of Religion, of Education fill the eye, but the form contributes nothing to the strength. The virtue of society is really the basis of its stability. The existence of society indicates the presence of virtue in its upholders. In complaining of the seeming and half death of society I neither wish nor dare to disparage the virtue, so much reverenced by all, of the hundreds of good men and good women who are the pride and honor of every social circle. It is very shallow to think the world full of vice because the conventions of society when measured by an ideal standard are little worth. Adam and John, Edith and Mary are generous, tenderhearted, and of scrupulous conscience whilst as yet they are entirely immersed in these poor forms and conventions. Mint, anise, and cummin do not make them unhappy for they have never discriminated these from truth and justice. They may attain much growth too before they shall become critical and impatient of all but what is real. By and by that unfolding will come also and then they will snap asunder many cords of mere leather and twine.

But those who desire to see a more virtuous state of society cannot afford to undervalue these present merits. They see a solid benefit in the common, well-meaning, private person. In each village, in each neighborhood, in each family connexion who does not discern some one individual on whose worth and good nature as on a main column the municipal, the ecclesiastical, the social order leans?

Thus Life preaches by conspicuous examples Being. But not only is the actual fabric of Society upheld by what real life it encloses but furthermore falsehood is a suicide, defeats its own end, for it is always unlovely, tedious, and barren. A man lives for display. Why? That he may attract of course love or respect, but now see how love and respect are always stealing away from the false to the true, for we are interested only by reality and the fact is, To Seem you must Be.

Children are sincere. The child is thoroughly in earnest; and the child's movements are all beautiful. A man as earnest as a child would attract us also. As the contemporaries of Columbus hungered to see the wild man so undoubtedly we should have the liveliest interest in a wild man who exhibited the wild virtues of the stock, man. But men in society do not interest us because they are tame. We know all they will do and man is like man as one steamboat is like another. Tame men are tedious, like the talking with a young fop who says *Yes Sir* indifferently to every sort of thing you say thinking *Yes Sir* to mean nothing.

From every man, even from great men as the world goes, a large deduction is to be made on account of this taming or conventions. His going to church does not interest me because all men go to church. His staying at home would until I see why he stays at home; if from vulgar reasons it is dulness still.

But he falls desperately in love. Ah, does he? Now I am awake. This is not conventional but the great epoch of the revelation of beauty to his soul. Now let me see every line he writes; every step he makes; the rosy light which is shed over books, papers, yes, and streets too; let me hear his confessions and his vows. There walks not on this planet the man sage or savage who is passionately in love whose deportment and thoughts, could they be witnessed or reported, would not instantly engage our interest. Such is the constant charm of reality. Our interest in men of genius,—what is it, but, (so to speak) interest in the wild man? for genius is only the listening to the soul and the utterance of the soul.

We are eager to know what Shakspear said at the Boar's Head in Eastcheap. We should like to see him in his own tenement bring wood to his fire or walking in his field. We would see what book he chose to entertain a solitary evening or refusing all books what he did. Rather would I know how he looked at the Supreme Being in some lonely hour of fear or gratitude, hear what he said, or know what he forbore to say.

I know that a natural association of ideas consecrates what is conventional and trivial in a great man. Boswellism scrapes all together and would know how the hero did what every body does and what he did as every body does it. But the philosopher drops all the conventional part and only studies the new and voluntary part of each man. As far as Sir Walter Scott aspired to be known for a fine gentleman so far our sympathies leave him. We know very well the height of that doll and do not suppose he was any finer gentleman than Lord Chesterfield or Beau Brummell. Our concern is only with the residue where the man Scott was warmed with a divine ray that clad with beauty every sheet of water, every bald hill in the country he looked upon and so reanimated the well-nigh obsolete feudal history and illustrated every hidden corner of a barren and disagreeable territory.

Scott seems to me not to have been a great poet but to have had one talent, a sort of *clairvoyance,* so that no man died to him but whatever he knew of the history of a house or a hamlet or a glen instantly reproduced the ghosts of the departed in form and habit as when they lived, the moment he looked on the spot. This reverence for great men I think betrays always our deep sympathy with the real and what approximates the real. Yet our love of greatness always seems to me the prophecy of greatness in the lover. We cleave to genius, to truth, to power because they are our own soul, and as we have not yet learned to know it within we at least worship it in others. But there is a higher vision awaiting the lovers of truth, the contemners of pretension. They shall not only receive but impart. They shall not only see but do. For Nature and the soul is but one in us all.

For what is Genius but this very love of reality? A soul disdaining shows and exposing shows out of love of sincere and enduring substance. "Some minds," said Schelling, "speak about things; some minds speak the things themselves." Genius is a spontaneous soul; one which does not accept from others but speaks from its own insight and to us therefore always appears creative. It makes; but making always rests in Being. Yet this should all men do and thus should all men be. Every man has acted, has spoken if but once in his lifetime from his character, from himself. Then he was in the right path.

And when I say that all men have genius and will at some time be as creative as the poet, the orator, the artist it is not because I think society shows now any great degree of reality and life. It is rather wonderful how little leaven is in the lump, how little original action, thought, or art there is. Ordinarily we speak of creators as a small class and intimate difference of kind. One can sketch with invention. Others can draw as well but cannot design. One can sing as he or she has learned. Another shows character, a certain sally of the heart in every note. One speaks always in set phrase. Another's conversation surprises with unheard of combinations at each turn.

I look upon this as difference in degree and that the powers of all are the same. The veriest plodder we can conceive as instantly soaring by trusting himself more. I call it self-distrust, a fear to launch away into the deep which they might freely and safely do. It is as if the dolphins should float on rafts or creep or squirm along the shore in fear to trust themselves to the element which is really native to them. The advice which Blind Willie the fiddler in Scott's tale of Redgauntlet gives to young Darsie Latimer who had executed an ostentatious flourish on his instrument "Ye maun learn to put the heart into it, man,—to put the heart into it," is good forever and for all.

What is really good is ever a new creation. It is our reverence for being over seeming that gives always so humble a place in society to the theatrical profession which consists in seeming. You cannot help pitying the performers at the opera in their fillets and shields and togas and being pained by their strained and unsuccessful exertions, remembering even their long toilette and personal mortification at making such a figure. There they stand, the same poor Johns and Antonios they were in the morning for all their gilt and pasteboard. But the moment the primadonna utters one tone or makes a gesture of natural passion it puts life into the dead scene. You pity them no more. It is not a ghost of departed things, not an old Greece and Rome but a Greece and Rome of this moment. It is living merit which takes ground with all other merit of whatever kind, with beauty, nobility, genius, power.

I believe, as I intimated in the beginning of this discourse, that the only medicine which voluntary effort can bring to the cure of Society is a wise exploring of the power of man. We want faith in Human Nature. I observe that very good and learned persons are shocked never more easily than by any broad assertion of the fathomless powers of a man. So very lowly are the popular ideas of the soul that it seems to men blasphemy to intimate any equality of nature and hope between themselves and one or two holy men whose biography is recorded in history. As if it were possible that this infinite essence with which we all aspire, round which as round a central fire we all are warmed could yet have been circumscribed and exhausted in a single life, in a few actions. We do not honor the great God by setting so quick a bound to this germinating, ever-creating life with which he fills us, and which we are. It shines in us, evermore holy and beautiful, inviting us upward from height to height, inviting us outward from object to object; always transforming the condition of the man into better conformity with his affections and thoughts; always bringing the beautiful to the true; so that the tendency forever is to make him who is just and brave, the delight of men and happy with the happiness of God. EL 295–309

Works and Days

Our nineteenth century is the age of tools. They grew out of our structure. "Man is the meter of all things," said Aristotle; "the hand is the instrument of instruments, and the mind is the form of forms." The human body is the magazine of inventions, the patent office, where are the models from which every hint was taken. All the tools and engines on earth are only extensions of its limbs and senses. One definition of man is "an intelligence served by organs." Machines can only second, not supply, his unaided senses. The body is a meter. The eye appreciates finer differences than art can expose. The apprentice clings to his foot-rule; a practised mechanic will measure by his thumb and his arm with equal precision; and a good surveyor will pace sixteen rods more accurately than another man can measure them by tape. The sympathy of eye and hand by which an Indian or a practised slinger hits his mark with a stone, or a wood-chopper or a carpenter swings his axe to a hair-line on his log, are examples; and there is no sense or organ which is not capable of exquisite performance.

Men love to wonder, and that is the seed of our science; and such is the mechanical determination of our age, and so recent are our best contrivances, that use has not dulled our joy and pride in them; and we pity our fathers for dying before steam and galvanism, sulphuric ether and ocean telegraphs, photograph and spectroscope arrived, as cheated out of half their human estate. These arts open great gates of a future, promising to make the world plastic and to lift human life out of its beggary to a godlike ease and power.

Our century to be sure had inherited a tolerable apparatus. We had the compass, the printing-press, watches, the spiral spring, the barometer, the telescope. Yet so many inventions have been added that life seems almost made over new; and as Leibnitz said of Newton, that "if he reckoned all that had been done by mathematicians from the beginning of the world down to Newton, and what had been done by him, his would be the better half," so one might say that the inventions of the last fifty years counterpoise those of the fifty centuries before them. For the vast production and manifold application of iron is new; and our common and indispensable utensils of house and farm are new; the sewing-machine, the power-loom, the McCormick reaper, the mowing-machines, gaslight, lucifer matches, and the immense productions of the laboratory, are new in this century, and one franc's worth of coal does the work of a laborer for twenty days.

Why need I speak of steam, the enemy of space and time, with its enormous strength and delicate applicability, which is made in hospitals to bring a bowl of gruel to a sick man's bed, and can twist beams of iron like candy-braids, and vies with the forces which upheaved and doubled over the geologic strata? Steam is an apt scholar and a strong-shouldered fellow, but it has not yet done all its work. It already walks about the field like a man, and will do anything required of it. It irrigates crops, and drags away a mountain. It must sew our shirts, it must drive our gigs; taught by Mr. Babbage, it must calculate interest and logarithms. Lord Chancellor Thurlow thought it might be made to draw bills and answers in chancery. If that were satire, it is yet coming to render many higher services of a mechanico-intellectual kind, and will leave the satire short of the fact.

How excellent are the mechanical aids we have applied to the human body, as in dentistry, in vaccination, in the rhinoplastic treatment; in the beautiful aid of ether, like a finer sleep; and in the boldest promiser of all,—the transfusion of the blood,—which, in Paris, it was claimed, enables a man to change his blood as often as his linen!

What of this dapper caoutchouc and gutta-percha, which make water-pipes and stomach-pumps, belting for mill-wheels, and diving-bells, and rain-proof coats for all climates, which teach us to defy the wet, and put every man on a footing with the beaver and the crocodile? What of the grand tools with which we engineer, like kobolds and enchanters, tunnelling Alps, canalling the American Isthmus, piercing the Arabian desert? In Massachusetts we fight the sea successfully with beach-grass and broom, and the blowing sand-barrens with pine plantations. The soil of Holland, once the most populous in Europe, is below the level of the sea. Egypt, where no rain fell for three thousand years, now, it is said, thanks Mehemet Ali's irrigations and planted forests for late-returning showers. The old Hebrew king said, "He makes the wrath of man to praise him." And there is no argument of theism better than the grandeur of ends brought about by paltry means. The chain of Western railroads from Chicago to the Pacific has planted cities and civilization in less time than it costs to bring an orchard into bearing.

What shall we say of the ocean telegraph, that extension of the eye and ear, whose sudden performance astonished mankind as if the intellect were taking the brute earth itself into training, and shooting the first thrills of life and thought through the unwilling brain?

There does not seem any limit to these new informations of the same Spirit that made the elements at first, and now, through man, works them. Art and power will go on as they have done,—will make day out of night, time out of space, and space out of time.

Invention breeds invention. No sooner is the electric telegraph devised than gutta-percha, the very material it requires, is found. The aëronaut is provided with gun-cotton, the very fuel he wants for his balloon. When commerce is vastly enlarged, California and Australia expose the gold it needs. When Europe is over-populated, America and Australia crave to be peopled; and so throughout, every chance is timed, as if Nature, who made the lock, knew where to find the key.

Another result of our arts is the new intercourse which is surprising us with new solutions of the embarrassing political problems. The intercourse is not new, but the scale is new. Our selfishness would have held slaves, or would have excluded from a quarter of the planet all that are not born on the soil of that quarter. Our politics are disgusting; but what can they help or hinder when from time to time the primal instincts are impressed on masses of mankind, when the nations are in exodus and flux? Nature loves to cross her stocks,—and German, Chinese, Turk, Russ and Kanaka were putting out to sea, and intermarrying race with race; and commerce took the hint, and ships were built capacious enough to carry the people of a county.

This thousand-handed art has introduced a new element into the state. The science of power is forced to remember the power of science. Civilization mounts and climbs. Malthus, when he stated that the mouths went on multiplying geometrically and the food only arithmetically, forgot to say that the human mind was also a factor in political economy, and that the augmenting wants of society would be met by an augmenting power of invention.

Yes, we have a pretty artillery of tools now in our social arrangements: we ride four times as fast as our fathers did; travel, grind, weave, forge, plant, till and excavate better. We have new shoes, gloves, glasses and gimlets; we have the calculus; we have the newspaper, which does its best to make every square acre of land and sea give an account of itself at your breakfast-table; we have money, and paper money; we have language,—the finest tool of all, and nearest to the mind. Much will have more. Man flatters himself that his command over Nature must increase. Things begin to obey him. We are to have the balloon yet, and the next war will be fought in the air. We may yet find a rose-water that will wash the negro white. He sees the skull of the English race changing from its Saxon type under the exigencies of American life.

Tantalus, who in old times was seen vainly trying to quench his thirst with a flowing stream which ebbed whenever he approached it, has been seen again lately. He is in Paris, in New York, in Boston. He is now in great spirits; thinks he shall reach it yet; thinks he shall bottle the wave. It is however getting a little doubtful. Things have an ugly look still. No matter how many centuries of culture have preceded, the new man always finds himself standing on the brink of chaos, always in a crisis.

Can anybody remember when the times were not hard, and money not scarce? Can anybody remember when sensible men, and the right sort of men, and the right sort of women, were plentiful? Tantalus begins to think steam a delusion, and galvanism no better than it should be.

Many facts concur to show that we must look deeper for our salvation than to steam, photographs, balloons or astronomy. These tools have some questionable properties. They are reagents. Machinery is aggressive. The weaver becomes a web, the machinist a machine. If you do not use the tools, they use you. All tools are in one sense edge-tools, and dangerous. A man builds a fine house; and now he has a master, and a task for life: he is to furnish, watch, show it, and keep it in repair, the rest of his days. A man has a reputation, and is no longer free, but must respect that. A man makes a picture or a book, and, if it succeeds, 't is often the worse for him. I saw a brave man the other day, hitherto as free as the hawk or the fox of the wilderness, constructing his cabinet of drawers for shells, eggs, minerals and mounted birds. It was easy to see that he was amusing himself with making pretty links for his own limbs.

Then the political economist thinks " 't is doubtful if all the mechanical inventions that ever existed have lightened the day's toil of one human being." The machine unmakes the man. Now that the machine is so perfect, the engineer is nobody. Every new step in improving the engine restricts one more act of the engineer,—unteaches him. Once it took Archimedes; now it only needs a fireman, and a boy to know the coppers, to pull up the handles or mind the water-tank. But when the engine breaks, they can do nothing.

What sickening details in the daily journals! I believe they have ceased to publish the Newgate Calendar and the Pirate's Own Book since the family newspapers, namely the New York Tribune and the London Times, have quite superseded them in the freshness as well as the horror of their records of crime. Politics were never more corrupt and brutal; and Trade, that pride and darling of our ocean, that educator of nations, that benefactor in spite of itself, ends in shameful defaulting, bubble and bankruptcy, all over the world.

Of course we resort to the enumeration of his arts and inventions as a measure of the worth of man. But if, with all his arts, he is a felon, we cannot assume the mechanical skill or chemical resources as the measure of worth. Let us try another gauge.

What have these arts done for the character, for the worth of mankind? Are men better? 'T is sometimes questioned whether morals have not declined as the arts have ascended. Here are great arts and little men. Here is greatness begotten of paltriness. We cannot trace the triumphs of civilization to such benefactors as we wish. The greatest meliorator of the world is selfish, huckstering Trade. Every victory over matter ought to recommend to man the worth of his nature. But now one wonders who did all this good. Look up the inventors. Each has his own knack; his genius is in veins and spots. But the great, equal, symmetrical brain, fed from a great heart, you shall not find. Every one has more to hide than he has to show, or is lamed by his excellence. 'T is too plain that with the material power the moral progress has not kept pace. It appears that we have not made a judicious investment. Works and days were offered us, and we took works.

The new study of the Sanskrit has shown us the origin of the old names of God,—Dyaus, Deus, Zeus, Zeu pater, Jupiter,—names of the sun, still recognizable through the modifications of our vernacular words, importing that the Day is the Divine Power and Manifestation, and indicating that those ancient men, in their attempts to express the Supreme Power of the universe, called him the Day, and that this name was accepted by all the tribes.

Hesiod wrote a poem which he called Works and Days, in which he marked the changes of the Greek year, instructing the husbandman at the rising of what constellation he might safely sow, when to reap, when to gather wood, when the sailor might launch his boat in security from storms, and what admonitions of the planets he must heed. It is full of economies for Grecian life, noting the proper age for marriage, the rules of household thrift and of hospitality. The poem is full of piety as well as prudence, and is adapted to all meridians by adding the ethics of works and of days. But he has not pushed his study of days into such inquiry and analysis as they invite.

A farmer said "he should like to have all the land that joined his own." Bonaparte, who had the same appetite, endeavored to make the Mediterranean a French lake. Czar Alexander was more expansive, and wished to call the Pacific *my ocean;* and the Americans were obliged to resist his attempts to make it a close sea. But if he had the earth for his pasture and the sea for his pond, he would be a pauper still. He only is rich who owns the day. There is no king, rich man, fairy or demon who possesses such power as that. The days are ever divine as to the first Aryans. They are of the least pretension and of the greatest capacity of anything that exists. They come and go like muffled and veiled figures, sent from a distant friendly party; but they say nothing, and if we do not use the gifts they bring, they carry them as silently away.

How the day fits itself to the mind, winds itself round it like a fine drapery, clothing all its fancies! Any holiday communicates to us its color. We wear its cockade and favors in our humor. Remember what boys think in the morning of "Election day," of the Fourth of July, of Thanksgiving or Christmas. The very stars in their courses wink to them of nuts and cakes, bonbons, presents and fire-works. Cannot memory still descry the old school-house and its porch, somewhat hacked by jack-knives, where you spun tops and snapped marbles; and do you not recall that life was then calendared by moments, threw itself into nervous knots of glittering hours, even as now, and not spread itself abroad an equable felicity? In college terms, and in years that followed, the young graduate, when the Commencement anniversary returned, though he were in a swamp, would see a festive light and find the air faintly echoing with plausive academic thunders. In solitude and in the country, what dignity distinguishes the holy time! The old Sabbath, or Seventh Day, white with the religions of unknown thousands of years, when this hallowed hour dawns out of the deep,—a clean page, which the wise may inscribe with truth, whilst the savage scrawls it with fetishes,—the cathedral music of history breathes through it a psalm to our solitude.

So, in the common experience of the scholar, the weathers fit his moods. A thousand tunes the variable wind plays, a thousand spectacles it brings, and each is the frame or dwelling of a new spirit. I used formerly to choose my time with some nicety for each favorite book. One author is good for winter, and one for the dog-days. The scholar must look long for the right hour for Plato's Timæus. At last the elect morning arrives, the early dawn,—a few lights conspicuous in the heaven, as of a world just created and still becoming,—and in its wide leisures we dare open that book.

There are days when the great are near us, when there is no frown on their brow, no condescension even; when they take us by the hand, and we share their thought. There are days which are the carnival of the year. The angels assume flesh, and repeatedly become visible. The imagination of the gods is excited and rushes on every side into forms. Yesterday not a bird peeped; the world was barren, peaked and pining: to-day 't is inconceivably populous; creation swarms and meliorates.

The days are made on a loom whereof the warp and woof are past and future time. They are majestically dressed, as if every god brought a thread to the skyey web. 'T is pitiful the things by which we are rich or poor,—a matter of coins, coats and carpets, a little more or less stone, or wood, or paint, the fashion of a cloak or hat; like the luck of naked Indians, of whom one is proud in the possession of a glass bead or a red feather, and the rest miserable in the want of it. But the treasures which Nature spent itself to amass,—the secular, refined, composite anatomy of man, which all strata go to form, which the prior races, from infusory and saurian, existed to ripen; the surrounding plastic natures; the earth with its foods; the intellectual, temperamenting air; the sea with its invitations; the heaven deep with worlds; and the answering brain and nervous structure replying to these; the eye that looketh into the deeps, which again look back to the eye, abyss to abyss;—these, not like a glass bead, or the coins or carpets, are given immeasurably to all.

This miracle is hurled into every beggar's hands. The blue sky is a covering for a market and for the cherubim and seraphim. The sky is the varnish or glory with which the Artist has washed the whole work,—the verge or confines of matter and spirit. Nature could no farther go. Could our happiest dream come to pass in solid fact,—could a power open our eyes to behold "millions of spiritual creatures walk the earth,"—I believe I should find that mid-plain on which they moved floored beneath and arched above with the same web of blue depth which weaves itself over me now, as I trudge the streets on my affairs.

It is singular that our rich English language should have no word to denote the face of the world. *Kinde* was the old English term, which, however, filled only half the range of our fine Latin word, with its delicate future tense,—*natura, about to be born,* or what German philosophy denotes as a *becoming.* But nothing expresses that power which seems to work for beauty alone. The Greek *Kosmos* did; and therefore, with great propriety, Humboldt entitles his book, which recounts the last results of science, *Cosmos.*

Such are the days,—the earth is the cup, the sky is the cover, of the immense bounty of Nature which is offered us for our daily aliment; but what a force of *illusion* begins life with us and attends us to the end! We are coaxed, flattered and duped from morn to eve, from birth to death; and where is the old eye that ever saw through the deception? The Hindoos represent Maia, the illusory energy of Vishnu, as one of his principal attributes. As if, in this gale of warring elements which life is, it was necessary to bind souls to human life as mariners in a tempest lash themselves to the mast and bulwarks of a ship, and Nature employed certain illusions as her ties and straps,—a rattle, a doll, an apple, for a child; skates, a river, a boat, a horse, a gun, for the growing boy; and I will not begin to name those of the youth and adult, for they are numberless. Seldom and slowly the mask falls and the pupil is permitted to see that all is one stuff, cooked and painted under many counterfeit appearances. Hume's doctrine was that the circumstances vary, the amount of happiness does not; that the beggar cracking fleas in the sunshine under a hedge, and the duke rolling by in his chariot; the girl equipped for her first ball, and the orator returning triumphant from the debate, had different means, but the same quantity of pleasant excitement.

This element of illusion lends all its force to hide the values of present time. Who is he that does not always find himself doing something less than his best task? "What are you doing?" "O, nothing; I have been doing thus, or I shall do so or so, but now I am only—" Ah! poor dupe, will you never slip out of the web of the master juggler,—never learn that as soon as the irrecoverable years have woven their blue glory between to-day and us these passing hours shall glitter and draw us as the wildest romance and the homes of beauty and poetry? How difficult to deal erect with them! The events they bring, their trade, entertainments and gossip, their urgent work, all throw dust in the eyes and distract attention. He is a strong man who can look them in the eye, see through this juggle, feel their identity, and keep his own; who can know surely that one will be like another to the end of the world, nor permit love, or death, or politics, or money, war or pleasure to draw him from his task.

The world is always equal to itself, and every man in moments of deeper thought is apprised that he is repeating the experiences of the people in the streets of Thebes or Byzantium. An everlasting Now reigns in Nature, which hangs the same roses on our bushes which charmed the Roman and the Chaldæan in their hanging-gardens. 'To what end, then,' he asks, 'should I study languages, and traverse countries, to learn so simple truths?'

History of ancient art, excavated cities, recovery of books and inscriptions,—yes, the works were beautiful, and the history worth knowing; and academies convene to settle the claims of the old schools. What journeys and measurements,—Niebuhr and Müller and Layard,—to identify the plain of Troy and Nimroud town! And your homage to Dante costs you so much sailing; and to ascertain the discoverers of America needs as much voyaging as the discovery cost. Poor child! that flexile clay of which these old brothers moulded their admirable symbols was not Persian, nor Memphian, nor Teutonic, nor local at all, but was common lime and silex and water and sunlight, the heat of the blood and the heaving of the lungs; it was that clay which thou heldest but now in thy foolish hands, and threwest away to go and seek in vain in sepulchres, mummy-pits and old book-shops of Asia Minor, Egypt and England. It was the deep to-day which all men scorn; the rich poverty which men hate; the populous, all-loving solitude which men quit for the tattle of towns. He lurks, *he* hides,—*he* who is success, reality, joy and power. One of the illusions is that the present hour is not the critical, decisive hour. Write it on your heart that every day is the best day in the year. No man has learned anything rightly until he knows that every day is Doomsday. 'T is the old secret of the gods that they come in low disguises. 'T is the vulgar great who come dizened with gold and jewels. Real kings hide away their crowns in their wardrobes, and affect a plain and poor exterior. In the Norse legend of our ancestors, Odin dwells in a fisher's hut and patches a boat. In the Hindoo legends, Hari dwells a peasant among peasants. In the Greek legend, Apollo lodges with the shepherds of Admetus, and Jove liked to rusticate among the poor Ethiopians. So, in our history, Jesus is born in a barn, and his twelve peers are fishermen. 'T is the very principle of science that Nature shows herself best in leasts; it was the maxim of Aristotle and Lucretius; and, in modern times, of Swedenborg and of Hahnemann. The order of changes in the egg determines the age of fossil strata. So it was the rule of our poets, in the legends of fairy lore, that the fairies largest in power were the least in size. In the Christian graces, humility stands highest of all, in the form of the Madonna; and in life, this is the secret of the wise. We owe to genius always the same debt, of lifting the curtain from the common, and showing us that divinities are sitting disguised in the seeming gang of gypsies and pedlers. In daily life, what distinguishes the master is the using those materials he has, instead of looking about for what are more renowned, or what others have used well. "A general," said Bonaparte, "always has troops enough, if he only knows how to employ those he has, and bivouacs with them." Do not refuse the employment which the hour brings you, for one more ambitious. The highest heaven of wisdom is alike near from every point, and thou must find it, if at all, by methods native to thyself alone.

That work is ever the more pleasant to the imagination which is not now required. How wistfully, when we have promised to attend the working committee, we look at the distant hills and their seductions!

The use of history is to give value to the present hour and its duty. That is good which commends to me my country, my climate, my means and materials, my associates. I knew a man in a certain religious exaltation who "thought it an honor to wash his own face." He seemed to me more sane than those who hold themselves cheap.

Zoölogists may deny that horse-hairs in the water change to worms, but I find that whatever is old corrupts, and the past turns to snakes. The reverence for the deeds of our ancestors is a treacherous sentiment. Their merit was not to reverence the old, but to honor the present moment; and we falsely make them excuses of the very habit which they hated and defied.

Another illusion is that there is not time enough for our work. Yet we might reflect that though many creatures eat from one dish, each, according to its constitution, assimilates from the elements what belongs to it, whether time, or space, or light, or water, or food. A snake converts whatever prey the meadow yields him into snake; a fox, into fox; and Peter and John are working up all existence into Peter and John. A poor Indian chief of the Six Nations of New York made a wiser reply than any philosopher, to some one complaining that he had not enough time. "Well," said Red Jacket, "I suppose you have all there is."

A third illusion haunts us, that a long duration, as a year, a decade, a century, is valuable. But an old French sentence says, "God works in moments,"—"*En peu d'heure Dieu labeure.*" We ask for long life, but 't is deep life, or grand moments, that signify. Let the measure of time be spiritual, not mechanical. Life is unnecessarily long. Moments of insight, of fine personal relation, a smile, a glance,—what ample borrowers of eternity they are! Life culminates and concentrates; and Homer said, "The gods ever give to mortals their apportioned share of reason only on one day."

I am of the opinion of the poet Wordsworth, that "there is no real happiness in this life but in intellect and virtue." I am of the opinion of Pliny that "whilst we are musing on these things, we are adding to the length of our lives." I am of the opinion of Glauco, who said, "The measure of life, O Socrates, is, with the wise, the speaking and hearing such discourses as yours."

He only can enrich me who can recommend to me the space between sun and sun. 'T is the measure of a man,—his apprehension of a day. For we do not listen with the best regard to the verses of a man who is only a poet, nor to his problems if he is only an algebraist; but if a man is at once acquainted with the geometric foundations of things and with their festal splendor, his poetry is exact and his arithmetic musical. And him I reckon the most learned scholar, not who can unearth for me the buried dynasties of Sesostris and Ptolemy, the Sothiac era, the Olympiads and consulships, but who can unfold the theory of this particular Wednesday. Can he uncover the ligaments concealed from all but piety, which attach the dull men and things we know to the First Cause? These passing fifteen minutes, men think, are time, not eternity; are low and subaltern, are but hope or memory; that is, the way *to* or the way *from* welfare, but not welfare. Can he show their tie? That interpreter shall guide us from a menial and eleemosynary existence into riches and stability. He dignifies the place where he is. This mendicant America, this curious, peering, itinerant, imitative America, studious of Greece and Rome, of England and Germany, will take off its dusty shoes, will take off its glazed traveller's-cap and sit at home with repose and deep joy on its face. The world has no such landscape, the æons of history no such hour, the future no equal second opportunity. Now let poets sing! now let arts unfold!

One more view remains. But life is good only when it is magical and musical, a perfect timing and consent, and when we do not anatomize it. You must treat the days respectfully, you must be a day yourself, and not interrogate it like a college professor. The world is enigmatical,—everything said, and everything known or done,—and must not be taken literally, but genially. We must be at the top of our condition to understand anything rightly. You must hear the bird's song without attempting to render it into nouns and verbs. Cannot we be a little abstemious and obedient? Cannot we let the morning be?

Everything in the universe goes by indirection. There are no straight lines. I remember well the foreign scholar who made a week of my youth happy by his visit. "The savages in the islands," he said, "delight to play with the surf, coming in on the top of the rollers, then swimming out again, and repeat the delicious manœuvre for hours. Well, human life is made up of such transits. There can be no greatness without abandonment. But here your very astronomy is an espionage. I dare not go out of doors and see the moon and stars, but they seem to measure my tasks, to ask how many lines or pages are finished since I saw them last. Not so, as I told you, was it in Belleisle. The days at Belleisle were all different, and only joined by a perfect love of the same object. Just to fill the hour,— that is happiness. Fill my hour, ye gods, so that I shall not say, whilst I have done this, 'Behold, also, an hour of my life is gone,'—but rather, 'I have lived an hour.'"

We do not want factitious men, who can do any literary or professional feat, as, to write poems, or advocate a cause, or carry a measure, for money; or turn their ability indifferently in any particular direction by the strong effort of will. No, what has been best done in the world,—the works of genius,—cost nothing. There is no painful effort, but it is the spontaneous flowing of the thought. Shakspeare made his Hamlet as a bird weaves its nest. Poems have been written between sleeping and waking, irresponsibly. Fancy defines herself:—

> "Forms that men spy
> With the half-shut eye
> In the beams of the setting sun, am I."

The masters painted for joy, and knew not that virtue had gone out of them. They could not paint the like in cold blood. The masters of English lyric wrote their songs so. It was a fine efflorescence of fine powers; as was said of the letters of the Frenchwoman,—"the charming accident of their more charming existence." Then the poet is never the poorer for his song. A song is no song unless the circumstance is free and fine. If the singer sing from a sense of duty or from seeing no way of escape, I had rather have none. Those only can sleep who do not care to sleep; and those only write or speak best who do not too much respect the writing or the speaking.

The same rule holds in science. The savant is often an amateur. His performance is a memoir to the Academy on fish-worms, tadpoles, or spiders' legs; he observes as other academicians observe; he is on stilts at a microscope, and his memoir finished and read and printed, he retreats into his routinary existence, which is quite separate from his scientific. But in Newton, science was as easy as breathing; he used the same wit to weigh the moon that he used to buckle his shoes; and all his life was simple, wise and majestic. So was it in Archimedes,—always self-same, like the sky. In Linnæus, in Franklin, the like sweetness and equality,— no stilts, no tiptoe; and their results are wholesome and memorable to all men.

In stripping time of its illusions, in seeking to find what is the heart of the day, we come to the quality of the moment, and drop the duration altogether. It is the depth at which we live and not at all the surface extension that imports. We pierce to the eternity, of which time is the flitting surface; and, really, the least acceleration of thought and the least increase of power of thought, make life to seem and to be of vast duration. We call it time; but when that acceleration and that deepening take effect, it acquires another and a higher name.

There are people who do not need much experimenting; who, after years of activity, say, We knew all this before; who love at first sight and hate at first sight; discern the affinities and repulsions; who do not care so much for conditions as others, for they are always in one condition and enjoy themselves; who dictate to others and are not dictated to; who in their consciousness of deserving success constantly slight the ordinary means of attaining it; who have self-existence and self-help; who are suffered to be themselves in society; who are great in the present; who have no talents, or care not to have them,—being that which was before talent, and shall be after it, and of which talent seems only a tool: this is character, the highest name at which philosophy has arrived.

'T is not important how the hero does this or this, but what he is. What he is will appear in every gesture and syllable. In this way the moment and the character are one.

It is a fine fable for the advantage of character over talent, the Greek legend of the strife of Jove and Phœbus. Phœbus challenged the gods, and said, "Who will outshoot the far-darting Apollo?" Zeus said, "I will." Mars shook the lots in his helmet, and that of Apollo leaped out first. Apollo stretched his bow and shot his arrow into the extreme west. Then Zeus rose, and with one stride cleared the whole distance, and said, "Where shall I shoot? there is no space left." So the bowman's prize was adjudged to him who drew no bow.

And this is the progress of every earnest mind; from the works of man and the activity of the hands to a delight in the faculties which rule them; from a respect to the works to a wise wonder at this mystic element of time in which he is conditioned; from local skills and the economy which reckons the amount of production *per* hour to the finer economy which respects the quality of what is done, and the right we have to the work, or the fidelity with which it flows from ourselves; then to the depth of thought it betrays, looking to its universality, or that its roots are in eternity, not in time. Then it flows from character, that sublime health which values one moment as another, and makes us great in all conditions, and as the only definition we have of freedom and power.

W VII, 155–185

2. Henry David Thoreau
(1817-1862)

LIVING AUTHENTICALLY

An appropriate transition from Emerson's writing to Thoreau's is provided by the address Emerson gave after the premature death of his younger friend. By that time the two men had ceased to be as close as they had once been, and there are places in the address where the tension between them comes to the surface. All the same, Emerson's words are based on twenty-five years of friendship and the opportunity to know his friend under every sort of circumstance—on forest walks and in drawing-room discussions, as a platform speaker and a member of the household, as an angry social critic and a scholarly naturalist. Originally addressed to Thoreau's fellow townsmen and then revised for publication, Emerson's portrait records memorably the life-style of the man who believed that the person's life was worthless unless it was lived with a style that was the natural product of personal conviction.

EMERSON ON THOREAU

He was born in Concord, Massachusetts, on the 12th of July, 1817. He was graduated at Harvard College in 1837, but without any literary distinction. An iconoclast in literature, he seldom thanked colleges for their service to him, holding them in small esteem, whilst yet his debt to them was important. After leaving the University, he joined his brother in teaching a private school, which he soon renounced. His father was a manufacturer of lead-pencils, and Henry applied himself for a time to this craft, believing he could make a better pencil than was then in use. After completing his experiments, he exhibited his work to chemists and artists in Boston, and having obtained their certificates to its excellence and to its equality with the best London manufacture, he returned home contented. His friends congratulated him that he had now opened his way to fortune. But he replied that he should never make another pencil. "Why should I? I would not do again what I have done once." He resumed his endless walks and miscellaneous studies, making every day some new acquaintance with Nature, though as yet never speaking of zoölogy or botany, since, though very studious of natural facts, he was incurious of technical and textual science. . . .

He declined to give up his large ambition of knowledge and action for any narrow craft or profession, aiming at a much more comprehensive calling, the art of living well. If he slighted and defied the opinions of others, it was only that he was more intent to reconcile his practice with his own belief. Never idle or self-indulgent, he preferred, when he wanted money, earning it by some piece of manual labor agreeable to him, as building a boat or a fence, planting, grafting, surveying or other short work, to any long engagements. With his hardy habits and few wants, his skill in wood-craft, and his powerful arithmetic, he was very competent to live in any part of the world. It would cost him less time to supply his wants than another. He was therefore secure of his leisure. . . .

A fine house, dress, the manners and talk of highly cultivated people were all thrown away on him. He much preferred a good Indian, and considered these refinements as impediments to conversation, wishing to meet his companion on the simplest terms. He declined invitations to dinner-parties, because there each was in every one's way, and he could not meet the individuals to any purpose. "They make their pride," he said, "in making their dinner cost much; I make my pride in making my dinner cost little." When asked at table what dish he preferred, he answered, "The nearest." He did not like the taste of wine, and never had a vice in his life. He said,—"I have a faint recollection of pleasure derived from smoking dried lily-stems, before I was a man. I had commonly a supply of these. I have never smoked anything more noxious."

He chose to be rich by making his wants few, and supplying them himself. In his travels, he used the railroad only to get over so much country as was unimportant to the present purpose, walking hundreds of miles, avoiding taverns, buying a lodging in farmers' and fishermen's houses, as cheaper, and more agreeable to him, and because there he could better find the men and the information he wanted.

There was somewhat military in his nature, not to be subdued, always manly and able, but rarely tender, as if he did not feel himself except in opposition. He wanted a fallacy to expose, a blunder to pillory, I may say required a little sense of victory, a roll of the drum, to call his powers into full exercise. It cost him nothing to say No; indeed he found it much easier than to say Yes. It seemed as if his first instinct on hearing a proposition was to controvert it, so impatient was he of the limitations of our daily thought. This habit, of course, is a little chilling to the social affections; and though the companion would in the end acquit him of any malice or untruth, yet it mars conversation. Hence, no equal companion stood in affectionate relations with one so pure and guileless. "I love

Henry," said one of his friends, "but I cannot like him; and as for taking his arm, I should as soon think of taking the arm of an elm-tree."

Yet, hermit and stoic as he was, he was really fond of sympathy, and threw himself heartily and childlike into the company of young people whom he loved, and whom he delighted to entertain, as he only could, with the varied and endless anecdotes of his experiences by field and river: and he was always ready to lead a huckleberry-party or a search for chestnuts or grapes. . . .

He was a speaker and actor of the truth, born such, and was ever running into dramatic situations from this cause. In any circumstance it interested all bystanders to know what part Henry would take, and what he would say; and he did not disappoint expectation, but used an original judgment on each emergency. . . .

He coldly and fully stated his opinion without affecting to believe that it was the opinion of the company. It was of no consequence if every one present held the opposite opinion. On one occasion he went to the University Library to procure some books. The librarian refused to lend them. Mr. Thoreau repaired to the President, who stated to him the rules and usages, which permitted the loan of books to resident graduates, to clergymen who were alumni, and to some others resident within a circle of ten miles' radius from the College. Mr. Thoreau explained to the President that the railroad had destroyed the old scale of distances,—that the library was useless, yes, and President and College useless, on the terms of his rules,—that the one benefit he owed to the College was its library,—that, at this moment, not only his want of books was imperative, but he wanted a large number of books, and assured him that he, Thoreau, and not the librarian, was the proper custodian of these. In short, the President found the petitioner so formidable, and the rules getting to look so ridiculous, that he ended by giving him a privilege which in his hands proved unlimited thereafter. . . .

His senses were acute, his frame well-knit and hardy, his hands strong and skilful in the use of tools. And there was a wonderful fitness of body and mind. He could pace sixteen rods more accurately than another man could measure them with rod and chain. He could find his path in the woods at night, he said, better by his feet than his eyes. He could estimate the measure of a tree very well by his eyes; he could estimate the weight of a calf or a pig, like a dealer. From a box containing a bushel or more of loose pencils, he could take up with his hands fast enough just a dozen pencils at every grasp. He was a good swimmer, runner, skater, boatman, and would probably outwalk most countrymen in a day's journey. . . .

He lived for the day, not cumbered and mortified by his memory. If he brought you yesterday a new proposition, he would bring you today another not less revolutionary. A very industrious man, and setting, like all highly organized men, a high value on his time, he seemed the only man of leisure in town, always ready for any excursion that promised well, or for conversation prolonged into late hours. His trenchant sense was never stopped by his rules of daily prudence, but was always up to the new occasion. . . .

He noted what repeatedly befell him, that, after receiving from a distance a rare plant, he would presently find the same in his own haunts. And those pieces of luck which happen only to good players happened to him. One day, walking with a stranger, who inquired where Indian arrowheads could be found, he replied, "Everywhere," and, stooping forward, picked one on the instant from the ground. At Mount Washington, in Tuckerman's Ravine, Thoreau had a bad fall, and sprained his foot. As he was in the act of getting up from his fall, he saw for the first time the leaves of the *Arnica mollis*. . . .

He remarked that the Flora of Massachusetts embraced almost all the important plants in America,—most of the oaks, most of the willows, the best pines, the ash, the maple, the beech, the nuts. He returned Kane's Arctic Voyage to a friend of whom he had borrowed it, with the remark, that "Most of the phenomena noted might be observed in Concord." . . . I think his fancy for referring everything to the meridian of Concord did not grow out of any ignorance or depreciation of other longitudes or latitudes, but was rather a playful expression of his conviction of the indifferency of all places, and that the best place for each is where he stands. He expressed it once in this wise: "I think nothing is to be hoped from you, if this bit of mold under your feet is not sweeter to you to eat than any other in this world, or in any world."

It was a pleasure and a privilege to walk with him. He knew the country like a fox or a bird, and passed through it as freely by paths of his own. He knew every track in the snow or on the ground, and what creature had taken this path before him. One must submit abjectly to such a guide, and the reward was great. Under his arm he carried an old music-book to press plants; in his pocket, his diary and pencil, a spy-glass for birds, microscope, jack-knife and twine. He wore a straw hat, stout shoes, strong gray trousers, to brave scrub-oaks and smilax, and to climb a tree for a hawk's or a squirrel's nest. He waded into the pool for the water-plants, and his strong legs were no insignificant part of his armor. On the day I speak of he looked for the Menyanthes, detected it across the wide pool, and, on examination of the florets, decided that it had been in flower five days. He drew out of his breast-pocket his diary, and read the names of all the plants that should bloom on this day, whereof he kept account as a banker when his notes fall due. The Cypripedium not due till tomorrow. He thought that, if waked up from a trance, in this swamp, he could tell by the plants what time of the year it was within two days. . . .

His interest in the flower or the bird lay very deep in his mind, was connected with Nature,—and the meaning of Nature was never attempted to be defined by him. He would not offer a memoir of his observations to the Natural History Society. "Why should I? To detach the description from its connections in my mind would make it no longer true or valuable to me: and they do not wish what belongs to it." . . .

No college ever offered him a diploma, or a professor's chair; no academy made him its corresponding secretary, its discoverer or even its member. Perhaps these learned bodies feared the satire of his presence. Yet so much knowledge of Nature's secret and genius few others possessed; none in a more large and religious synthesis. For not a particle of respect had he to the opinions of any man or body of men, but homage solely to the truth itself; and as he discovered everywhere among doctors some learning of courtesy, it discredited them. He grew to be revered and admired by his townsmen, who had at first known him only as an oddity. The farmers who employed him as a surveyor soon discovered his rare accuracy and skill, his knowledge of their lands, of trees, of birds, of Indian remains and the like, which enabled him to tell every farmer more than he knew before of his own farm; so that he began to feel a little as if Mr. Thoreau had better rights in his land than he. . . .

Thoreau was sincerity itself, and might fortify the convictions of prophets in the ethical laws by his holy living. It was an affirmative experience which refused to be set aside. A truth-speaker he, capable of the most deep and strict conversation; a physician to the wounds of any soul; a friend, knowing not only the secret of friendship, but almost worshipped by those few persons who resorted to him as their confessor and prophet, and knew the deep value of his mind and great heart. He thought that without religion or devotion of some kind nothing great was ever accomplished: and he thought that the bigoted sectarian had better bear this in mind. . . .

There is a flower known to botanists, one of the same genus with our summer plant called "Life-Everlasting," a *Gnaphalium* like that, which grows on the most inaccessible cliffs of the Tyrolese mountains, where the chamois dare hardly venture, and which the hunter, tempted by its beauty, and by his love (for it is immensely valued by the Swiss maidens), climbs the cliffs to gather, and is sometimes found dead at the foot, with the flower in his hand. It is called by botanists the *Gnaphalium leontopodium*, but by the Swiss *Edelweisse*, which signifies *Noble Purity*. Thoreau seemed to me living in the hope to gather this plant, which belonged to him of right. The scale on which his studies proceeded was so large as to require longevity, and we were the less prepared for his sudden disappearance. The country knows not yet, or in the least part, how great a son it has lost. It seems an injury that he should leave in the midst his broken task which none else can finish, a kind of indignity to so noble a soul that he should depart out of Nature before yet he has been really shown to his peers for what he is. But he, at least, is content. His soul was made for the noblest society; he had in a short life exhausted the capabilities of this world; wherever there is knowledge, wherever there is virtue, wherever there is beauty, he will find a home.

SOCIETY AND ALIENATION

Supporting the natural independence of mind that Emerson describes in his address was a careful analysis that Thoreau made of life in a competitive and acquisitive society. Watching the farmers and tradesmen and factory workers of New England struggle for years to earn the money to amass the goods that would provide security and comfort, he decided that the means were overwhelming the ends that they were meant to serve. He called on his readers to look to their own situations and see whether the central business of living wasn't being buried under the demands of *making a living. In all too many cases, he believed, the latter task had long ago stopped serving the former and had become instead a self-serving system in which each act was necessitated by the requirements of the system itself. He illustrated this problem with the example of the friend who suggested that Thoreau, who liked to travel, save up some money and take the train trip to nearby Fitchburg. Thoreau's reaction was to inquire what sort of a "saving" that would be:*

I say to my friend, Suppose we try who will get there first. The distance is thirty miles; the fare ninety cents. That is almost a day's wages [for a manual laborer]. . . . Well, I start now on foot, and get there before night; I have travelled at that rate by the week together. You will in the meantime have earned your fare, and arrive there some time to-morrow, or possibly this evening, if you are lucky enough to get a job in season. Instead of going to Fitchburg, you will be working here the greater part of the day. And so, if the railroad reached round the world, I think that I should keep ahead of you; and as for seeing the country and getting experience of that kind, I should have to cut your acquaintance altogether.[1]

If changes in wages, fares, and travel time have undercut Thoreau's example, his main point remains as valid as ever: what is the point in a life spent getting ready to live, and what is the sense in the expenditure of energy in accumulating the equipment for a journey that will never be made because of the need to devote the time to keeping the equipment in repair? The same sort of self-destructive service to a system meant to serve man was the basis of his despair over those whose quest for social and personal security rendered them incapable of speaking out against injustice.

I would fain say something, not so much concerning the Chinese and Sandwich Islanders as you who read these pages, who are said to live in New England; something about your condition, especially your outward condition or circumstances in this world, in this town, what it is, whether it is necessary that it be as bad as it is, whether it cannot be improved as well as not. I have travelled a good deal in Concord; and everywhere, in

---

[1] *Walden,* pp. 58–59.

shops, and offices, and fields, the inhabitants have appeared to me to be doing penance in a thousand remarkable ways. . . .

The twelve labors of Hercules were trifling in comparison with those which my neighbors have undertaken; for they were only twelve, and had an end; but I could never see that these men slew or captured any monster or finished any labor. They have no friend Iolaus to burn with a hot iron the root of the hydra's head, but as soon as one head is crushed, two spring up.

I see young men, my townsmen, whose misfortune it is to have inherited farms, houses, barns, cattle, and farming tools; for these are more easily acquired than got rid of. Better if they had been born in the open pasture and suckled by a wolf, that they might have seen with clearer eyes what field they were called to labor in. Who made them serfs of the soil? Why should they eat their sixty acres, when man is condemned to eat only his peck of dirt? Why should they begin digging their graves as soon as they are born? They have got to live a man's life, pushing all these things before them, and get on as well as they can. How many a poor immortal soul have I met well-nigh crushed and smothered under its load, creeping down the road of life, pushing before it a barn seventy-five feet by forty, its Augean stables never cleansed, and one hundred acres of land, tillage, mowing, pasture, and wood-lot. The portionless, who struggle with no such unnecessary inherited encumbrances, find it labor enough to subdue and cultivate a few cubic feet of flesh.

But men labor under a mistake. The better part of the man is soon plowed into the soil for compost. By a seeming fate, commonly called necessity, they are employed, as it says in an old book, laying up treasures which moth and rust will corrupt and thieves break through and steal. It is a fool's life, as they will find when they get to the end of it, if not before. *"Economy," Walden W II, 4–6*

I am wont to think that men are not so much the keepers of herds as herds are the keepers of men, the former are so much the freer. Men and oxen exchange work; but if we consider necessary work only, the oxen will be seen to have greatly the advantage, their farm is so much the larger. Man does some of his part of the exchange work in his six weeks of haying, and it is no boy's play. Certainly no nation that lived simply in all respects, that is, no nation of philosophers, would commit so great a blunder as to use the labor of animals. True, there never was and is not likely, soon to be a nation of philosophers, nor am I certain it is desirable that there should be. However, *I* should never have broken a horse or bull and taken him to board for any work he might do for me, for fear I should become a horse-man or a herds-man merely; and if society seems to be the gainer by so doing, are we certain that what is one man's gain is not another's loss, and that the stable-boy has equal cause with his master to be satisfied? Granted that some public works would not have been constructed without this aid, and let man share the glory of such with the ox and horse; does it follow that he could not have accomplished works yet more worthy of himself in that case?

"Economy," Walden W II, 62–63

It is very evident what mean and sneaking lives many of you live, for my sight has been whetted by experience; always on the limits, trying to get into business and trying to get out of debt, a very ancient slough, called by the Latins *aes alienum,* another's brass, for some of their coins were made of brass; still living, and dying, and buried by this other's brass; always promising to pay, promising to pay, to-morrow, and dying to-day, insolvent: seeking to curry favor, to get custom, by how many modes, only not state-prison offenses; lying, flattering, voting, contracting yourselves into a nutshell of civility, or dilating into an atmosphere of thin and vaporous generosity, that you may persuade your neighbor to let you make his shoes, or his hat, or his coat, or his carriage, or import his groceries for him; making yourselves sick, that you may lay up something against a sick day, something to be tucked away in an old chest, or in a stocking behind the plastering, or, more safely, in the brick bank; no matter where, no matter how much or how little. . . .

The mass of men lead lives of quiet desperation. What is called resignation is confirmed desperation. From the desperate city you go into the desperate country, and have to console yourself with the bravery of minks and muskrats. A stereotyped but unconscious despair is concealed even under what are called the games and amusements of mankind. There is no play in them, for this comes after work. But it is a characteristic of wisdom not to do desperate things.

When we consider what, to use the words of the catechism, is the chief end of man, and what are the true necessaries and means of life, it appears as if men had deliberately chosen the common mode of living because they preferred it to any other. Yet they honestly think there is no choice left. But alert and healthy natures remember that the sun rose clear. It is never too late to give up our prejudices.

"Economy," Walden W II, 7–9

Our life is frittered away by detail. An honest man has hardly need to count more than his ten fingers, or in extreme cases he may add his ten toes, and lump the rest. Simplicity, simplicity, simplicity! I say, let your affairs be as two or three, and not a hundred or a thousand; instead of a million count half a dozen, and keep your accounts on your thumb-nail. In the midst of this chopping sea of civilized life, such are the clouds and storms and quicksands and thousand-and-one items to be allowed for, that a man has to live, if he would not founder and go to the bottom and not make his port at all, by dead reckoning, and he must be a great calculator indeed who succeeds. Simplify, simplify. Instead of three meals a day, if it be necessary eat but one; instead of a hundred dishes, five; and reduce other things in proportion. Our life is like a German Confederacy, made up of petty states, with its boundary forever fluctuating, so that even a German cannot tell you how it is bounded at any moment. . . .

Men think that it is essential that the *Nation* have commerce, and export ice, and talk through a telegraph, and ride thirty miles an hour, without a doubt, whether *they* do or not; but whether we should live like baboons or like men, is a little uncertain. If we do not get out sleepers, and forge rails, and devote days and nights to the work, but go to tinkering upon our *lives* to improve *them,* who will build railroads? And if railroads are not built, how shall we get to heaven in season? But if we stay at home and mind our business, who will want railroads? We do not ride on the railroad; it rides upon us. . . .

Why should we live with such hurry and waste of life? We are determined to be starved before we are hungry. Men say that a stitch in time saves nine, and so they take a thousand stitches to-day to save nine tomorrow. As for *work,* we haven't any of any consequence. We have the Saint Vitus' dance, and cannot possibly keep our heads still. . . .

Hardly a man takes a half-hour's nap after dinner, but when he wakes he holds up his head and asks, "What's the news?" as if the rest of mankind had stood his sentinels. Some give directions to be waked every half-hour, doubtless for no other purpose; and then, to pay for it, they tell what they have dreamed. After a night's sleep the news is as indispensable as the breakfast. "Pray tell me anything new that has happened to a man anywhere on this globe,"—and he reads it over his coffee and rolls, that a man has had his eyes gouged out this morning on the Wachito River; never dreaming the while that he lives in the dark unfathomed mammoth cave of this world, and has but the rudiment of an eye himself.

"*Where I Lived and What I Lived For," Walden* W II, 101–104

As with our colleges, so with a hundred "modern improvements;" there is an illusion about them; there is not always a positive advance. The devil goes on exacting compound interest to the last for his early share and numerous succeeding investments in them. Our inventions are wont to be pretty toys, which distract our attention from serious things. They are but improved means to an unimproved end, an end which it was already but too easy to arrive at; as railroads lead to Boston or New York. We are in great haste to construct a magnetic telegraph from Maine to Texas; but Maine and Texas, it may be, have nothing important to communicate. Either is in such a predicament as the man who was earnest to be introduced to a distinguished deaf woman, but when he was presented, and one end of her ear trumpet was put into his hand, had nothing to say. As if the main object were to talk fast and not to talk sensibly. We are eager to tunnel under the Atlantic and bring the Old World some weeks nearer to the New; but perchance the first news that will leak through into the broad, flapping American ear will be that the Princess Adelaide has the whooping cough.

"Economy," *Walden* W II, 57–58

Most men appear never to have considered what a house is, and are actually though needlessly poor all their lives because they think that they must have such a one as their neighbors have. As if one were to wear any sort of coat which the tailor might cut out for him, or, gradually leaving off palm-leaf hat or cap of woodchuck skin, complain of hard times because he could not afford to buy him a crown! It is possible to invent a house still more convenient and luxurious than we have, which yet all would admit that man could not afford to pay for. Shall we always study to obtain more of these things, and not sometimes to be content with less? Shall the respectable citizen thus gravely teach, by precept and example, the necessity of the young man's providing a certain number of superfluous glow-shoes, and umbrellas, and empty guest chambers for empty guests, before he dies? Why should not our furniture be as simple as the Arab's or the Indian's? When I think of the benefactors of the race, whom we have apotheosized as messengers from heaven, bearers of divine gifts to man, I do not see in my mind any retinue at their heels, any car-load of fashionable furniture. Or what if I were to allow—would it not be a singular allowance?—that our furniture should be more complex than the Arab's, in proportion as we are morally and intellectually his superiors! At present our houses are cluttered and defiled with it, and a good housewife would sweep out the greater part into the dust hole, and not leave her morning's work undone. Morning work! By the blushes of Aurora and the music of Memnon, what should be man's *morning work* in this world? I had three pieces of limestone on my desk, but I was terrified to find that they required to be dusted daily, when the furniture of my mind was all undusted still, and I threw them out the window in disgust. How, then, could I have a furnished house? I would rather sit in the open air, for no dust gathers on the grass, unless where man has broken ground. "Economy," *Walden* W II, 39–40

When I converse with the freest of my neighbors, I perceive that, whatever they may say about the magnitude and seriousness of the question, and their regard for the public tranquillity, the long and the short of the matter is, that they cannot spare the protection of the existing government, and they dread the consequences of disobedience to it to their property and families. For my own part, I should not like to think that I ever rely on the protection of the State. But, if I deny the authority of the State when it presents its tax-bill, it will soon take and waste all my property, and so harass me and my children without end. This is hard.

This makes it impossible for a man to live honestly and at the same time comfortably in outward respects. It will not be worth the while to accumulate property; that would be sure to go again. You must hire or squat somewhere, and raise but a small crop, and eat that soon. You must live within yourself, and depend upon yourself, always tucked up and ready for a start, and not have many affairs.

"Civil Disobedience" W IV, 373

Practically speaking, the opponents to a reform in Massachusetts are not a hundred thousand politicians at the South, but a hundred thousand merchants and farmers here, who are more interested in commerce and agriculture than they are in humanity and are not prepared to do justice to the slave and to Mexico, *cost what it may*. I quarrel not with far-off foes, but with those who, near at home, co-operate with, and do the bidding of those far away, and without whom the latter would be harmless. We are accustomed to say, that the mass of men are unprepared; but improvement is slow, because the few are not materially wiser or better than the many. It is not so important that many should be as good as you, as that there be some absolute goodness somewhere; for that will leaven the whole lump. There are thousands who are *in opinion* opposed to slavery and to the war, who yet in effect do nothing to put an end to them; who, esteeming themselves children of Washington and Franklin, sit down with their hands in their pockets, and say that they know not what to do, and do nothing; who even postpone the question of freedom to the question of free-trade, and quietly read the prices-current along with the latest advices from Mexico, after dinner, and, it may be, fall asleep over them both. What is the price-current of an honest man and patriot to-day? They hesitate, and they regret, and sometimes they petition; but they do nothing in earnest and with effect. They will wait, well disposed, for others to remedy the evil, that they may no longer have it to regret. At most, they give only a cheap vote, and a feeble countenance and Godspeed, to the right, as it goes by them. There are nine hundred and ninety-nine patrons of virtue to one virtuous man; but it is easier to deal with the real possessor of a thing than with the temporary guardian of it.

All voting is a sort of gaming, like chequers or backgammon, with a slight moral tinge to it, a playing with right and wrong, with moral questions; and betting naturally accompanies it. The character of the voters is not staked. I cast my vote, perchance, as I think right; but I am not vitally concerned that that right should prevail. I am willing to leave it to the majority. Its obligation, therefore, never exceeds that of expediency. Even voting *for the right* is *doing* nothing for it. It is only expressing to men feebly your desire that it should prevail. A wise man will not leave the right to the mercy of chance, nor wish it to prevail through the power of the majority. There is but little virtue in the action of masses of men. When the majority shall at length vote for the abolition of slavery, it will be because they are indifferent to slavery, or because there is but little slavery left to be abolished by their vote. *They* will then be the only slaves. Only *his* vote can hasten the abolition of slavery who asserts his own freedom by his vote.   "*Civil Disobedience*" W IV, 362–364

Can there not be a government in which majorities do not virtually decide right and wrong, but conscience?—in which majorities decide only those questions to which the rule of expediency is applicable? Must the citizen ever for a moment, or in the least degree, resign his conscience to the legislator? Why has every man a conscience, then? I think that we should be men first, and subjects afterward. It is not desirable to cultivate a respect for the law, so much as for the right. The only obligation which I have a right to assume, is to do at any time what I think right. It is truly enough said, that a corporation has no conscience; but a corporation of conscientious men is a corporation *with* a conscience. Law never made men a whit more just; and, by means of their respect for it, even the well-disposed are daily made the agents of injustice. A common and natural result of an undue respect for law is, that you may see a file of soldiers, colonel, captain, corporal, privates, powder-monkeys and all, marching in admirable order over hill and dale to the wars, against their wills, aye, against their common sense and consciences, which makes it very steep marching indeed, and produces a palpitation of the heart. They have no doubt that it is a damnable business in which they are concerned; they are all peaceably inclined. Now, what are they? Men at all? or small moveable forts and magazines, at the service of some unscrupulous man in power? Visit the Navy Yard, and behold a marine, such a man as an American government can make, or such as it can make a man with its black arts,—a mere shadow and reminiscence of humanity, a man laid out alive and standing, and already, as one may say, buried under arms with funeral accompaniments, though it may be

> "Not a drum was heard, nor a funeral note,
>   As his corse to the ramparts we hurried;
> Not a soldier discharged his farewell shot
>   O'er the grave where our hero we buried."

The mass of men serve the State thus, not as men mainly, but as machines, with their bodies. They are the standing army, and the militia, jailers, constables, *posse comitatus,* &c. In most cases there is no free exercise whatever of the judgment or of the moral sense; but they put themselves on a level with wood and earth and stones; and wooden men can perhaps be manufactured that will serve the purpose as well. Such command no more respect than men of straw, or a lump of dirt. They have the same sort of worth only as horses and dogs. Yet such as these even are commonly esteemed good citizens. Others, as most legislators, politicians, lawyers, ministers, and office-holders, serve the State chiefly with their heads; and, as they rarely make any moral distinctions, they are as likely to serve the devil, without *intending* it, as God. A very few, as heroes, patriots, martyrs, reformers in the great sense, and *men*, serve the State with their consciences also, and so necessarily resist it for the most part; and they are commonly treated by it as enemies.

"*Civil Disobedience*" W IV, 358–360

I have paid no poll-tax for six years. I was put into a jail once on this account, for one night; and, as I stood considering the walls of solid stone, two or three feet thick, the door of wood and iron, a foot thick, and the iron grating which strained the light, I could not help being struck with the foolishness of that institution which treated me as if I were mere flesh and blood and bones, to be locked up. I wondered that it should have concluded at length that this was the best use it could put me to, and had never thought to avail itself of my services in some way. I saw that, if there was a wall of stone between me and my townsmen, there was a still more difficult one to climb or break through, before they could get to be as free as I was. I did not for a moment feel confined, and the walls seemed a great waste of stone and mortar. I felt as if I alone of all my townsmen had paid my tax. They plainly did not know how to treat me, but behaved like persons who are underbred. In every threat and in every compliment there was a blunder; for they thought that my chief desire was to stand the other side of that stone wall. I could not but smile to see how industriously they locked the door on my meditations, which followed them out again without let or hindrance, and *they* were really all that was dangerous. As they could not reach me, they had resolved to punish my body; just as boys, if they cannot come at some person against whom they have a spite, will abuse his dog. I saw that the State was half-witted, that it was timid as a lone woman with her silver spoons, and that it did not know its friends from its foes, and I lost all my remaining respect for it, and pitied it. . . .

I have never declined paying the highway tax, because I am as desirous of being a good neighbor as I am of being a bad subject; and, as for supporting schools, I am doing my part to educate my fellow-countrymen now. It is for no particular item in the tax-bill that I refuse to pay it. I simply wish to refuse allegiance to the State, to withdraw and stand aloof from it effectually. I do not care to trace the course of my dollar, if I could, till it buys a man, or a musket to shoot one with,—the dollar is innocent,—but I am concerned to trace the effects of my allegiance. In fact, I quietly declare war with the State, after my fashion, though I will still make what use and get what advantage of her I can, as is usual in such cases. "*Civil Disobedience*" W IV, 375, 380–381

Some years ago, the State met me in behalf of the church, and commanded me to pay a certain sum toward the support of a clergyman whose preaching my father attended, but never I myself. "Pay," it said, "or be locked up in the jail." I declined to pay. But, unfortunately another man saw fit to pay it. I did not see why the schoolmaster should be taxed to support the priest, and not the priest the schoolmaster: for I was not the State's schoolmaster, but I supported myself by voluntary subscription. I did not see why the lyceum should not present its tax-bill, and have the State to back its demand, as well as the church. However, at the request of the selectmen, I condescended to make some such statement as this in writing:—"Know all men by these presents, that I, Henry Thoreau, do not wish to be regarded as a member of any incorporated society which I have not joined." This I gave to the town-clerk; and he has it. The State, having thus learned that I did not wish to be regarded as a member of that church, has never made a like demand on me since; though it said that it must adhere to its original presumption that time. If I had known how to name them, I should then have signed off in detail from all the societies which I never signed on to; but I did not know where to find a complete list. *"Civil Disobedience"* W IV, 374–375

The very simplicity and nakedness of man's life in the primitive ages imply this advantage, at least, that they left him still but a sojourner in nature. When he was refreshed with food and sleep, he contemplated his journey again. He dwelt, as it were, in a tent in this world, and was either threading the valleys, or crossing the plains, or climbing the mountain-tops. But lo! men have become the tools of their tools. The man who independently plucked the fruits when he was hungry is become a farmer; and he who stood under a tree for shelter, a housekeeper. We now no longer camp as for a night, but have settled down on earth and forgotten heaven. We have adopted Christianity merely as an improved method of *agri*-culture. We have built for this world a family mansion, and for the next a family tomb. The best works of art are the expression of man's struggle to free himself from this condition, but the effect of our art is merely to make this low state comfortable and that higher state to be forgotten. There is actually no place in this village for a work of *fine* art, if any had come down to us, to stand, for our lives, our houses and streets, furnish no proper pedestal for it. There is not a nail to hang a picture on, nor a shelf to receive the bust of a hero or a saint. When I consider how our houses are built and paid for, or not paid for, and their internal economy managed and sustained, I wonder that the floor does not give way under the visitor while he is admiring the gewgaws upon the mantelpiece, and let him through into the cellar to some solid and honest though earthy foundation. I cannot but perceive that this so-called rich and refined life is a thing jumped at, and I do not get on in the enjoyment of the *fine* arts which adorn it, my attention being wholly occupied with the jump; for I remember that the greatest genuine leap, due to human muscles alone, on record, is that of certain wandering Arabs, who are said to have cleared twenty-five feet on level ground. Without factitious support, man is sure to come to earth again beyond that distance. The first question which I am tempted to put to the proprietor of such great impropriety is, Who bolsters you? Are you one of the ninety-seven who fail, or the three who succeed? Answer me these questions, and then perhaps I may look at your baubles and find them ornamental. The cart before the horse is neither beautiful nor useful. Before we can adorn our houses with beautiful objects the walls must be stripped, and our lives must be stripped, and beautiful housekeeping and beautiful living be laid for a foundation: now, a taste for the beautiful is most cultivated out of doors, where there is no house and no housekeeper.

"*Economy,*" *Walden* W II, 41–42

Furniture! Thank God, I can sit and I can stand without the aid of a furniture warehouse. What man but a philosopher would not be ashamed to see his furniture packed in a cart and going up country exposed to the light of heaven and the eyes of men, a beggarly account of empty boxes? That is Spaulding's furniture. I could never tell from inspecting such a load whether it belonged to a so-called rich man or a poor one; the owner always seemed poverty-stricken. Indeed, the more you have of such things the poorer you are. Each load looks as if it contained the contents of a dozen shanties; and if one shanty is poor, this is a dozen times as poor. Pray, for what do we *move* ever but to get rid of our furniture, our *exuviæ;* at last to go from this world to another newly furnished, and leave this to be burned? It is the same as if all these traps were buckled to a man's belt, and he could not move over the rough country where our lines are cast without dragging them,—dragging his trap. He was a lucky fox that left his tail in the trap. The muskrat will gnaw his third leg off to be free. No wonder man has lost his elasticity. How often he is at a dead set! "Sir, if I may be so bold, what do you mean by a dead set?" If you are a seer, whenever you meet a man you will see all that he owns, ay, and much that he pretends to disown, behind him, even to his kitchen furniture and all the trumpery which he saves and will not burn, and he will appear to be harnessed to it and making what headway he can. I think that the man is at a dead set who has got through a knot-hole or gateway where his sledge load of furniture cannot follow him. I cannot but feel compassion when I hear some trig, compact-looking man, seemingly free, all girded and ready, speak of his "furniture," as whether it is insured or not. "But what shall I do with my furniture?" My gay butterfly is entangled in a spider's web then. Even those who seem for a long while not to have any, if you inquire more narrowly you will find have some stored in somebody's barn. I look upon England to-day as an old gentleman who is travelling with a great deal of baggage, trumpery which has accumulated from long housekeeping, which he has not the courage to burn; great trunk, little trunk, bandbox, and bundle. Throw away the first three at least. It would surpass the powers of a well man nowadays to take up his bed and walk, and I should certainly advise a sick one to lay down his bed and run. When I have met an immigrant tottering under a bundle which contained his all,—looking like an enormous wen which had grown out of the nape of his neck,—I have pitied him, not because that was his all, but because he had all *that* to carry. If I have got to drag my trap, I will take care that it be a light one and do not nip me in a vital part. But perchance it would be wisest never to put one's paw into it.

I would observe, by the way, that it costs me nothing for curtains, for I have no gazers to shut out but the sun and moon, and I am willing that they should look in. The moon will not sour milk nor taint meat of mine, nor will the sun injure my furniture or fade my carpet; and if he is sometimes too warm a friend, I find it still better economy to retreat behind some curtain which nature has provided, than to add a single item to the details of housekeeping. A lady once offered me a mat, but as I had no room to spare within the house, nor time to spare within or without to shake it, I declined it, preferring to wipe my feet on the sod before my door. It is best to avoid the beginnings of evil.

Not long since I was present at the auction of a deacon's effects, for his life had not been ineffectual:—

"The evil that men do lives after them."

As usual, a great proportion was trumpery which had begun to accumulate in his father's day. Among the rest was a dried tapeworm. And now, after lying half a century in his garret and other dust holes, these things were not burned; instead of a *bonfire*, or purifying destruction of them, there was an *auction*, or increasing of them. The neighbors eagerly collected to view them, bought them all, and carefully transported them to their garrets and dust holes, to lie there till their estates are settled, when they will start again. When a man dies he kicks the dust.

The customs of some savage nations might, perchance, be profitably imitated by us, for they at least go through the semblance of casting their slough annually; they have the idea of the thing, whether they have the reality or not. Would it not be well if we were to celebrate such a "busk," or "feast of first fruits," as Bartram describes to have been the custom of the Mucclasse Indians? "When a town celebrates the busk," says he, "having previously provided themselves with new clothes, new pots, pans, and other household utensils and furniture, they collect all their worn out clothes and other despicable things, sweep and cleanse their houses, squares, and the whole town, of their filth, which with all the remaining grain and other old provisions they cast together into one common heap, and consume it with fire. After having taken medicine, and fasted for three days, all the fire in the town is extinguished. During this fast they abstain from the gratification of every appetite and passion whatever. A general amnesty is proclaimed; all malefactors may return to their town."

"On the fourth morning, the high priest, by rubbing dry wood together, produces new fire in the public square, from whence every habitation in the town is supplied with the new and pure flame."

They then feast on the new corn and fruits, and dance and sing for three days, "and the four following days they receive visits and rejoice with their friends from neighboring towns who have in like manner purified and prepared themselves."

The Mexicans also practised a similar purification at the end of every fifty-two years, in the belief that it was time for the world to come to an end.

I have scarcely heard of a truer sacrament, that is, as the dictionary defines it, "outward and visible sign of an inward and spiritual grace," than this, and I have no doubt that they were originally inspired directly from Heaven to do thus, though they have no Biblical record of the revelation. *"Economy," Walden W II, 72–76*

We are apt to speak vaguely sometimes, as if a divine life were to be grafted on to or built over this present as a suitable foundation. This might do if we could so build over our old life as to exclude from it all the warmth of our affection, and addle it, as the thrush builds over the cuckoo's egg, and lays her own atop, and hatches that only; but the fact is, we—so there is the partition—hatch them both, and the cuckoo's always by a day first, and that young bird crowds the young thrushes out of the nest. No. Destroy the cuckoo's egg, or build a new nest.

Change is change. No new life occupies the old bodies;—they decay. *It* is born, and grows, and flourishes. Men very pathetically inform the old, accept and wear it. Why put it up with the almshouse when you may go to heaven? It is embalming,—no more. Let alone your ointments and your linen swathes, and go into an infant's body. You see in the catacombs of Egypt the result of that experiment,—that is the end of it.

I do believe in simplicity. It is astonishing as well as sad, how many trivial affairs even the wisest man thinks he must attend to in a day; how singular an affair he thinks he must omit. When the mathematician would solve a difficult problem, he first frees the equation of all incumbrances, and reduces it to its simplest terms. So simplify the problem of life, distinguish the necessary and the real. Probe the earth to see where your main roots run. I would stand upon facts. Why not see,—use our eyes? Do men know nothing? I know many men who, in common things, are not to be deceived; who trust no moonshine; who count their money correctly, and know how to invest it; who are said to be prudent and knowing, who yet will stand at a desk the greater part of their lives, as cashiers in banks, and glimmer and rust and finally go out there. If they *know* anything, what under the sun do they do that for? Do they know what *bread* is? or what it is for? Do they know what life is? If they *knew* something, the places which know them now would know them no more forever.

This, our respectable daily life, in which the man of common sense, the Englishman of the world, stands so squarely, and on which our institutions are founded, is in fact the veriest illusion, and will vanish like the baseless fabric of a vision; but that faint glimmer of reality which sometimes illuminates the darkness of daylight for all men, reveals something more solid and enduring than adamant, which is in fact the corner-stone of the world. *Letter to H. G. O. Blake, 3/27/48 Corr 214–215*

My neighbors tell me of their adventures with famous gentlemen and ladies, what notabilities they met at the dinner-table; but I am no more interested in such things than in the contents of the Daily Times. The interest and the conversation are about costume and manners chiefly; but a goose is a goose still, dress it as you will. They tell me of California and Texas, of England and the Indies, of the Hon. Mr.—— of Georgia or Massachusetts, all transient and fleeting phenomena, till I am ready to leap from their court-yard like the Mameluke bey. I delight to come to my bearings—not walk in procession with pomp and parade, in a conspicuous place, but to walk even with the Builder of the universe, if I may,—not to live in this restless, nervous, bustling, trivial Nineteenth Century, but stand or sit thoughtfully while it goes by. What are men celebrating? They are all on a committee of arrangements, and hourly expect a speech from somebody. God is only the president of the day, and Webster is his orator. I love to weigh, to settle, to gravitate toward that which most strongly and rightfully attracts me,—not hang by the beam of the scale and try to weigh less,—not suppose a case, but take the case that is; to travel the only path I can, and that on which no power can resist me. It affords me no satisfaction to commence to spring an arch before I have got a solid foundation. Let us not play at kittly-benders. There is a solid bottom everywhere. We read that the traveller asked the boy if the swamp before him had a hard bottom. The boy replied that it had. But presently the traveller's horse sank in up to the girths, and he observed to the boy, "I thought you said that this bog had a hard bottom." "So it has," answered the latter, "but you have not got half way to it yet." So it is with the bogs and quicksands of society; but he is an old boy that knows it. *"Conclusion," Walden W II, 362–363*

I perceive that we inhabitants of New England live this mean life that we do because our vision does not penetrate the surface of things. We think that that *is* which *appears* to be. If a man should walk through this town and see only the reality, where, think you, would the "Mill-dam" go to? If he should give us an account of the realities he beheld there, we should not recognize the place in his description. Look at a meeting-house, or a court-house, or a jail, or a shop, or a dwelling-house, and say what that thing really is before a true gaze, and they would all go to pieces in your account of them. Men esteem truth remote, in the outskirts of the system, behind the farthest star, before Adam and after the last man. In eternity there is indeed something true and sublime. But all these times and places and occasions are now and here. God himself culminates in the present moment, and will never be more divine in the lapse of all the ages. And we are enabled to apprehend at all what is sublime and noble only by the perpetual instilling and drenching of the reality that surrounds us. The universe constantly and obediently answers to our conceptions; whether we travel fast or slow, the track is laid for us. Let us spend our lives in conceiving then. The poet or the artist never yet had so fair and noble a design but some of his posterity at least could accomplish it.

Let us spend one day as deliberately as Nature, and not be thrown off the track by every nutshell and mosquito's wing that falls on the rails. Let us rise early and fast, or break fast, gently and without perturbation; let company come and let company go, let the bells ring and the children cry,—determined to make a day of it. Why should we knock under and go with the stream? Let us not be upset and overwhelmed in that terrible rapid and whirlpool called a dinner, situated in the meridian shallows. Weather this danger and you are safe, for the rest of the way is down hill. With unrelaxed nerves, with morning vigor, sail by it, looking another way, tied to the mast like Ulysses. If the engine whistles, let it whistle till it is hoarse for its pains. If the bell rings, why should we run? We will consider what kind of music they are like. Let us settle ourselves, and work and wedge our feet downward through the mud and slush of opinion, and prejudice, and tradition, and delusion, and appearance, that alluvion which covers the globe, through Paris and London, through New York and Boston and Concord, through Church and State, through poetry and philosophy and religion, till we come to a hard bottom and rocks in place, which we can call *reality*, and say, This is, and no mistake; and then begin, having a point d'appui, below freshet and frost and fire, a place where you might found a wall or a state, or set a lamp-post safely, or perhaps a gauge, not a Nilometer, but a Realometer, that future ages might know how deep a freshet of shams and appearances had gathered from time to time. If you stand right fronting and face to face to a fact, you will see the sun glimmer on both its surfaces, as if it were a cimeter, and feel its sweet edge dividing you through the heart and marrow, and so you will happily conclude your mortal career. Be it life or death, we crave only reality. If we are really dying, let us hear the rattle in our throats and feel cold in the extremities; if we are alive, let us go about our business.

"Where I Lived and What I Lived For," *Walden* W II, 108–109

THE BUSINESS AT HAND: LIVING

Thoreau called the first chapter of Walden *"Economy," a term and concept dear to his fellow New Englanders and one that gave him the opportunity for a double-edged kind of irony. On the one hand he included detailed records of his expenses, which together with his commentary on them called attention to how easily the truly independent person could support himself: "Yes, I did eat $8.74, all told," he admitted with tongue-in-cheek in his account of his first eight months in his cabin at Walden Pond; "but I should not thus unblushingly publish my guilt, if I did not know that most of my readers were equally guilty with myself, and that their deeds would look no better in print." On the other hand, his focus on economy called into question the relative value of what was gained in the business world. In his intent here he was like Emerson, who had written in his journal, "Economy does not consist in saving the coal but in using the time whilst it burns" (JMN V 319, May 4, 1837). To people bent on saving coal (and on earning the money to buy coal), Thoreau's activities could only look most unbusinesslike. But to Thoreau himself it was otherwise. The business that took him to Walden Pond and then away again two years later into new ventures was the business of living—of finding joy and meaning in the hours and days allotted to him. He saw his own endeavors as parallel to, but infinitely more rewarding than, those of his neighbors who spent their lives working to pay for a journey that they never took. Thus it is that his descriptions of the way in which he spent a day and the narrative of his time at Walden Pond go beyond the condition of simple accounts of events and become records of an existence redeemed from triviality and illuminated by the significance that Emerson had said was inherent in any life truly lived.*

If I should attempt to tell how I have desired to spend my life in years past, it would probably surprise those of my readers who are somewhat acquainted with its actual history; it would certainly astonish those who know nothing about it. I will only hint at some of the enterprises which I have cherished.

In any weather, at any hour of the day or night, I have been anxious to improve the nick of time, and notch it on my stick too; to stand on the meeting of two eternities, the past and future, which is precisely the present moment; to toe that line. You will pardon some obscurities, for there are more secrets in my trade than in most men's, and yet not voluntarily kept, but inseparable from its very nature. I would gladly tell all that I know about it, and never paint "No Admittance" on my gate. . . .

So many autumn, ay, and winter days, spent outside the town, trying to hear what was in the wind, to hear and carry it express! I well-nigh sunk all my capital in it, and lost my own breath into the bargain, running in the face of it. If it had concerned either of the political parties, depend upon it, it would have appeared in the Gazette with the earliest intelligence. At other times watching from the observatory of some cliff or tree, to telegraph any new arrival; or waiting at evening on the hill-tops for the sky to fall, that I might catch something, though I never caught much, and that, manna-wise, would dissolve again in the sun.

For a long time I was reporter to a journal, of no very wide circulation, whose editor has never yet seen fit to print the bulk of my contributions, and, as is too common with writers, I got only my labor for my pains. However, in this case my pains were their own reward.

For many years I was self-appointed inspector of snow-storms and rain-storms, and did my duty faithfully, surveyor, if not of highways, then of forest paths and all across-lot routes, keeping them open, and ravines bridged and passable at all seasons, where the public heel had testified to their utility.

I have looked after the wild stock of the town, which give a faithful herdsman a good deal of trouble by leaping fences; and I have had an eye to the unfrequented nooks and corners of the farm; though I did not always know whether Jonas or Solomon worked in a particular field today; that was none of my business. I have watered the red huckleberry, the sand cherry and the nettle-tree, the red pine and the black ash, the white grape and the yellow violet, which might have withered else in dry seasons.

In short, I went on thus for a long time (I may say it without boasting), faithfully minding my business, till it became more and more evident that my townsmen would not after all admit me into the list of town officers, nor make my place a sinecure with a moderate allowance. My accounts, which I can swear to have kept faithfully, I have, indeed, never got audited, still less accepted, still less paid and settled. However, I have not set my heart on that. . . .

Finding that my fellow-citizens were not likely to offer me any room in the court house, or any curacy or living anywhere else, but I must shift for myself, I turned my face more exclusively than ever to the woods, where I was better known. I determined to go into business at once, and not wait to acquire the usual capital, using such slender means as I had already got. My purpose in going to Walden Pond was not to live cheaply nor to live dearly there, but to transact some private business with the fewest obstacles; to be hindered from accomplishing which for want of a little common sense, a little enterprise and business talent, appeared not so sad as foolish. *"Economy," Walden* W II, 18–21

I went to the woods because I wished to live deliberately, to front only the essential facts of life, and see if I could not learn what it had to teach, and not, when I came to die, discover that I had not lived. I did not wish to live what was not life, living is so dear; nor did I wish to practise resignation, unless it was quite necessary. I wanted to live deep and suck out all the marrow of life, to live so sturdily and Spartan-like as to put to rout all that was not life, to cut a broad swath and shave close, to drive life into a corner, and reduce it to its lowest terms, and, if it proved to be mean, why then to get the whole and genuine meanness of it, and publish its meanness to the world; or if it were sublime, to know it by experience, and be able to give a true account of it in my next excursion. . . .

Where I lived was as far off as many a region viewed nightly by astronomers. We are wont to imagine rare and delectable places in some remote and more celestial corner of the system, behind the constellation of Cassiopeia's Chair, far from noise and disturbance. I discovered that my house actually had its site in such a withdrawn, but forever new and unprofaned, part of the universe. If it were worth the while to settle in those parts near to the Pleiades or the Hyades, to Aldebaran or Altair, then I was really there, or at an equal remoteness from the life which I had left behind, dwindled and twinkling with as fine a ray to my nearest neighbor, and to be seen only in moonless nights by him.

Every morning was a cheerful invitation to make my life of equal simplicity, and I may say innocence, with Nature herself. I have been as sincere a worshipper of Aurora as the Greeks. I got up early and bathed in the pond; that was a religious exercise, and one of the best things which I did. They say that characters were engraven on the bathing tub of King Tching-thang to this effect: "Renew thyself completely each day; do it again, and again, and forever again." I can understand that. Morning brings back the heroic ages. I was as much affected by the faint hum of a mosquito making its invisible and unimaginable tour through my apartment at earliest dawn, when I was sitting with door and windows open, as I could be by any trumpet that ever sang of fame. It was Homer's requiem; itself an Iliad and Odyssey in the air, singing its own wrath and wanderings. There was something cosmical about it; a standing advertisement, till forbidden, of the everlasting vigor and fertility of the world. The morning, which is the most memorable season of the day, is the awakening hour. Then there is least somnolence in us; and for an hour, at least, some part of us awakes which slumbers all the rest of the day and night. Little is to be expected of that day, if it can be called a day, to which we are not awakened by our Genius, but by the mechanical nudgings of some servitor, are not awakened by our own newly acquired force and aspirations from within, accompanied by the undulations of celestial music, instead of factory bells, and a fragrance filling the air—to a higher life than we fell asleep from; and thus the darkness bear its fruit, and prove itself to be good, no less than the light. That man who does not believe that each day contains an earlier, more sacred, and auroral hour than he has yet profaned, has despaired of life, and is pursuing a descending and darkening way. . . .

To him whose elastic and vigorous thought keeps pace with the sun, the day is a perpetual morning. It matters not what the clocks say or the attitudes and labors of men. Morning is when I am awake and there is a dawn in me. Moral reform is the effort to throw off sleep. Why is it that men give so poor an account of their day if they have not been slumbering? They are not such poor calculators. If they had not been overcome with drowsiness, they would have performed something. The millions are awake enough for physical labor; but only one in a million is awake enough for effective intellectual exertion, only one in a hundred millions to a poetic or divine life. To be awake is to be alive. I have never yet met a man who was quite awake. How could I have looked him in the face?

We must learn to reawaken and keep ourselves awake, not by mechanical aids, but by an infinite expectation of the dawn, which does not forsake us in our soundest sleep. I know of no more encouraging fact than the unquestionable ability of man to elevate his life by a conscious endeavor. It is something to be able to paint a particular picture, or to carve a statue, and so to make a few objects beautiful; but it is far more glorious to carve and paint the very atmosphere and medium through which we look, which morally we can do. To affect the quality of the day, that is the highest of arts. Every man is tasked to make his life, even in its details, worthy of the contemplation of his most elevated and critical hour.   "*Where I Lived and What I Lived For*," *Walden* W II, 97–100

Mr Blake,

I must endeavor to pay some of my debts to you.

To begin where we left off then.

The presumption is that *we* are always the same; our opportunities & Nature herself fluctuating. Look at mankind. No great difference between two, apparently; perhaps the same height and breadth and weight; and yet to the man who sits most E. this life is a weariness, routine, dust and ashes, and he drowns his imaginary cares (!) (a sort of friction among his vital organs), in a bowl. But to the man who sits most W., his *contemporary* (!) it is a field for all noble endeavors, an elysium, the dwelling place of heroes & knights. The former complains that he has a thousand affairs to attend to; but he does not realize, that his affairs, (though they may be a thousand,) and he are one.

Men & boys are learning all kinds of trades but how to make *men* of themselves. They learn to make houses, but they are not so well housed, they are not so contented in their houses, as the woodchucks in their holes. What is the use of a house if you haven't got a tolerable planet to put it on? If you can not tolerate the planet it is on? Grade the ground first. If a man believes and expects great things of himself, it makes no

The Business at Hand: Living

odds where you put him, or what you show him, (of course, you cannot put him anywhere nor show him anything), he will be surrounded by grandeur. He's in the condition of a healthy & hungry man, who says to himself—How sweet this crust is!

If he despairs of himself, then Tophet is his dwelling place, and he is in the condition of a sick man who is disgusted with the fruits of finest flavor.

Whether he sleeps or wakes, whether he runs or walks, whether he uses a microscope or a telescope, or his naked eye, a man never discovers anything, never overtakes anything or leaves anything behind, but himself. Whatever he says or does he merely reports himself. If he is in love, he *loves;* if he is in heaven he *enjoys,* if he is in hell he *suffers.* It is his condition that determines his locality.

The principal, the only thing a man makes is his condition, or fate. Though commonly he does not know it, nor put up a sign to this effect, "My own destiny made & mended here." [not *yours*] He is a masterworkman in this business. He works 24 hours a day at it and gets it done. Whatever else he neglects or botches, no man was ever known to neglect this work. A great many pretend to make *shoes* chiefly, and would scout the idea that they make the hard times which they experience.

Each reaching and aspiration is an instinct with which all nature consists & cooperates, and therefore it is not in vain. But alas! each relaxing and desperation is an instinct too. To be active, well, happy, implies rare courage. To be ready to fight in a duel or a battle implies desperation, or that you hold your life cheap.

If you take this life to be simply what old religious folks pretend, (I mean the effete, gone to seed in a drought, mere human galls stung by the Devil once), then all your joy & serenity is reduced to grinning and bearing it. The fact is, you have got to take the world on your shoulders like Atlas and put along with it. You will do this for an idea's sake, and your success will be in proportion to your devotion to ideas. It may make your back ache occasionally, but you will have the satisfaction of hanging it or twirling it to suit yourself. Cowards suffer, heroes enjoy. After a long day's walk with it, pitch it into a hollow place, sit down and eat your luncheon. Unexpectedly, by some immortal thoughts, you will be compensated. The bank whereon you sit will be a fragrant and flowery one, and your world in the hollow a sleek and light gazelle.

Where is the "Unexplored land" but in our own untried enterprises? To an adventurous spirit any place,—London, New York, Worcester, or his own yard, is "unexplored land," to seek which Freemont & Kane travel so far. To a sluggish & defeated spirit even the Great Basin & the Polaris are trivial places. If they ever get there (& indeed they are there now) they will want to sleep & give it up, just as they always do. These are the regions of the Known & of the Unknown. What is the use of going right over the old track again? There is an adder in the path which your own feet have worn. You must make tracks into the Unknown. That is what you have your board & clothes for. Why do you ever mend your clothes, unless that, wearing them, you may mend your ways?

Let us sing. *Letter to H. G. O. Blake, 5/20/60 Corr 579–580*

One young man of my acquaintance, who has inherited some acres, told me that he thought he should live as I did, *if he had the means.* I would not have any one adopt *my* mode of living on any account; for, beside that before he has fairly learned it I may have found out another for myself, I desire that there may be as many different persons in the world as possible; but I would have each one be very careful to find out and pursue *his own* way, and not his father's or his mother's or his neighbor's instead. The youth may build or plant or sail, only let him not be hindered from doing that which he tells me he would like to do. It is by a mathematical point only that we are wise, as the sailor or the fugitive slave keeps the polestar in his eye; but that is sufficient guidance for all our life. We may not arrive at our port within a calculable period, but we would preserve the true course. *"Economy," Walden* W II, 78–79

Some are dinning in our ears that we Americans, and moderns generally, are intellectual dwarfs compared with the ancients, or even the Elizabethan men. But what is that to the purpose? A living dog is better than a dead lion. Shall a man go and hang himself because he belongs to the race of pygmies, and not be the biggest pygmy that he can? Let every one mind his own business, and endeavor to be what he was made.

Why should we be in such desperate haste to succeed and in such desperate enterprises? If a man does not keep pace with his companions, perhaps it is because he hears a different drummer. Let him step to the music which he hears, however measured or far away. It is not important that he should mature as soon as an apple tree or an oak. Shall he turn his spring into summer? If the condition of things which we were made for is not yet, what were any reality which we can substitute?

"Conclusion," Walden W II, 358–359

The greater part of what my neighbors call good I believe in my soul to be bad, and if I repent of anything, it is very likely to be my good behavior. What demon possessed me that I behaved so well? You may say the wisest thing you can, old man,—you who have lived seventy years, not without honor of a kind,—I hear an irresistible voice which invites me away from all that. One generation abandons the enterprises of another like stranded vessels. *"Economy," Walden* W II, 11–12

It is essential that a man confine himself to pursuits . . . which lie next to and conduce to his life, which do not go against the grain, either of his will or his imagination. The scholar finds in his experience some studies to be most fertile and radiant with light, others dry, barren, and

dark. If he is wise, he will not persevere in the last, as a plant in a cellar will strive toward the light. He will confine the observations of his mind as closely as possible to the experience or life of his senses. His thought must live with and be inspired with the life of the body.
Journal entry W XI, 16–17

But all this is very selfish, I have heard some of my townsmen say. I confess that I have hitherto indulged very little in philanthropic enterprises. I have made some sacrifices to a sense of duty, and among others have sacrificed this pleasure also. There are those who have used all their arts to persuade me to undertake the support of some poor family in the town; and if I had nothing to do—for the devil finds employment for the idle—I might try my hand at some such pastime as that. However, when I have thought to indulge myself in this respect, and lay their Heaven under an obligation by maintaining certain poor persons in all respects as comfortably as I maintain myself, and have even ventured so far as to make them the offer, they have one and all unhesitatingly preferred to remain poor. While my townsmen and women are devoted in so many ways to the good of their fellows, I trust that one at least may be spared to other and less humane pursuits. You must have a genius for charity as well as for anything else. As for Doing-good, that is one of the professions which are full. Moreover, I have tried it fairly, and, strange as it may seem, am satisfied that it does not agree with my constitution. Probably I should not consciously and deliberately forsake my particular calling to do the good which society demands of me, to save the universe from annihilation; and I believe that a like but infinitely greater steadfastness elsewhere is all that now preserves it. But I would not stand between any man and his genius; and to him who does this work, which I decline, with his whole heart and soul and life, I would say, Persevere, even if the world call it doing evil, as it is most likely they will.
"Economy," Walden W II, 80–81

It is not a man's duty, as a matter of course, to devote himself to the eradication of any, even the most enormous wrong; he may still properly have other concerns to engage him; but it is his duty, at least, to wash his hands of it, and, if he gives it no thought longer, not to give it practically his support. If I devote myself to other pursuits and contemplations, I must first see, at least, that I do not pursue them sitting upon another man's shoulders. I must get off him first, that he may pursue his contemplations too.
"Civil Disobedience" W IV, 365

Pursue, keep up with, circle round and round your life as a dog does his master's chaise. Do what you love. Know your own bone; gnaw at it, bury it, unearth it, and gnaw it [still. Do not be too] moral. You may cheat yourself out of much life so. Aim above morality. Be not *simply* good—be good for something.—All fables indeed have their morals, but the innocent enjoy the story.

Let nothing come between you and the light. Respect men as brothers only. When you travel to the celestial city, carry no letter of introduction. When you knock ask to see God—none of the servants. In what concerns you much do not think that you have companions—know that you are alone in the world. *Letter to H. G. O. Blake, 3/27/48 Corr 216–217*

The heavens are as deep as our aspirations are high. So high as a tree aspires to grow, so high it will find an atmosphere suited to it. Every man should stand for a force which is perfectly irresistible. How can any man be weak who dares *to be* at all? Even the tenderest plants force their way up through the hardest earth, and the crevices of rocks; but a man no material power can resist. What a wedge, what a beetle, what a catapult, is an *earnest* man! What can resist him?

It is a momentous fact that a man may be *good*, or he may be *bad*; his life may be *true*, or it may be *false*; it may be either a shame or a glory to him. The good man builds himself up; the bad man destroys himself.

But whatever we do we must do confidently (if we are timid, let us, then, act timidly), not expecting more light, but having light enough. If we confidently expect more, then let us wait for it. But what is this which we have? Have we not already waited? Is this the beginning of time? Is there a man who does not see clearly beyond, though only a hair's breadth beyond where he at any time stands?

If one hesitates in his path, let him not proceed. Let him respect his doubts, for doubts, too, may have some divinity in them. That we have but little faith is not sad, but that we have but little faithfulness. By faithfulness faith is earned. When, in the progress of a life, a man swerves, though only by an angle infinitely small, from his proper and allotted path (and this is never done quite unconsciously even at first; in fact, that was his broad and scarlet sin,—ah, he knew of it more than he can tell), then the drama of his life turns to tragedy, and makes haste to its fifth act. When once we thus fall behind ourselves, there is no accounting for the obstacles which rise up in our path, and no one is so wise as to advise, and no one so powerful as to aid us while we abide on that ground. Such are cursed with *duties*, and the *neglect of their duties*. For such the decalogue was made, and other far more voluminous and terrible codes.

These departures,—who have not made them?—for they are as faint as the parallax of a fixed star, and at the commencement we say they are nothing,—that is, they originate in a kind of sleep and forgetfulness of the soul when it is naught. A man cannot be too circumspect in order to keep in the straight road, and be sure that he sees all that he may at any time see, that so he may distinguish his true path.

Letter to H. G. O. Blake, 5/2/48 Corr 220–221

When first I took up my abode in the woods, that is, began to spend my nights as well as days there, which, by accident, was on Independence Day, or the Fourth of July, 1845, my house was not finished for winter, but was merely a defence against the rain, without plastering or chimney, the walls being of rough, weather-stained boards, with wide chinks, which made it cool at night. The upright white hewn studs and freshly planed door and window casings gave it a clean and airy look, especially in the morning, when its timbers were saturated with dew, so that I fancied that by noon some sweet gum would exude from them. To my imagination it retained throughout the day more or less of this auroral character, reminding me of a certain house on a mountain which I had visited a year before. This was an airy and unplastered cabin, fit to entertain a travelling god, and where a goddess might trail her garments. The winds which passed over my dwelling were such as sweep over the ridges of mountains, bearing the broken strains, or celestial parts only, of terrestrial music. The morning wind forever blows, the poem of creation is uninterrupted; but few are the ears that hear it. Olympus is but the outside of the earth everywhere.
"Where I Lived and What I Lived For," *Walden* W II, 94

No face which we can give to a matter will stead us so well at last as the truth. This alone wears well. For the most part, we are not where we are, but in a false position. Through an infirmity of our natures, we suppose a case, and put ourselves into it, and hence are in two cases at the same time, and it is doubly difficult to get out. In sane moments we regard only the facts, the case that is. Say what you have to say, not what you ought. Any truth is better than make-believe. Tom Hyde, the tinker, standing on the gallows, was asked if he had anything to say. "Tell the tailors," said he, "to remember to make a knot in their thread before they take the first stitch." His companion's prayer is forgotten.

However mean your life is, meet it and live it; do not shun it and call it hard names. It is not so bad as you are. It looks poorest when you are richest. The fault-finder will find faults even in paradise. Love your life, poor as it is. You may perhaps have some pleasant, thrilling, glorious hours, even in a poor-house. The setting sun is reflected from the windows of the alms-house as brightly as from the rich man's abode; the snow melts before its door as early in the spring. I do not see but a quiet mind may live as contentedly there, and have as cheering thoughts, as in a palace. *"Conclusion," Walden* W II, 360–361

Any prospect of awakening or coming to life to a dead man makes indifferent all times and places. The place where that may occur is always the same, and indescribably pleasant to all our senses. For the most part we allow only outlying and transient circumstances to make our occasions. They are, in fact, the cause of our distraction. Nearest to all things is that power which fashions their being. *Next* to us the grandest laws are continually being executed. *Next* to us is not the workman whom we have hired, with whom we love so well to talk, but the workman whose work we are. "Solitude," *Walden* W II, 148

Nature never makes haste; her systems revolve at an even pace. The bud swells imperceptibly, without hurry or confusion, as though the short spring days were an eternity. All her operations seem separately, for the time, the single object for which all things tarry. Why, then, should man hasten as if anything less than eternity were allotted for the least deed? Let him consume never so many eons, so that he go about the meanest task well, though it be but the paring of his nails. *Journal entry* W VII, 92

There was an artist in the city of Kouroo who was disposed to strive after perfection. One day it came into his mind to make a staff. Having considered that in an imperfect work time is an ingredient, but into a perfect work time does not enter, he said to himself, It shall be perfect in all respects, though I should do nothing else in my life. He proceeded instantly to the forest for wood, being resolved that it should not be made of unsuitable material; and as he searched for and rejected stick after stick, his friends gradually deserted him, for they grew old in their works and died, but he grew not older by a moment. His singleness of purpose and resolution, and his elevated piety, endowed him, without his knowledge, with perennial youth. As he made no compromise with Time, Time kept out of his way, and only sighed at a distance because he could not overcome him. Before he had found a stick in all respects suitable the city of Kouroo was a hoary ruin, and he sat on one of its mounds to peel the stick. Before he had given it the proper shape the dynasty of the Candahars was at an end, and with the point of the stick he wrote the name of the last of that race in the sand, and then resumed his work. By the time he had smoothed and polished the staff Kalpa was no longer the pole-star; and ere he had put on the ferule and the head adorned with precious stones, Brahma had awoke and slumbered many times. But why do I stay to mention these things? When the finishing stroke was put to his work, it suddenly expanded before the eyes of the astonished artist into the fairest of all the creations of Brahma. He had made a new system in making a staff, a world with full and fair proportions; in which, though the old cities and dynasties had passed away, fairer and more glorious ones had taken their places. And now he saw by the heap of shavings still fresh at his feet, that, for him and his work, the former lapse of time had been an illusion, and that no more time had elapsed than is required for a single scintillation from the brain of Brahma to fall on and inflame the tinder of a mortal brain. The material was pure, and his art was pure; how could the result be other than wonderful?

"Conclusion," *Walden* W II, 359–360

It would be worth the while to build [a house] still more deliberately than I did, considering, for instance, what foundation a door, a window, a cellar, a garret, have in the nature of man, and perchance never raising any superstructure until we found a better reason for it than our temporal necessities even. There is some of the same fitness in a man's building his own house that there is in a bird's building its own nest. Who knows but if men constructed their dwellings with their own hands, and provided food for themselves and families simply and honestly enough, the poetic faculty would be universally developed, as birds universally sing when they are so engaged? But alas! we do like cowbirds and cuckoos, which lay their eggs in nests which other birds have built, and cheer no traveller with their chattering and unmusical notes. Shall we forever resign the pleasure of construction to the carpenter? What does architecture amount to in the experience of the mass of men? I never in all my walks came across man engaged in so simple and natural an occupation as building his house. We belong to the community. It is not the tailor alone who is the ninth part of a man; it is as much the preacher, and the merchant, and the farmer. Where is this division of labor to end? and what object does it finally serve? No doubt another *may* also think for me; but it is not therefore desirable that he should do so to the exclusion of my thinking for myself. *"Economy," Walden* W II, 50–51

> "Direct your eye right inward, and you'll find
> A thousand regions in your mind
> Yet undiscovered. Travel them, and be
> Expert in home-cosmography."

What does Africa,—what does the West stand for? Is not our own interior white on the chart? black though it may prove, like the coast, when discovered. Is it the source of the Nile, or the Niger, or the Mississippi, or a Northwest Passage around this continent, that we would find? Are these the problems which most concern mankind? Is Franklin the only man who is lost, that his wife should be so earnest to find him? Does Mr. Grinnell know where he himself is? Be rather the Mungo Park, the Lewis and Clark and Frobisher, of your own streams and oceans; explore your own higher latitudes,—with shiploads of preserved meats to support you, if they be necessary; and pile the empty cans sky-high for a sign. Were preserved meats invented to preserve meat merely? Nay, be a Columbus to whole new continents and worlds within you, opening new channels, not of trade, but of thought. Every man is the lord of a realm beside which the earthly empire of the Czar is but a petty state, a hummock left by the ice. . . . What was the meaning of that South-Sea Exploring Expedition, with all its parade and expense, but an indirect recognition of the fact that there are continents and seas in the moral world to which every man is an isthmus or an inlet, yet unexplored by him, but that it is easier to sail many thousand miles through cold and storm and cannibals, in a government ship, with five hundred men and boys to assist one, than it is to explore the private sea, the Atlantic and Pacific Ocean of one's being alone.— . . . England and France, Spain and Portugal, Gold Coast and Slave Coast, all front on this private sea; but no bark from them has ventured out of sight of land, though it is without doubt the direct way to India. If you would learn to speak all tongues and conform to the customs of all nations, if you would travel farther than all travellers, be naturalized in all climes, and cause the Sphinx to dash her head against a stone, even obey the precept of the old philosopher, and Explore thyself. Herein are demanded the eye and the nerve. Only the defeated and deserters go to the wars, cowards that run away and enlist. Start now on that farthest western way, which does not pause at the Mississippi or the Pacific, nor conduct toward a worn-out China or Japan, but leads on direct, a tangent to this sphere, summer and winter, day and night, sun down, moon down, and at last earth down too.

"*Conclusion*," *Walden* W II, 353–355

I sometimes wonder that we can be so frivolous, I may almost say, as to attend to the gross but somewhat foreign form of servitude called Negro Slavery, there are so many keen and subtle masters that enslave both North and South. It is hard to have a Southern overseer; it is worse to have a Northern one; but worst of all when you are the slave-driver of yourself. Talk of a divinity in man! Look at the teamster on the highway, wending to market by day or night; does any divinity stir within him? His highest duty to fodder and water his horses! What is his destiny to him compared with the shipping interests? Does not he drive for Squire Make-a-stir? How godlike, how immortal, is he? See how he cowers and sneaks, how vaguely all the day he fears, not being immortal nor divine, but the slave and prisoner of his own opinion of himself, a fame won by his own deeds. Public opinion is a weak tyrant compared with our own private opinion. What a man thinks of himself, that it is which determines, or rather indicates, his fate. Self-emancipation even in the West Indian provinces of the fancy and imagination,—what Wilberforce is there to bring that about? Think, also, of the ladies of the land weaving toilet cushions against the last day, not to betray too green an interest in their fates! As if you could kill time without injuring eternity.

"*Economy*," *Walden* W II, 8

Will you live? or will you be embalmed? Will you live, though it be astride of a sunbeam; or will you repose safely in the catacombs for a thousand years? In the former case, the worst accident that can happen is that you may break your neck. Will you break your heart, your soul, to save your neck? Necks and pipe-stems are fated to be broken. Men make a great ado about the folly of demanding too much of life (or of eternity?), and of endeavoring to live according to that demand. It is much

ado about nothing. No harm ever came from that quarter. I am not afraid that I shall exaggerate the value and significance of life, but that I shall not be up to the occasion which it is. I shall be sorry to remember that I was there, but noticed nothing remarkable,—not so much as a prince in disguise; lived in the golden age a hired man; visited Olympus even, but fell asleep after dinner, and did not hear the conversation of the gods. I lived in Judæa eighteen hundred years ago, but I never knew that there was such a one as Christ among my contemporaries!
Letter to H. G. O. Blake, 4/3/50 Corr 257–258

I almost shrink from the arduousness of meeting men erectly day by day. Be resolutely and faithfully what you are; be humbly what you aspire to be. Be sure you give men the best of your wares, though they be poor enough, and the gods will help you to lay up a better store for the future. Man's noblest gift to man is his sincerity, for it embraces his integrity also. Let him not dole out of himself anxiously, to suit their weaker or stronger stomachs, but make a clean gift of himself, and empty his coffers at once. I would be in society as in the landscape; in the presence of nature there is no reserve, nor effrontery.
Journal entry W VII, 174–175

If thy neighbor hail thee to inquire how goes the world, feel thyself put to thy trumps to return a true and explicit answer. Plant the feet firmly, and, will he nill he, dole out to him with strict and conscientious impartiality his modicum of response. *Journal entry W VII, 40*

Men are very generally spoiled by being so civil and well-disposed. You can have no profitable conversation with them, they are so conciliatory, determined to agree with you. They exhibit such long-suffering and kindness in a short interview. I would meet with some provoking strangeness, so that we may be guest and host and refresh one another. It is possible for a man wholly to disappear and be merged in his manners. . . . A cross man, a coarse man, an eccentric man, a silent, a man who does not drill well—of him there is some hope. Your gentlemen, they are all alike. They utter their opinions as if it was not a man that uttered them. *Journal entry W VIII, 328–329*

Many a traveller came out of his way to see me and the inside of my house, and, as an excuse for calling, asked for a glass of water. I told them that I drank at the pond, and pointed thither, offering to lend them a dipper. Far off as I lived, I was not exempted from that annual visitation which occurs, methinks, about the first of April, when everybody is on the move; and I had my share of good luck, though there were some curious specimens among my visitors. Half-witted men from the almshouse and elsewhere came to see me; but I endeavored to make them exercise all the wit they had, and make their confessions to me; in such cases making wit the theme of our conversation; and so was compensated. Indeed, I found some of them to be wiser than the so-called *overseers* of the poor and selectmen of the town, and thought it was time that the tables were turned. With respect to wit, I learned that there was not much difference between the half and the whole. One day, in particular, an inoffensive, simple-minded pauper, whom with others I had often seen used as fencing stuff, standing or sitting on a bushel in the fields to keep cattle and himself from straying, visited me, and expressed a wish to live as I did. He told me, with the utmost simplicity and truth, quite superior, or rather *inferior*, to anything that is called humility, that he was "deficient in intellect." These were his words. The Lord had made him so, yet he supposed the Lord cared as much for him as for another. "I have always been so," said he, "from my childhood; I never had much mind; I was not like other children; I am weak in the head. It was the Lord's will, I suppose." And there he was to prove the truth of his words. He was a metaphysical puzzle to me. I have rarely met a fellow-man on such promising ground,—it was so simple and sincere and so true all that he said. *"Visitors," Walden* W II, 167–168

Men frequently say to me, "I should think you would feel lonesome down there, and want to be nearer to folks, rainy and snowy days and nights especially." I am tempted to reply to such,—This whole earth which we inhabit is but a point in space. How far apart, think you, dwell the two most distant inhabitants of yonder star, the breadth of whose disk cannot be appreciated by our instruments? Why should I feel lonely? Is not our planet in the Milky Way? This which you put seems to me not to be the most important question. What sort of space is that which separates a man from his fellows and makes him solitary? I have found that no exertion of the legs can bring two minds much nearer to one another. What do we want most to dwell near to? Not to many men surely, the depot, the post-office, the bar-room, the meeting-house, the school-house, the grocery, Beacon Hill, or the Five Points, where men most congregate, but to the perennial source of our life, whence in all our experience we have found that to issue, as the willow stands near the water and sends out its roots in that direction. This will vary with different natures, but this is the place where a wise man will dig his cellar.
"Solitude," Walden W II, 147–148

I left the woods for as good a reason as I went there. Perhaps it seemed to me that I had several more lives to live, and could not spare any more time for that one. It is remarkable how easily and insensibly we fall into a particular route, and make a beaten track for ourselves. I had not lived there a week before my feet wore a path from my door to the pond-side; and though it is five or six years since I trod it, it is still quite distinct. It is true, I fear, that others may have fallen into it, and so helped to keep it open. The surface of the earth is soft and impressible by the feet of men; and so with the paths which the mind travels. How worn and dusty, then, must be the highways of the world, how deep the ruts of tradition and conformity! I did not wish to take a cabin passage, but rather to go before the mast and on the deck of the world, for there I could best see the moonlight amid the mountains. I do not wish to go below now.

I learned this, at least, by my experiment: that if one advances confidently in the direction of his dreams, and endeavors to live the life which he has imagined, he will meet with a success unexpected in common hours. He will put some things behind, will pass an invisible boundary; new, universal, and more liberal laws will begin to establish themselves around and within him; or the old laws be expanded, and interpreted in his favor in a more liberal sense, and he will live with the license of a higher order of beings. In proportion as he simplifies his life, the laws of the universe will appear less complex, and solitude will not be solitude, nor poverty poverty, nor weakness weakness. If you have built castles in the air, your work need not be lost; that is where they should be. Now put the foundations under them.   *"Conclusion," Walden* W II, 355–356

NATURE AS SETTING AND SYMBOL

Although Thoreau's famous experiment of living alone at Walden Pond lasted only two years, his whole adult life was spent living close to nature. His surveying work and his walks through Concord's woods and fields—not to mention the long walking trips he took to Maine, Cape Cod, and Canada—combined with his scientific study of botany to give him that wonderful familiarity with growing things that Emerson commented on in his eulogy. But Thoreau regarded such information as but a route to a higher kind of understanding, an insight into the process of growth itself. In this process he saw an analogy with the actualization of his own inner being, and so the humblest facts and occurrences seemed to him rich with significance. To live meant to be alive to the world around him: to see, to hear, to taste and smell and touch natural objects with senses unclouded by preconception. "I have heard," he wrote in his journal, "that there is a Society for the Diffusion of Useful Knowledge. It is said that knowledge is power and the like. Methinks there is equal need of a Society for the Diffusion of Useful Ignorance, for what is most of our boasted so-called knowledge but a conceit that we know something, which robs us of the advantages of our actual ignorance." (Journal entry, 2/9/51)[1] As he grew older, the moments of spontaneous insight seem to have become rarer, and he became more willing to settle for the pleasures of a more prosaic kind of understanding of nature. But to the very end of his life, he viewed nature as his domain—at once the setting for meaningful life and a symbol of the process of living itself.

But while we are confined to books, though the most select and classic, and read only particular written languages, which are themselves but dialects and provincial, we are in danger of forgetting the language which all things and events speak without metaphor, which alone is copious and standard. Much is published, but little printed. The rays which stream through the shutter will be no longer remembered when the shutter is wholly removed. No method nor discipline can supersede the necessity of being forever on the alert. What is a course of history or philosophy, or poetry, no matter how well selected, or the best society, or the most admirable routine of life, compared with the discipline of looking always at what is to be seen? Will you be a reader, a student merely, or a seer? Read your fate, see what is before you, and walk on into futurity.

I did not read books the first summer; I hoed beans. Nay, I often did better than this. There were times when I could not afford to sacrifice the bloom of the present moment to any work, whether of the head or hands.

[1] *Writings*, VIII, 150.

I love a broad margin to my life. Sometimes, in a summer morning, having taken my accustomed bath, I sat in my sunny doorway from sunrise till noon, rapt in a revery, amidst the pines and hickories and sumachs, in undisturbed solitude and stillness, while the birds sang around or flitted noiseless through the house, until by the sun falling in at my west window, or the noise of some travellers' wagon on the distant highway, I was reminded of the lapse of time. I grew in those seasons like corn in the night, and they were far better than any work of the hands would have been. They were not time subtracted from my life, but so much over and above my usual allowance.

"Sounds," *Walden* W II, 123–124

I believe that there is a subtle magnetism in Nature, which, if we unconsciously yield to it, will direct us aright. It is not indifferent to us which way we walk. There is a right way; but we are very liable from heedlessness and stupidity to take the wrong one. We would fain take that walk, never yet taken by us through this actual world, which is perfectly symbolical of the path which we love to travel in the interior and ideal world; and sometimes, no doubt, we find it difficult to choose our direction, because it does not yet exist distinctly in our idea.

When I go out of the house for a walk, uncertain as yet whither I will bend my steps, and submit myself to my instinct to decide for me, I find, strange and whimsical as it may seem, that I finally and inevitably settle southwest, toward some particular wood or meadow or deserted pasture or hill in that direction. . . .

Eastward I go only by force; but westward I go free. Thither no business leads me. It is hard for me to believe that I shall find fair landscapes or sufficient wildness and freedom behind the eastern horizon. . . .

The West of which I speak is but another name for the Wild; and what I have been preparing to say is, that in Wildness is the preservation of the World. Every tree sends its fibres forth in search of the Wild. The cities import it at any price. Men plow and sail for it. From the forest and wilderness come the tonics and barks which brace mankind. Our ancestors were savages. The story of Romulus and Remus being suckled by a wolf is not a meaningless fable. The founders of every state which has risen to eminence have drawn their nourishment and vigor from a similar wild source. It was because the children of the Empire were not suckled by the wolf that they were conquered and displaced by the children of the northern forests who were.

I believe in the forest, and in the meadow, and in the night in which the corn grows. We require an infusion of hemlock spruce or arbor-vitæ in our tea. . . .

Life consists with wildness. The most alive is the wildest. Not yet subdued to man, its presence refreshes him. One who pressed forward incessantly and never rested from his labors, who grew fast and made infinite demands on life, would always find himself in a new country or wilderness, and surrounded by the raw material of life. He would be climbing over the prostrate stems of primitive forest-trees.

Hope and the future for me are not in lawns and cultivated fields, not in towns and cities, but in the impervious and quaking swamps. When, formerly, I have analyzed my partiality for some farm which I had contemplated purchasing, I have frequently found that I was attracted solely by a few square rods of impermeable and unfathomable bog,—a natural sink in one corner of it. That was the jewel which dazzled me. I derive more of my subsistence from the swamps which surround my native town than from the cultivated gardens in the village. . . . When I would re-create myself, I seek the darkest wood, the thickest and most interminable and, to the citizen, most dismal, swamp. I enter a swamp as a sacred place, a *sanctum sanctorum*. There is the strength, the marrow, of Nature. The wildwood covers the virgin mould, and the same soil is good for men and for trees. A man's health requires as many acres of meadow to his prospect as his farm does loads of muck. There are the strong meats on which he feeds. A town is saved, not more by the righteous men in it than by the woods and swamps that surround it.

"*Walking,*" *Walden* W V, 226–229 passim

As I came home through the woods with my string of fish, trailing my pole, it being now quite dark, I caught a glimpse of a woodchuck stealing across my path, and felt a strange thrill of savage delight, and was strongly tempted to seize and devour him raw; not that I was hungry then, except for that wildness which he represented. Once or twice, however, while I lived at the pond, I found myself ranging the woods, like a half-starved hound, with a strange abandonment, seeking some kind of venison which I might devour, and no morsel could have been too savage for me. The wildest scenes had become unaccountably familiar. I found in myself, and still find, an instinct toward a higher, or, as it is named, spiritual life, as do most men, and another toward a primitive rank and savage one, and I reverence them both. I love the wild not less than the good. The wildness and adventure that are in fishing still recommended it to me. I like sometimes to take rank hold on life and spend my day more as the animals do. "*Higher Laws,*" *Walden* W II, 232

Sometimes, after staying in a village parlor till the family had all retired, I have returned to the woods, and, partly with a view to the next day's dinner, spent the hours of midnight fishing from a boat by moonlight, serenaded by owls and foxes, and hearing, from time to time, the creaking note of some unknown bird close at hand. These experiences were very memorable and valuable to me,—anchored in forty feet of water, and twenty or thirty rods from the shore, surrounded sometimes by thousands of small perch and shiners, dimpling the surface with their tails in the moonlight, and communicating by a long flaxen line with mysterious nocturnal fishes which had their dwelling forty feet below, or sometimes dragging sixty feet of line about the pond as I drifted in the gentle night breeze, now and then feeling a slight vibration along it, indicative of some life prowling about its extremity, of dull uncertain blundering purpose there, and slow to make up its mind. At length you slowly raise, pulling hand over hand, some horned pout squeaking and squirming to the upper air. It was very queer, especially in dark nights, when your thoughts had wandered to vast and cosmogonal themes in other spheres, to feel this faint jerk, which came to interrupt your dreams and link you to Nature again. It seemed as if I might next cast my line upward into the air, as well as downward into this element, which was scarcely more dense. Thus I caught two fishes as it were with one hook.

"The Ponds," Walden W II, 194–195

Few phenomena gave me more delight than to observe the forms which thawing sand and clay assume in flowing down the sides of a deep cut on the railroad through which I passed on my way to the village, a phenomenon not very common on so large a scale, though the number of freshly exposed banks of the right material must have been greatly multiplied since railroads were invented. The material was sand of every degree of fineness and of various rich colors, commonly mixed with a little clay. When the frost comes out in the spring, and even in a thawing day in the winter, the sand begins to flow down the slopes like lava, sometimes bursting out through the snow and overflowing it where no sand was to be seen before. Innumerable little streams overlap and interlace one with another, exhibiting a sort of hybrid product, which obeys half way the law of currents, and half way that of vegetation. As it flows it takes the forms of sappy leaves or vines, making heaps of pulpy sprays a foot or more in depth, and resembling, as you look down on them, the laciniated, lobed, and imbricated thalluses of some lichens; or you are reminded of coral, of leopards' paws or birds' feet, of brains or lungs or bowels, and excrements of all kinds. It is a truly *grotesque* vegetation, whose forms and color we see imitated in bronze, a sort of architectural foliage more ancient and typical than acanthus, chicory, ivy, vine, or any vegetable leaves; destined perhaps, under some circumstances, to become a puzzle to future geologists. The whole cut impressed me as if it were a cave with its stalactites laid open to the light. The various shades of the sand are singularly rich and agreeable, embracing the different iron colors, brown, gray, yellowish, and reddish. When the flowing mass reaches the drain at the foot of the bank it spreads out flatter into *strands,* the separate streams losing their semi-cylindrical form and gradually becoming more flat and broad, running together as they are more moist, till they form an almost flat *sand,* still variously and beautifully shaded, but in which you can trace the original forms of vegetation; till at length, in the water itself, they are converted into *banks,* like those formed off the mouths of rivers, and the forms of vegetation are lost in the ripple-marks on the bottom.

The whole bank, which is from twenty to forty feet high, is sometimes overlaid with a mass of this kind of foliage, or sandy rupture, for a quarter of a mile on one or both sides, the produce of one spring day. What makes this sand foliage remarkable is its springing into existence thus suddenly. When I see on the one side the inert bank,—for the sun acts on one side first,—and on the other this luxuriant foliage, the creation of an hour, I am affected as if in a peculiar sense I stood in the laboratory of the Artist who made the world and me,—had come to where he was still at work, sporting on this bank, and with excess of energy strewing his fresh designs about. I feel as if I were nearer to the vitals of the globe, for this sandy overflow is something such a foliaceous mass as the vitals of the animal body. You find thus in the very sands an anticipation of the vegetable leaf. No wonder that the earth expresses itself outwardly in leaves, it so labors with the idea inwardly. The atoms have already learned this law, and are pregnant by it. The overhanging leaf sees here its prototype. *Internally,* whether in the globe or animal body, it is a moist thick *lobe,* a word especially applicable to the liver and lungs and the *leaves* of fat (λείβω, *labor, lapsus,* to flow or slip downward, a lapsing; λοβός, *globus,* lobe, globe; also lap, flap, and many other words); *externally,* a dry thin *leaf,* even as the *f* and *v* are a pressed and dried *b*. The radicals of *lobe* are *lb,* the soft mass of the *b* (single-lobed, or B, double-lobed), with the liquid *l* behind it pressing it forward. In globe, *glb,* the guttural *g* adds to the meaning the capacity of the throat. The feathers and wings of birds are still drier and thinner leaves. Thus, also, you pass from the lumpish grub in the earth to the airy and fluttering butterfly. The very globe continually transcends and translates itself, and becomes winged in its orbit. Even ice begins with delicate crystal leaves, as if it had flowed into moulds which the fronds of waterplants have impressed on the watery mirror. The whole tree itself is but one leaf, and rivers are still vaster leaves whose pulp is intervening earth, and towns and cities are the ova of insects in their axils.

When the sun withdraws the sand ceases to flow, but in the morning the streams will start once more and branch and branch again into a myriad of others. You here see perchance how blood-vessels are formed. If you look closely you observe that first there pushes forward from the thawing mass a stream of softened sand with a drop-like point, like the ball of the finger, feeling its way slowly and blindly downward, until at last with more heat and moisture, as the sun gets higher, the moist fluid portion, in its effort to obey the law to which the most inert also yields, separates from the latter and forms for itself a meandering channel or artery within that, in which is seen a little silvery stream glancing like lightning from one stage of pulpy leaves or branches to another, and ever and anon swallowed up in the sand. It is wonderful how rapidly yet perfectly the sand organizes itself as it flows, using the best material its mass affords to form the sharp edges of its channel. Such are the sources of rivers. In the silicious matter which the water deposits is perhaps the bony system, and in the still finer soil and organic matter the fleshy fibre or cellular tissue. What is man but a mass of thawing clay? The ball of the human finger is but a drop congealed. The fingers and toes flow to their extent from the thawing mass of the body. Who knows what the human body would expand and flow out to under a more genial heaven? Is not the hand a spreading *palm* leaf with its lobes and veins? The ear may be regarded, fancifully, as a lichen, *Umbilicaria*, on the side of the head, with its lobe or drop. The lip—*labium*, from *labor* (?)—laps or lapses from the sides of the cavernous mouth. The nose is a manifest congealed drop or stalactite. The chin is a still larger drop, the confluent dripping of the face. The cheeks are a slide from the brows into the valley of the face, opposed and diffused by the cheek bones. Each rounded lobe of the vegetable leaf, too, is a thick and now loitering drop, larger or smaller; the lobes are the fingers of the leaf; and as many lobes as it has, in so many directions it tends to flow, and more heat or other genial influences would have caused it to flow yet farther.

Thus it seemed that this one hillside illustrated the principle of all the operations of Nature. The Maker of this earth but patented a leaf. What Champollion will decipher this hieroglyphic for us, that we may turn over a new leaf at last? This phenomenon is more exhilarating to me than the luxuriance and fertility of vineyards. True, it is somewhat excrementitious in its character, and there is no end to the heaps of liver, lights, and bowels, as if the globe were turned wrong side outward; but this suggests at least that Nature has some bowels, and there again is mother of humanity. This is the frost coming out of the ground; this is Spring. It precedes the green and flowery spring, as mythology precedes regular poetry. I know of nothing more purgative of winter fumes and indigestions. It convinces me that Earth is still in her swaddling-clothes, and stretches forth baby fingers on every side. Fresh curls spring from the baldest brow. There is nothing inorganic. These foliaceous heaps lie along the bank like the slag of a furnace, showing that Nature is "in full blast" within. The earth is not a mere fragment of dead history, stratum upon stratum like the leaves of a book, to be studied by geologist and antiquaries chiefly, but living poetry like the leaves of a tree, which precede flowers and fruit,—not a fossil earth, but a living earth; compared with whose great central life all animal and vegetable life is merely parasitic.

Its throes will heave our exuviæ from their graves. You may melt your metals and cast them into the most beautiful moulds you can; they will never excite me like the forms which this molten earth flows out into. And not only it, but the institutions upon it are plastic like clay in the hands of the potter. *"Spring," Walden* W II, 336–341

After a still winter night I awoke with the impression that some question had been put to me, which I had been endeavoring in vain to answer in my sleep, as what—how—when—where? But there was dawning Nature, in whom all creatures live, looking in at my broad windows with serene and satisfied face, and no question on *her* lips. I awoke to an answered question, to Nature and daylight.
"The Pond in Winter," Walden W II, 312

The life in us is like the water in the river. It may rise this year higher than man has ever known it, and flood the parched uplands; even this may be the eventful year, which will drown out all our muskrats. It was not always dry land where we dwell. I see far inland the banks which the stream anciently washed, before science began to record its freshets. Everyone has heard the story which has gone the rounds of New England, of a strong and beautiful bug which came out of the dry leaf of an old table of apple-tree wood, which had stood in a farmer's kitchen for sixty years, first in Connecticut, and afterward in Massachusetts,—from an egg deposited in the living tree many years earlier still, as appeared by counting the annual layers beyond it; which was heard gnawing out for several weeks, hatched perchance by the heat of an urn. Who does not feel his faith in a resurrection and immortality strengthened by hearing of this? Who knows what beautiful and winged life, whose egg has been buried for ages under many concentric layers of woodenness in the dead dry life of society, deposited at first in the alburnum of the green and living tree, which has been gradually converted into the semblance of its well-seasoned tomb,—heard perchance gnawing out now for years by the astonished family of man, as they sat round the festive board,—may unexpectedly come forth from amidst society's most trivial and hand-selled furniture, to enjoy its perfect summer life at last!
"Conclusion," Walden W II, 366–367

TWO SELECTIONS

The foregoing excerpts from Thoreau's writing illustrate his talent across the spectrum of nonfiction, from the highly personal to the abstractly philosophical. The final two selections will illustrate at somewhat greater length two other aspects of his literary powers—narration and persuasion. The first is the account of his arrival and sojourn at Walden Pond, where he built himself a small cabin and conducted his famous experiment in self-dependence. The second is the speech, delivered just three years before his death, in behalf of John Brown, the radical abolitionist who would shortly be hanged for his attempt to initiate a slave rebellion in the year before the Civil War broke out. The tone of the two pieces is as different as their purposes. The first alternates between relaxed informativeness and irony, as it describes his ability to live well on very little. The second soars angrily, as he calls to his fellow townsmen to wake up to the realities of the moral and political situation on the eve of the Civil War. It was characteristic of Thoreau that the latter piece was delivered to an audience that he himself had summoned to the Town Hall, going around the town door to door for that purpose. It was also characteristic that he got an audience, for as Emerson said, people were fascinated by Thoreau and always anxious (both ready and a little fearful) to hear what he had to say. The Walden narrative too was a response to the interest expressed by people who were fascinated by the phenomenon of Thoreau's self-sufficiency and could not help seeing in it an ironic commentary on their own complicated lives.

LIFE AT WALDEN POND

Near the end of March, 1845, I borrowed an axe and went down to the woods by Walden Pond, nearest to where I intended to build my house, and began to cut down some tall, arrowy white pines, still in their youth, for timber. It is difficult to begin without borrowing, but perhaps it is the most generous course thus to permit your fellow-men to have an interest in your enterprise. The owner of the axe, as he released his hold on it, said that it was the apple of his eye; but I returned it sharper than I received it. It was a pleasant hillside where I worked, covered with pine woods, through which I looked out on the pond, and a small open field in the woods where pines and hickories were springing up. The ice in the pond was not yet dissolved, though there were some open spaces, and it was all dark-colored and saturated with water. There were some slight flurries of snow during the days that I worked there; but for the most part when I came out on to the railroad, on my way home, its yellow sand-heap stretched away gleaming in the hazy atmosphere, and the rails shone in the spring sun, and I heard the lark and pewee and other birds already come to commence another year with us. They were pleasant spring days, in which the winter of man's discontent was thawing as well as the earth, and the life that had lain torpid began to stretch itself. One day, when my axe had come off and I had cut a green hickory for a wedge, driving it with a stone, and had placed the whole to soak in a pond-hole in order to swell the wood, I saw a striped snake run into the water, and he lay on the bottom, apparently without inconvenience, as long as I stayed there, or more than a quarter of an hour: perhaps because he had not yet fairly come out of the torpid state. It appeared to me that for a like reason men remain in their present low and primitive condition; but if they should feel the influence of the spring of springs arousing them, they would of necessity rise to a higher and more ethereal life. I had previously seen the snakes in frosty mornings in my path with portions of their bodies still numb and inflexible, waiting for the sun to thaw them. On the 1st of April it rained and melted the ice, and in the early part of the day, which was very foggy, I heard a stray goose groping about over the pond and cackling as if lost, or like the spirit of the fog.

So I went on for some days cutting and hewing timber, and also studs and rafters, all with my narrow axe, not having many communicable or scholar-like thoughts singing to myself,—

> Men say they know many things;
> But lo! they have taken wings,—
> The arts and sciences,
> And a thousand appliances;
> The wind that blows
> Is all that any body knows.

I hewed the main timbers six inches square, most of the studs on two sides only, and the rafters and floor timbers on one side, leaving the rest of the bark on, so that they were just as straight and much stronger than sawed ones. Each stick was carefully mortised or tenoned by its stump, for I had borrowed other tools by this time. My days in the woods were not very long ones; yet I usually carried my dinner of bread and butter, and read the newspaper in which it was wrapped, at noon, sitting amid the green pine boughs which I had cut off, and to my bread was imparted some of their fragrance, for my hands were covered with a thick coat of pitch. Before I had done I was more the friend than the foe of the pine tree, though I had cut down some of them, having become better acquainted with it. Sometimes a rambler in the wood was attracted by the sound of my axe, and we chatted pleasantly over the chips which I had made.

By the middle of April, for I made no haste in my work, but rather made the most of it, my house was framed and ready for the raising. I had already bought the shanty of James Collins, an Irishman who worked on the Fitchburg Railroad, for boards. James Collins' shanty was considered an uncommonly fine one. When I called to see it he was not at home. I walked about the outside, at first unobserved from within, the window was so deep and high. It was of small dimensions, with a peaked cottage roof, and not much else to be seen, the dirt being raised five feet all around as if it were a compost heap. The roof was the soundest part, though a good deal warped and made brittle by the sun. Doorsill there was none, but a perennial passage for the hens under the door-board. Mrs. C. came to the door and asked me to view it from the inside. The hens were driven in by my approach. It was dark, and had a dirt floor for the most part, dank, clammy, and aguish, only here a board and there a board which would not bear removal. She lighted a lamp to show me the inside of the roof and the walls, and also that the board floor extended under the bed, warning me not to step into the cellar, a sort of dust hole two feet deep. In her own words, they were "good boards overhead, good boards all around, and a good window,"—of two whole squares originally, only the cat had passed out that way lately. There was a stove, a bed, and a place to sit, an infant in the house where it was born, a silk parasol, gilt-framed looking-glass, and a patent new coffee-mill nailed to an oak sapling, all told. The bargain was soon concluded, for James had in the meanwhile returned. I to pay four dollars and twenty-five cents tonight, he to vacate at five to-morrow morning, selling to nobody else meanwhile: I to take possession at six. It were well, he said, to be there early, and anticipate certain indistinct but wholly unjust claims on the score of ground rent and fuel. This he assured me was the only encumbrance. At six I passed him and his family on the road. One large bundle held their all,—bed, coffee-mill, looking-glass, hens,—all but the cat; she took to the woods and became a wild cat, and, as I learned afterward, trod in a trap set for woodchucks, and so became a dead cat at last.

I took down this dwelling the same morning, drawing the nails, and removed it to the pond-side by small cartloads, spreading the boards on the grass there to bleach and warp back again in the sun. One early thrush gave me a note or two as I drove along the woodland path. I was informed treacherously by a young Patrick that neighbor Seeley, an Irishman, in the intervals of the carting, transferred the still tolerable, straight, and drivable nails, staples, and spikes to his pocket, and then stood when I came back to pass the time of day, and look freshly up, unconcerned, with spring thoughts, at the devastation; there being a dearth of work, as he said. He was there to represent spectatordom, and help make this seemingly insignificant event one with the removal of the gods of Troy.

I dug my cellar in the side of a hill sloping to the south, where a woodchuck had formerly dug his burrow, down through sumach and blackberry roots, and the lowest stain of vegetation, six feet square by seven deep, to a fine sand where potatoes would not freeze in any winter. The sides were left shelving, and not stoned; but the sun having never shone on them, the sand still keeps its place. It was but two hours' work. I took particular pleasure in this breaking of ground, for in almost all latitudes men dig into the earth for an equable temperature. Under the most splendid house in the city is still to be found the cellar where they store their roots as of old, and long after the superstructure has disappeared posterity remark its dent in the earth. The house is still but a sort of porch at the entrance of a burrow.

At length, in the beginning of May, with the help of some of my acquaintances, rather to improve so good an occasion for neighborliness than from any necessity, I set up the frame of my house. No man was ever more honored in the character of his raisers than I. They are destined, I trust, to assist at the raising of loftier structures one day. I began to occupy my house on the 4th of July, as soon as it was boarded and roofed, for the boards were carefully feather-edged and lapped, so that it was perfectly impervious to rain, but before boarding I laid the foundation of a chimney at one end, bringing two cartloads of stones up the hill from the pond in my arms. I built the chimney after my hoeing in the fall, before a fire became necessary for warmth, doing my cooking in the meanwhile out of doors on the ground, early in the morning: which mode I still think is in some respects more convenient and agreeable than the usual one. When it stormed before my bread was baked, I fixed a few boards over the fire, and sat under them to watch my loaf, and passed some pleasant hours in that way. In those days, when my hands were much employed, I read but little, but the least scraps of paper which lay on the ground, my holder, or tablecloth, afforded me as much entertainment, in fact answered the same purpose as the Iliad. . . .   W II, 45–50

Before I finished my house, wishing to earn ten or twelve dollars by some honest and agreeable method, in order to meet my unusual expenses, I planted about two acres and a half of light and sandy soil near it chiefly with beans, but also a small part with potatoes, corn, peas, and turnips. The whole lot contains eleven acres, mostly growing up to pines and hickories, and was sold the preceding season for eight dollars and eight cents an acre. One farmer said that it was "good for nothing but to raise cheeping squirrels on." I put no manure whatever on this land, not being the owner, but merely a squatter, and not expecting to cultivate so much again, and I did not quite hoe it all once. I got out several cords of stumps in plowing, which supplied me with fuel for a long time, and left small circles of virgin mould, easily distinguishable through the summer by the greater luxuriance of the beans there. The dead and for the most part unmerchantable wood behind my house, and the driftwood from the pond, have supplied the remainder of my fuel. I was obliged to hire a team and a man for the plowing, though I held the plow myself. My farm outgoes for the first season were, for implements, seed, work, etc., $14.72½. The seed corn was given me. This never costs anything to speak of, unless you plant more than enough. I got twelve bushels of beans, and eighteen bushels of potatoes, beside some peas and sweet corn. The yellow corn and turnips were too late to come to anything. My whole income from the farm was

	$23 44
Deducting the outgoes	14 72½
There are left	$8 71½,

beside produce consumed and on hand at the time this estimate was made of the value of $4.50,—the amount on hand much more than balancing a little grass which I did not raise. All things considered, that is, considering the importance of a man's soul and of to-day, notwithstanding the short time occupied by my experiment, nay, partly even because of its transient character, I believe that that was doing better than any farmer in Concord did that year.

The next year I did better still, for I spaded up all the land which I required, about a third of an acre, and I learned from the experience of both years, not being in the least awed by many celebrated works on husbandry, Arthur Young among the rest, that if one would live simply and eat only the crop which he raised, and raise no more than he ate, and not exchange it for an insufficient quantity of more luxurious and expensive things, he would need to cultivate only a few rods of ground, and that it would be cheaper to spade up that than to use oxen to plow it, and to select a fresh spot from time to time than to manure the old, and he could do all his necessary farm work as it were with his left hand at odd hours in the summer; and thus he would not be tied to an ox, or horse, or cow, or pig, as at present. I desire to speak impartially on this point, and as one not interested in the success or failure of the present economical and social arrangements. I was more independent than any farmer in Concord, for I was not anchored to a house or farm, but could follow the bent of my genius, which is a very crooked one, every moment. Beside being better off than they already, if my house had been burned or my crops had failed, I should have been nearly as well off as before. . . .

W II, 60–62

Before winter I built a chimney, and shingled the sides of my house, which were already impervious to rain, with imperfect and sappy shingles made of the first slice of the log, whose edges I was obliged to straighten with a plane.

I have thus a tight shingled and plastered house, ten feet wide by fifteen long, and eight-feet posts, with a garret and a closet, a large window on each side, two trap-doors, one door at the end, and a brick fireplace opposite. The exact cost of my house, paying the usual price for such materials as I used, but not counting the work, all of which was done by myself, was as follows; and I give the details because very few are able to tell exactly what their houses cost, and fewer still, if any, the separate cost of the various materials which compose them:—

Boards	$8 03½,	mostly shanty boards.
Refuse shingles for roof and sides . .	4 00	
Laths	1 25	
Two second-hand windows with glass .	2 43	
One thousand old brick	4 00	
Two casks of lime	2 40	That was high.
Hair	0 31	More than I needed.
Mantle-tree iron	0 15	
Nails	3 90	
Hinges and screws	0 14	
Latch	0 10	
Chalk	0 01	
Transportation	1 40	{ I carried a good part on my back.
In all	$28 12½	

These are all the materials, excepting the timber, stones, and sand, which I claimed by squatter's right. I have also a small woodshed adjoining, made chiefly of the stuff which was left after building the house.

I intend to build me a house which will surpass any on the main street in Concord in grandeur and luxury, as soon as it pleases me as much and will cost me no more than my present one.

I thus found that the student who wishes for a shelter can obtain one for a lifetime at an expense not greater than the rent which he now pays annually. If I seem to boast more than is becoming, my excuse is that I brag for humanity rather than for myself; and my shortcomings and inconsistencies do not affect the truth of my statement. . . . W II, 52–55

By surveying, carpentry, and day-labor of various other kinds in the village in the meanwhile, for I have as many trades as fingers, I had earned $13.34. The expense of food for eight months, namely, from July 4th to March 1st, the time when these estimates were made, though I lived there more than two years,—not counting potatoes, a little green corn, and some peas, which I had raised, nor considering the value of what was on hand at the last date,—was

Rice	$1 73½	
Molasses	1 73	Cheapest form of the saccharine.
Rye meal	1 04¾	
Indian meal	0 99¾	Cheaper than rye.
Pork	0 22	
Flour	0 8	Costs more than Indian meal, both money and trouble.
Sugar	0 80	
Lard	0 65	
Apples	0 25	
Dried apple	0 22	
Sweet potatoes	0 10	
One pumpkin	0 6	
One watermelon	0 2	
Salt	0 3	

{ All experiments which failed. }

Yes, I did eat $8.74, all told; but I should not thus unblushingly publish my guilt if I did not know that most of my readers were equally guilty with myself, and that their deeds would look no better in print. The next year I sometimes caught a mess of fish for my dinner, and once I went so far as to slaughter a woodchuck which ravaged my bean-field,—effect his transmigration, as a Tartar would say,—and devour him, partly for experiment's sake; but though it afforded me a momentary enjoyment, notwithstanding a musky flavor, I saw that the longest use would not make that a good practice, however it might seem to have your woodchucks ready dressed by the village butcher.

Clothing and some incidental expenses within the same dates, though little can be inferred from this item, amounted to

$8 40¾

Oil and some household utensils . . . 2 00

So that all of the pecuniary outgoes, excepting for washing and mending, which for the most part were done out of the house, and their bills have not yet been received,—and these are all and more than all the ways by which money necessarily goes out in this part of the world,—were

House	$28 12½
Farm one year	14 72½
Food eight months	8 74
Clothing, etc., eight months	8 40¾
Oil, etc., eight months	2 00
In all	61 99¾

I address myself now to those of my readers who have a living to get. And to meet this I have for farm produce sold

                              Earned by day-labor $23 34
                                                                    13 34
                              In all $36 78,

which subtracted from the sum of the outgoes leaves a balance of $25.21¾ on the one side,—this being very nearly the means with which I started, and the measure of expenses to be incurred,—and on the other, beside the leisure and independence and health thus secured, a comfortable house for me as long as I choose to occupy it.   W II, 65–67

For more than five years I maintained myself thus solely by the labor of my hands, and I found that, by working about six weeks in a year, I could meet all the expenses of living. The whole of my winters, as well as most of my summers, I had free and clear for study. I have thoroughly tried school-keeping, and found that my expenses were in proportion, or rather out of proportion, to my income, for I was obliged to dress and train, not to say think and believe, accordingly, and I lost my time into the bargain. As I did not teach for the good of my fellow-men, but simply for a livelihood, this was a failure. I have tried trade but I found that it would take ten years to get under way in that, and that then I should probably be on my way to the devil. I was actually afraid that I might by that time be doing what is called a good business. When formerly I was looking about to see what I could do for a living, some sad experience in conforming to the wishes of friends being fresh in my mind to tax my ingenuity, I thought often and seriously of picking huckleberries; that surely I could do, and its small profits might suffice,—for my greatest skill has been to want but little,—so little capital it required, so little distraction from my wonted moods, I foolishly thought. While my acquaintances went unhesitatingly into trade or the professions, I contemplated this occupation as most like theirs; ranging the hills all summer to pick the berries which came in my way, and thereafter carelessly dispose of them; so, to keep the flocks of Admetus. I also dreamed that I might gather the wild herbs, or carry evergreens to such villagers as loved to be reminded of the woods, even to the city, by hay-cart loads. But I have since learned that trade curses everything it handles; and though you trade in messages from heaven, the whole curse of trade attaches to the business.

As I preferred some things to others, and especially valued my freedom, as I could fare hard and yet succeed well, I did not wish to spend my time in earning rich carpets or other fine furniture, or delicate cookery, or a house in the Grecian or the Gothic style just yet. If there are any to whom it is no interruption to acquire these things, and who know how to use them when acquired, I relinquish to them the pursuit. Some are "industrious," and appear to love labor for its own sake, or perhaps because it keeps them out of worse mischief; to such I have at present nothing to say. Those who would not know what to do with more leisure than they now enjoy, I might advise to work twice as hard as they do,—work till they pay for themselves, and get their free papers. For myself I found that the occupation of a day-laborer was the most independent of any, especially as it required only thirty or forty days in a year to support one. The laborer's day ends with the going down of the sun, and he is then free to devote himself to his chosen pursuit, independent of his labor; but his employer, who speculates from month to month, has no respite from one end of the year to the other.

In short, I am convinced, both by faith and experience, that to maintain one's self on this earth is not a hardship but a pastime, if we will live simply and wisely; as the pursuits of the simpler nations are still the sports of the more artificial. It is not necessary that a man should earn his living by the sweat of his brow, unless he sweats easier than I do.

W II, 76–78

A Plea for Captain John Brown

I trust that you will pardon me for being here. I do not wish to force my thoughts upon you, but I feel forced myself. Little as I know of Captain Brown, I would fain do my part to correct the tone and the statements of the newspapers, and of my countrymen generally, respecting his character and actions. It costs us nothing to be just. We can at least express our sympathy with, and admiration of, him and his companions, and that is what I now propose to do.

First, as to his history. I will endeavor to omit, as much as possible, what you have already read. I need not describe his person to you, for probably most of you have seen and will not soon forget him. I am told that his grandfather, John Brown, was an officer in the Revolution; that he himself was born in Connecticut about the beginning of this century, but early went with his father to Ohio. I heard him say that his father was a contractor who furnished beef to the army there, in the war of 1812; that he accompanied him to the camp, and assisted him in that employment seeing a good deal of military life,—more, perhaps, than if he had been a soldier; for he was often present at the councils of the officers. Especially, he learned by experience how armies are supplied and maintained in the field,—a work which, he observed, requires at least as much experience and skill as to lead them in battle. He said that few persons had any conception of the cost, even the pecuniary cost, of firing a single bullet in war. He saw enough, at any rate, to disgust him with a military life; indeed, to excite in him a great abhorrence of it; so much so, that though he was tempted by the offer of some petty office in the army, when he was about eighteen, he not only declined that, but he also refused to train when warned, and was fined for it. He then resolved that he would never have anything to do with any war, unless it were a war for liberty.

When the troubles in Kansas began, he sent several of his sons thither to strengthen the party of the Free State men, fitting them out with such weapons as he had; telling them that if the troubles should increase, and there should be need of him, he would follow, to assist them with his hand and counsel. This, as you all know, he soon after did; and it was through his agency, far more than any other's, that Kansas was made free.

For a part of his life he was a surveyor, and at one time he was engaged in wool-growing, and he went to Europe as an agent about that business. There, as everywhere, he had his eyes about him, and made many original observations. He said, for instance, that he saw why the soil of England was so rich, and that of Germany (I think it was) so poor, and he thought of writing to some of the crowned heads about it. It was because in England the peasantry live on the soil which they cultivate, but in Germany they are gathered into villages at night. It is a pity that he did not make a book of his observations.

I should say that he was an old-fashioned man in his respect for the Constitution, and his faith in the permanence of this Union. Slavery he deemed to be wholly opposed to these, and he was its determined foe.

He was by descent and birth a New England farmer, a man of great common sense, deliberate and practical as that class is, and tenfold more so. He was like the best of those who stood at Concord Bridge once, on Lexington Common, and on Bunker Hill, only he was firmer and higher principled than any that I have chanced to hear of as there. It was no abolition lecturer that converted him. Ethan Allen and Stark, with whom he may in some respects be compared, were rangers in a lower and less important field. They could bravely face their country's foes, but he had the courage to face his country herself when she was in the wrong. A Western writer says, to account for his escape from so many perils, that he was concealed under a "rural exterior;" as if, in that prairie land, a hero should, by good rights, wear a citizen's dress only.

He did not go to the college called Harvard, good old Alma Mater as she is. He was not fed on the pap that is there furnished. As he phrased it, "I know no more of grammar than one of your calves." But he went to the great university of the West, where he sedulously pursued the study of Liberty, for which he had early betrayed a fondness, and having taken many degrees, he finally commenced the public practice of Humanity in Kansas, as you all know. Such were *his humanities,* and not any study of grammar. He would have left a Greek accent slanting the wrong way, and righted up a falling man.

He was one of that class of whom we hear a great deal, but, for the most part, see nothing at all,—the Puritans. It would be in vain to kill him. He died lately in the time of Cromwell, but he reappeared here. Why should he not? Some of the Puritan stock are said to have come over and settled in New England. They were a class that did something else than celebrate their forefathers' day, and eat parched corn in remembrance of that time. They were neither Democrats nor Republicans, but men of simple habits, straightforward, prayerful; not thinking much of rulers who did not fear God, not making many compromises, nor seeking after available candidates.

"In his camp," as one has recently written, and as I have myself heard him state, "he permitted no profanity; no man of loose morals was suffered to remain there, unless, indeed, as a prisoner of war. 'I would rather,' said he, 'have the small-pox, yellow fever, and cholera, all together in my camp, than a man without principle. . . . It is a mistake, sir, that our people make, when they think that bullies are the best fighters, or that they are the fit men to oppose these Southerners. Give me men of good principles,—Godfearing men,—men who respect themselves, and with a dozen of them I will oppose any hundred such men as these Buford ruffians.'" He said that if one offered himself to be a soldier under him, who was forward to tell what he could or would do if he could only get sight of the enemy, he had but little confidence in him.

He was never able to find more than a score or so of recruits whom he would accept, and only about a dozen, among them his sons, in whom he had perfect faith. When he was here, some years ago, he showed to a few a little manuscript book,—his "orderly book" I think he called it,—containing the names of his company in Kansas, and the rules by which they bound themselves; and he stated that several of them had already sealed the contract with their blood. When some one remarked that, with the addition of a chaplain, it would have been a perfect Cromwellian troop, he observed that he would have been glad to add a chaplain to the list, if he could have found one who could fill that office worthily. It is easy enough to find one for the United States army. I believe that he had prayers in his camp morning and evening, nevertheless.

He was a man of Spartan habits, and at sixty was scrupulous about his diet at your table, excusing himself by saying that he must eat sparingly and fare hard, as became a soldier, or one who was fitting himself for difficult enterprises, a life of exposure.

A man of rare common sense and directness of speech, as of action; a transcendentalist above all, a man of ideas and principles,—that was what distinguished him. Not yielding to a whim or transient impulse, but carrying out the purpose of a life. I noticed that he did not overstate anything, but spoke within bounds. I remember, particularly, how, in his speech here, he referred to what his family had suffered in Kansas, without ever giving the least vent to his pent-up fire. It was a volcano with an ordinary chimney-flue. Also referring to the deeds of certain Border

Ruffians, he said, rapidly paring away his speech, like an experienced soldier, keeping a reserve of force and meaning, "They had a perfect right to be hung." He was not in the least a rhetorician, was not talking to Buncombe or his constituents anywhere, had no need to invent anything but to tell the simple truth, and communicate his own resolution; therefore he appeared incomparably strong, and eloquence in Congress and elsewhere seemed to me at a discount. It was like the speeches of Cromwell compared with those of an ordinary king.

As for his tact and prudence, I will merely say, that at a time when scarcely a man from the Free States was able to reach Kansas by any direct route, at least without having his arms taken from him, he, carrying what imperfect guns and other weapons he could collect, openly and slowly drove an ox-cart through Missouri, apparently in the capacity of a surveyor, with his surveying compass exposed in it, and so passed unsuspected, and had ample opportunity to learn the designs of the enemy. For some time after his arrival he still followed the same profession. When, for instance, he saw a knot of the ruffians on the prairie, discussing, of course, the single topic which then occupied their minds, he would, perhaps, take his compass and one of his sons, and proceed to run an imaginary line right through the very spot on which that conclave had assembled, and when he came up to them, he would naturally pause and have some talk with them, learning their news, and, at last, all their plans perfectly; and having thus completed his real survey he would resume his imaginary one, and run on his line till he was out of sight.

When I expressed surprise that he could live in Kansas at all, with a price set upon his head, and so large a number, including the authorities, exasperated against him, he accounted for it by saying, "It is perfectly well understood that I will not be taken." Much of the time for some years he has had to skulk in swamps, suffering from poverty and from sickness, which was the consequence of exposure, befriended only by Indians and a few whites. But though it might be known that he was lurking in a particular swamp, his foes commonly did not care to go in after him. He could even come out into a town where there were more Border Ruffians than Free State men, and transact some business, without delaying long, and yet not be molested; for, said he, "no little handful of men were willing to undertake it, and a large body could not be got together in season."

As for his recent failure, we do not know the facts about it. It was evidently far from being a wild and desperate attempt. His enemy, Mr. Vallandigham, is compelled to say that "it was among the best planned and executed conspiracies that ever failed."

Not to mention his other successes, was it a failure, or did it show a want of good management, to deliver from bondage a dozen human beings, and walk off with them by broad daylight, for weeks if not months, at a leisurely pace, through one State after another, for half the length of the North, conspicuous to all parties, with a price set upon his head, going into a court-room on his way and telling what he had done, thus convincing Missouri that it was not profitable to try to hold slaves in his neighborhood?—and this, not because the government menials were lenient, but because they were afraid of him.

Yet he did not attribute his success, foolishly, to "his star," or to any magic. He said, truly, that the reason why such greatly superior numbers quailed before him was, as one of his prisoners confessed, because they *lacked a cause*,—a kind of armor which he and his party never lacked. When the time came, few men were found willing to lay down their lives in defense of what they knew to be wrong; they did not like that this should be their last act in this world.

But to make haste to *his* last act, and its effects.

The newspapers seem to ignore, or perhaps are really ignorant, of the fact that there are at least as many as two or three individuals to a town throughout the North who think much as the present speaker does about him and his enterprise. I do not hesitate to say that they are an important and growing party. We aspire to be something more than stupid and timid chattels, pretending to read history and our Bibles, but desecrating every house and every day we breathe in. Perhaps anxious politicians may prove that only seventeen white men and five negroes were concerned in the late enterprise; but their very anxiety to prove this might suggest to themselves that all is not told. Why do they still dodge the truth? They are so anxious because of a dim consciousness of the fact, which they do not distinctly face, that at least a million of the free inhabitants of the United States would have rejoiced if it had succeeded. They at most only criticise the tactics. Though we wear no crape, the thought of that man's position and probable fate is spoiling many a man's day here at the North for other thinking. If any one who has seen him here can pursue successfully any other train of thought, I do not know what he is made of. If there is any such who gets his usual allowance of sleep, I will warrant him to fatten easily under any circumstances which do not touch his body or purse. I put a piece of paper and a pencil under my pillow, and when I could not sleep I wrote in the dark.

On the whole, my respect for my fellow-men, except as one may outweigh a million, is not being increased these days. I have noticed the cold-blooded way in which newspaper writers and men generally speak of this event, as if an ordinary malefactor, though one of unusual "pluck,"—as the Governor of Virginia is reported to have said, using the language of the cock-pit, "the gamest man he ever saw,"—had been caught, and were about to be hung. He was not dreaming of his foes when the governor thought he looked so brave. It turns what sweetness I have to gall, to hear, or hear of, the remarks of some of my neighbors. When we heard at first that he was dead, one of my townsmen observed that "he died as the fool dieth;" which, pardon me, for an instant suggested a likeness in him dying to my neighbor living. Others, craven-hearted, said disparagingly, that "he threw his life away," because he resisted the government. Which way have they thrown *their* lives, pray?—such as would praise a man for attacking singly an ordinary band of thieves or murderers. I hear another ask, Yankee-like, "What will he gain by it?" as if he expected to fill his pockets by this enterprise. Such a one has no idea of gain but in this worldly sense. If it does not lead to a "surprise" party, if he does not get a new pair of boots, or a vote of thanks, it must be a failure. "But he won't gain anything by it." Well, no, I don't suppose he could get four-and-sixpence a day for being hung, take the year round; but then he stands a chance to save a considerable part of his soul,—and *such* a soul!—when *you* do not. No doubt you can get more in your market for a quart of milk than for a quart of blood, but that is not the market that heroes carry their blood to.

Such do not know that like the seed is the fruit, and that, in the moral world, when good seed is planted, good fruit is inevitable, and does not depend on our watering and cultivating; that when you plant, or bury, a hero in his field, a crop of heroes is sure to spring up. This is a seed of such force and vitality, that it does not ask our leave to germinate.

The momentary charge at Balaklava, in obedience to a blundering command, proving what a perfect machine the soldier is, has, properly enough, been celebrated by a poet laureate; but the steady, and for the most part successful, charge of this man, for some years, against the legions of Slavery, in obedience to an infinitely higher command, is as much more memorable than that as an intelligent and conscientious man is superior to a machine. Do you think that that will go unsung?

"Served him right,"—"A dangerous man,"—"He is undoubtedly insane." So they proceed to live their sane, and wise, and altogether admirable lives, reading their Plutarch a little, but chiefly pausing at that feat of Putnam, who was let down into a wolf's den; and in this wise they nourish themselves for brave and patriotic deeds some time or other. The Tract Society could afford to print that story of Putnam. You might open the district schools with the reading of it, for there is nothing about Slavery or the Church in it; unless it occurs to the reader that some pastors are *wolves* in sheep's clothing. "The American Board of Commissioners for Foreign Missions," even, might dare to protest against *that* wolf. I have heard of boards, and of American boards, but it chances that I never heard of this particular lumber till lately. And yet I hear of Northern men, and women, and children, by families, buying a "life-membership" in such societies as these. A life-membership in the grave! You can get buried cheaper than that.

Our foes are in our midst and all about us. There is hardly a house but is divided againt itself, for our foe is the all but universal woodenness of both head and heart, the want of vitality in man, which is the effect of our vice; and hence are begotten fear, superstition, bigotry, persecution, and slavery of all kinds. We are mere figure-heads upon a hulk, with livers in the place of hearts. The curse is the worship of idols, which at length changes the worshiper into a stone image himself; and the New Englander is just as much an idolator as the Hindoo. This man was an exception, for he did not set up even a political graven image between him and his God.

A church that can never have done with excommunicating Christ while it exists! Away with your broad and flat churches, and your narrow and tall churches! Take a step forward, and invent a new style of out-houses. Invent a salt that will save you, and defend our nostrils.

The modern Christian is a man who has consented to say all the prayers in the liturgy, provided you will let him go straight to bed and sleep quietly afterward. All his prayers begin with "Now I lay me down to sleep," and he is forever looking forward to the time when he shall go to his "*long* rest." He has consented to perform certain old-established charities, too, after a fashion, but he does not wish to hear of any new-fangled ones; he doesn't wish to have any supplementary articles added to the contract, to fit it to the present time. He shows the whites of his eyes on the Sabbath, and the blacks all the rest of the week. The evil is not merely a stagnation of blood, but a stagnation of spirit. Many, no doubt, are well disposed, but sluggish by constitution and by habit, and they cannot conceive of a man who is actuated by higher motives than they are. Accordingly they pronounce this man insane, for they know that *they* could never act as he does, as long as they are themselves.

We dream of foreign countries, of other times and races of men, placing them at a distance in history or space; but let some significant event like the present occur in our midst, and we discover, often, this distance and this strangeness between us and our nearest neighbors. *They* are our Austrias, and Chinas, and South Sea Islands. Our crowded society becomes well spaced all at once, clean and handsome to the eye,—a city of magnificent distances. We discover why it was that we never got beyond compliments and surfaces with them before; we become aware of as many versts between us and them as there are between a wandering Tartar and a Chinese town. The thoughtful man becomes a hermit in the thoroughfares of the market-place. Impassable seas suddenly find their level between us, or dumb steppes stretch themselves out there. It is the difference of constitution, of intelligence, and faith, and not streams and mountains, that make the true and impassable boundaries between individuals and between states. None but the like-minded can come plenipotentiary to our court.

I read all the newspapers I could get within a week after this event, and I do not remember in them a single expression of sympathy for these men. I have since seen one noble statement, in a Boston paper, not editorial. Some voluminous sheets decided not to print the full report of Brown's words to the exclusion of other matter. It was as if a publisher should reject the manuscript of the New Testament, and print Wilson's last speech. The same journal which contained this pregnant news was chiefly filled, in parallel columns, with the reports of the political conventions that were being held. But the descent to them was too steep. They should have been spared this contrast,—been printed in an extra, at least. To turn from the voices and deeds of earnest men to the *cackling* of political conventions! Office-seekers and speech-makers, who do not so much as lay an honest egg, but wear their breasts bare upon an egg of chalk! Their great game is the game of straws, or rather that universal aboriginal game of the platter, at which the Indians cried *hub, bub!* Exclude the reports of religious and political conventions, and publish the words of a living man.

But I object not so much to what they have omitted as to what they have inserted. Even the *Liberator* called it "a misguided, wild, and apparently insane—effort." As for the herd of newspapers and magazines, I do not chance to know an editor in the country who will deliberately print anything which he knows will ultimately and permanently reduce the number of his subscribers. They do not believe that it would be expedient. How then can they print truth? If we do not say pleasant things, they argue, nobody will attend to us. And so they do like some traveling auctioneers, who sing an obscene song, in order to draw a crowd around them. Republican editors, obliged to get their sentences ready for the morning edition, and accustomed to look at everything by the twilight of politics, express no admiration, nor true sorrow even, but call these men "deluded fanatics,"—"mistaken men,"—"insane," or "crazed." It suggests what a *sane* set of editors we are blessed with, *not* "mistaken men;" who know very well on which side their bread is buttered, at least.

A man does a brave and humane deed, and at once, on all sides, we hear people and parties declaring, "I didn't do it, nor countenance him to do it, in any conceivable way. It can't be fairly inferred from my past career." I, for one, am not interested to hear you define your position. I don't know that I ever was or ever shall be. I think it is mere egotism, or impertinent at this time. Ye needn't take so much pains to wash your skirts of him. No intelligent man will ever be convinced that he was any creature of yours. He went and came, as he himself informs us, "under the auspices of John Brown and nobody else." The Republican party does not perceive how many his *failure* will make to vote more correctly than they would have them. They have counted the votes of Pennsylvania & Co., but they have not correctly counted Captain Brown's vote. He has taken the wind out of their sails,—the little wind they had,—and they may as well lie to and repair.

What though he did not belong to your clique! Though you may not approve of his method or his principles, recognize his magnanimity. Would you not like to claim kindredship with him in that, though in no other thing he is like, or likely, to you? Do you think that you would lose your reputation so? What you lost at the spile, you would gain at the bung.

If they do not mean all this, they do not speak the truth, and say what they mean. They are simply at their old tricks still.

"It was always conceded to him," *says one who calls him crazy,* "that he was a conscientious man, very modest in his demeanor, apparently inoffensive, until the subject of Slavery was introduced, when he would exhibit a feeling of indignation unparalleled."

The slave-ship is on her way, crowded with its dying victims; new cargoes are being added in mid-ocean; a small crew of slaveholders, countenanced by a large body of passengers, is smothering four millions under the hatches, and yet the politician asserts that the only proper way by which deliverance is to be obtained is by "the quiet diffusion of the sentiments of humanity," without any "outbreak." As if the sentiments of humanity were ever found unaccompanied by its deeds, and you could disperse them, all finished to order, the pure article, as easily as water with a watering-pot, and so lay the dust. What is that that I hear cast overboard? The bodies of the dead that have found deliverance. That is the way we are "diffusing" humanity, and its sentiments with it.

Prominent and influential editors, accustomed to deal with politicians, men of an infinitely lower grade, say, in their ignorance, that he acted "on the principle of revenge." They do not know the man. They must enlarge themselves to conceive of him. I have no doubt that the time will come when they will begin to see him as he was. They have got to conceive of a man of faith and of religious principle, and not a politician or an Indian; of a man who did not wait till he was personally interfered with or thwarted in some harmless business before he gave his life to the cause of the oppressed.

If Walker may be considered the representative of the South, I wish I could say that Brown was the representative of the North. He was a superior man. He did not value his bodily life in comparison with ideal things. He did not recognize unjust human laws, but resisted them as he was bid. For once we are lifted out of the trivialness and dust of politics into the region of truth and manhood. No man in America has ever stood up so persistently and effectively for the dignity of human nature, knowing himself for a man, and the equal of any and all governments. In that sense he was the most American of us all. He needed no babbling lawyer, making false issues, to defend him. He was more than a match for all the judges that American voters, or office-holders of whatever grade, can create. He could not have been tried by a jury of his peers, because his peers did not exist. When a man stands up serenely against the condemnation and vengeance of mankind, rising above them literally *by a whole body,*—even though he were of late the vilest murderer, who has settled that matter with himself,—the spectacle is a sublime one,—didn't ye know it, ye *Liberators,* ye *Tribunes,* ye *Republicans?*—and we become criminal in comparison. Do yourselves the honor to recognize him. He needs none of your respect.

As for the Democratic journals, they are not human enough to affect me at all. I do not feel indignation at anything they may say.

I am aware that I anticipate a little,—that he was still, at the last accounts, alive in the hands of his foes; but that being the case, I have all along found myself thinking and speaking of him as physically dead.

I do not believe in erecting statues to those who still live in our hearts, whose bones have not yet crumbled in the earth around us, but I would rather see the statue of Captain Brown in the Massachusetts State-House yard than that of any other man whom I know. I rejoice that I live in this age, that I am his contemporary.

What a contrast, when we turn to that political party which is so anxiously shuffling him and his plot out of its way, and looking around for some available slaveholder, perhaps, to be its candidate at least for one who will execute the Fugitive Slave Law, and all those other unjust laws which he took up arms to annul!

Insane! A father and six sons, and one son-in-law, and several more men besides,—as many at least as twelve disciples,—all struck with insanity at once; while the sane tyrant holds with a firmer grip than ever his four millions of slaves, and a thousand sane editors, his abettors, are saving their country and their bacon! Just as insane were his efforts in Kansas. Ask the tyrant who is his most dangerous foe, the sane man or the insane? Do the thousands who know him best, who have rejoiced at his deeds in Kansas, and have afforded him material aid there, think him insane? Such a use of this word is a mere trope with most who persist in using it, and I have no doubt that many of the rest have already in silence retracted their words.

Read his admirable answers to Mason and others. How they are dwarfed and defeated by the contrast! On the one side, half-brutish, half-timid questioning; on the other, truth, clear as lightning, crashing into their obscene temples. They are made to stand with Pilate, and Gessler and the Inquisition. How ineffectual their speech and action! and what a void their silence! They are but helpless tools in this great work. It was no human power that gathered them about this preacher.

What have Massachusetts and the North sent a few *sane* representatives to Congress for, of late years?—to declare with effect what kind of sentiments? All their speeches put together and boiled down—and probably they themselves will confess it—do not match for manly directness and force, and for simple truth, the few casual remarks of crazy John Brown on the floor of the Harper's Ferry engine-house,—that man whom you are about to hang, to send to the other world, though not to represent *you* there. No, he was not our representative in any sense. He was too fair a specimen of a man to represent the like of us. Who, then, *were* his constituents? If you read his words understandingly you will find out. In his case there is no idle eloquence, no made, nor maiden speech, no compliments to the oppressor. Truth is his inspirer, and earnestness the polisher of his sentences. He could afford to lose his Sharps rifles, while he retained his faculty of speech,—a Sharps rifle of infinitely surer and longer range.

And the New York *Herald* reports the conversation *verbatim!* It does not know of what undying words it is made the vehicle.

I have no respect for the penetration of any man who can read the report of that conversation and still call the principal in it insane. It has the ring of a saner sanity than an ordinary discipline and habits of life, than an ordinary organization, secure. Take any sentence of it,—"Any questions that I can honorably answer, I will; not otherwise. So far as I am myself concerned, I have told everything truthfully. I value my word, sir." The few who talk about his vindictive spirit, while they really admire his heroism, have no test by which to detect a noble man, no amalgam to combine with his pure gold. They mix their own dross with it.

It is a relief to turn from these slanders to the testimony of his more truthful, but frightened jailers and hangmen. Governor Wise speaks far more justly and appreciatingly of him than any Northern editor, or politician, or public personage, that I chance to have heard from. I know that you can afford to hear him again on this subject. He says: "They are themselves mistaken who take him to be a madman. . . . He is cool, collected, and indomitable, and it is but just to him to say that he was humane to his prisoners. . . . And he inspired me with great trust in his integrity as a man of truth. He is a fanatic, vain and garrulous" (I leave that part to Mr. Wise), "but firm, truthful, and intelligent. His men, too, who survive, are like him. . . . Colonel Washington says that he was the coolest and firmest man he ever saw in defying danger and death. With one son dead by his side, and another shot through, he felt the pulse of his dying son with one hand, and held his rifle with the other, and commanded his men with the utmost composure, encouraging them to be firm, and to sell their lives as dear as they could. Of the three white prisoners, Brown, Stevens, and Coppoc, it was hard to say which was most firm."

Almost the first Northern men whom the slaveholder has learned to respect!

The testimony of Mr. Vallandigham, though less valuable, is of the same purport, that "it is vain to underrate either the man or his conspiracy. . . . He is the farthest possible removed from the ordinary ruffian, fanatic, or madman."

"All is quiet at Harper's Ferry," say the journals. What is the character of that calm which follows when the law and the slaveholder prevail? I regard this event as a touchstone designed to bring out, with glaring distinctness, the character of this government. We needed to be thus assisted to see it by the light of history. It needed to see itself. When a government puts forth its strength on the side of injustice, as ours to maintain slavery and kill the liberators of the slave, it reveals itself a merely brute force, or worse, a demoniacal force. It is the head of the Plug-Uglies. It is more manifest than ever that tyranny rules. I see this government to be effectually allied with France and Austria in oppressing mankind. There sits a tyrant holding fettered four millions of slaves; here comes their heroic liberator. This most hypocritical and diabolical government looks up from its seat on the gasping four millions, and inquires with an assumption of innocence: "What do you assault me for? Am I not an honest man? Cease agitation on this subject, or I will make a slave of you, too, or else hang you."

We talk about a *representative* government; but what a monster of a government is that where the noblest faculties of the mind, and the *whole* heart, are not *represented*. A semi-human tiger or ox, stalking over the earth, with its heart taken out and the top of its brain shot away. Heroes have fought well on their stumps when their legs were shot off, but I never heard of any good done by such a government as that.

The only government that I recognize—and it matters not how few are at the head of it, or how small its army—is that power that establishes justice in the land, never that which establishes injustice. What shall we think of a government to which all the truly brave and just men in the land are enemies, standing between it and those whom it oppresses? A government that pretends to be Christian and crucifies a million Christs every day!

Treason! Where does such treason take its rise? I cannot help thinking of you as you deserve, ye governments. Can you dry up the fountains of thought? High treason, when it is resistance to tyranny here below, has its origin in, and is first committed by, the power that makes and forever recreates man. When you have caught and hung all these human rebels, you have accomplished nothing but your own guilt, for you have not struck at the fountainhead. You presume to contend with a foe against whom West Point cadets and rifled cannon *point* not. Can all the art of the cannon-founder tempt matter to turn against its maker? Is the form in which the founder thinks he casts it more essential than the constitution of it and of himself?

The United States have a coffle of four millions of slaves. They are determined to keep them in this condition; and Massachusetts is one of the confederated overseers to prevent their escape. Such are not all the inhabitants of Massachusetts, but such are they who rule and are obeyed here. It was Massachusetts, as well as Virginia, that put down this insurrection at Harper's Ferry. She sent the marines there, and she will have *to pay the penalty of her sin.*

Suppose that there is a society in this State that out of its own purse and magnanimity saves all the fugitive slaves that run to us, and protects our colored fellow-citizens, and leaves the other work to the government, so called. Is not that government fast losing its occupation, and becoming contemptible to mankind? If private men are obliged to perform the offices of government, to protect the weak and dispense justice, then the government becomes only a hired man, or clerk, to perform menial or indifferent services. Of course, that is but the shadow of a government whose existence necessitates a Vigilant Committee. What should we think of the Oriental Cadi even, behind whom worked in secret a Vigilant Committee? But such is the character of our Northern States generally; each has its Vigilant Committee. And, to a certain extent, these crazy governments recognize and accept this relation. They say, virtually, "We'll be glad to work for you on these terms, only don't make a noise about it." And thus the government, its salary being insured, withdraws into the back shop, taking the Constitution with it, and bestows most of its labor on repairing that. When I hear it at work sometimes, as I go by, it reminds me, at best, of those farmers who in winter contrive to turn a penny by following the cooperating business. And what kind of spirit is their barrel made to hold? They speculate in stocks, and bore holes in mountains, but they are not competent to lay out even a decent highway. The only *free* road, the Underground Railroad, is owned and managed by the Vigilant Committee. *They* have tunneled under the whole breadth of the land. Such a government is losing its power and respectability as surely as water runs out of a leaky vessel, and is held by one that can contain it.

I hear many condemn these men because they were so few. When were the good and the brave ever in a majority? Would you have had him wait till that time came?—till you and I came over to him? The very fact that he had no rabble or troop of hirelings about him would alone distinguish him from ordinary heroes. His company was small indeed, because few could be found worthy to pass muster. Each one who there laid down his life for the poor and oppressed was a picked man, culled out of many thousands, if not millions; apparently a man of principle, of rare courage, and devoted humanity; ready to sacrifice his life at any moment for the benefit of his fellow-man. It may be doubted if there were as many more their equals in these respects in all the country,—I speak of his followers only,—for their leader, no doubt, scoured the land far and wide, seeking to swell his troop. These alone were ready to step between the oppressor and the oppressed. Surely they were the very best men you could select to be hung. That was the greatest compliment which this country could pay them. They were ripe for her gallows. She has tried a long time, she has hung a good many, but never found the right one before.

When I think of him, and his six sons, and his son-in-law, not to enumerate the others, enlisted for this fight, proceeding coolly, reverently, humanely to work, for months if not years, sleeping and waking upon it, summering and wintering the thought, without expecting any reward but a good conscience, while almost all America stood ranked on the other side,—I say again that it affects me as a sublime spectacle. If he had had any journal advocating *"his cause,"* any organ, as the phrase is, monotonously and wearisomely playing the same old tune, and then passing round the hat, it would have been fatal to his efficiency. If he had acted in any way so as to be let alone by the government, he might have been suspected. It was the fact that the tyrant must give place to him, or he to the tyrant, that distinguished him from all the reformers of the day that I know.

It was his peculiar doctrine that a man has a perfect right to interfere by force with the slave-holder, in order to rescue the slave. I agree with him. They who are continually shocked by slavery have some right to be shocked by the violent death of the slave-holder, but no others. Such will be more shocked by his life than by his death. I shall not be forward to think him mistaken in his method who quickest succeeds to liberate the slave. I speak for the slave when I say that I prefer the philanthropy of Captain Brown to that philanthropy which neither shoots me nor liberates me. At any rate, I do not think it is quite sane for one to spend his whole life in talking or writing about this matter, unless he is continuously inspired, and I have not done so. A man may have other affairs to attend to. I do not wish to kill nor to be killed, but I can foresee circumstances in which both these things would be by me unavoidable. We preserve the so-called peace of our community by deeds of petty violence every day. Look at the policeman's billy and handcuffs! Look at the jail! Look at the gallows! Look at the chaplain of the regiment! We are hoping only to live safely on the outskirts of *this* provisional army. So we defend ourselves and our hen-roosts, and maintain slavery. I know that the mass of my countrymen think that the only righteous use that can be made of Sharps rifles and revolvers is to fight duels with them, when we are insulted by other nations, or to hunt Indians, or shoot fugitive slaves with them, or the like. I think that for once the Sharps rifles and the revolvers were employed in a righteous cause. The tools were in the hands of one who could use them.

The same indignation that is said to have cleared the temple once will clear it again. The question is not about the weapon, but the spirit in which you use it. No man has appeared in America, as yet, who loved his fellow-man so well, and treated him so tenderly. He lived for him. He took up his life and he laid it down for him. What sort of violence is that which is encouraged, not by soldiers, but by peaceable citizens, not so much by laymen as by ministers of the Gospel, not so much by the fighting sects as by the Quakers, and not so much by Quaker men as by Quaker women?

This event advertises me that there is such a fact as death,—the possibility of a man's dying. It seems as if no man had ever died in America before; for in order to die you must first have lived. I don't believe in the hearses, and palls, and funerals that they have had. There was no death in the case, because there had been no life; they merely rotted or sloughed off, pretty much as they had rotted or sloughed along. No temple's veil was rent, only a hole dug somewhere. Let the dead bury their dead. The best of them fairly ran down like a clock. Franklin,—Washington,—they were let off without dying; they were merely missing one day. I hear a good many pretend that they are going to die; or that they have died, for aught that I know. Nonsense! I'll defy them to do it. They haven't got life enough in them. They'll deliquesce like fungi, and keep a hundred eulogists mopping the spot where they left off. Only half a dozen or so have died since the world began. Do you think that you are going to die, sir? No, there's no hope of you. You haven't got your lesson yet. You've got to stay after school. We make a needless ado about capital punishment,—taking lives, when there is no life to take. *Memento mori!* We don't understand that sublime sentence which some worthy got sculptured on his gravestone once. We've interpreted it in a groveling and sniveling sense; we've wholly forgotten how to die.

But be sure you do die nevertheless. Do your work, and finish it. If you know how to begin, you will know when to end.

These men, in teaching us how to die, have at the same time taught us how to live. If this man's acts and words do not create a revival, it will be the severest possible satire on the acts and words that do. It is the best news that America has ever heard. It has already quickened the feeble pulse of the North, and infused more and more generous blood into her veins and heart than any number of years of what is called commercial and political prosperity could. How many a man who was lately contemplating suicide has now something to live for!

One writer says that Brown's peculiar monomania made him to be "dreaded by the Missourians as a supernatural being." Sure enough, a hero in the midst of us cowards is always so dreaded. He is just that thing. He shows himself superior to nature. He has a spark of divinity in him.

> "Unless above himself he can
> Erect himself, how poor a thing is man!"

Newspaper editors argue also that it is a proof of his *insanity* that he thought he was appointed to do this work which he did,—that he did not suspect himself for a moment! They talk as if it were impossible that a man could be "divinely appointed" in these days to do any work whatever; as if vows and religion were out of date as connected with any man's daily work; as if the agent to abolish slavery could only be somebody appointed by the President, or by some political party. They talk as if a man's death were a failure, and his continued life, be it of whatever character, were a success.

When I reflect to what a cause this man devoted himself, and how religiously, and then reflect to what cause his judges and all who condemn him so angrily and fluently devote themselves, I see that they are as far apart as the heavens and earth are asunder.

The amount of it is, our *"leading men"* are a harmless kind of folk, and they know *well enough* that *they* were not divinely appointed, but elected by the votes of their party.

Who is it whose safety requires that Captain Brown be hung? Is it indispensable to any Northern man? Is there no resource but to cast this man also to the Minotaur? If you do not wish it, say so distinctly. While these things are being done, beauty stands veiled and music is a screeching lie. Think of him,—of his rare qualities!—such a man as it takes ages to make, and ages to understand; no mock hero, nor the representative of any party. A man such as the sun may not rise upon again in this benighted land. To whose making went the costliest material, the finest adamant; sent to be the redeemer of those in captivity; and the only use to which you can put him is to hang him at the end of a rope! You who pretend to care for Christ crucified, consider what you are about to do to him who offered himself to be the saviour of four millions of men.

Any man knows when he is justified, and all the wits in the world cannot enlighten him on that point. The murderer always knows that he is justly punished; but when a government takes the life of a man without the consent of his conscience, it is an audacious government, and is taking a step toward its own dissolution. Is it not possible that an individual may be right and a government wrong? Are laws to be enforced simply because they were made? or declared by any number of men to be good, if they are *not* good? Is there any necessity for a man's being a tool to perform a deed of which his better nature disapproves? Is it the intention of law-makers that *good* men shall be hung ever? Are judges to interpret the law according to the letter, and not the spirit? What right have *you* to enter into a compact with yourself that you *will* do thus or so, against the light within you? Is it for *you* to *make up* your mind,—to form any resolution whatever,—and not accept the convictions that are forced upon you, and which ever pass your understanding? I do not believe in lawyers, in that mode of attacking or defending a man, because you descend to meet the judge on his own ground, and, in cases of the highest importance, it is of no consequence whether a man breaks a human law or not. Let lawyers decide trivial cases. Business men may arrange that among themselves. If they were the interpreters of the everlasting laws which rightfully bind man, that would be another thing. A counterfeiting law-factory, standing half in a slave land and half in a free! What kind of laws for free men can you expect from that?

I am here to plead his cause with you. I plead not for his life, but for his character,—his immortal life; and so it becomes your cause wholly, and is not his in the least. Some eighteen hundred years ago Christ was crucified; this morning, perchance, Captain Brown was hung. These are the two ends of a chain which is not without its links. He is not Old Brown any longer; he is an angel of light.

I see now that it was necessary that the bravest and humanest man in all the country should be hung. Perhaps he saw it himself. I *almost fear* that I may yet hear of his deliverance, doubting if a prolonged life, if *any* life, can do as much good as his death.

"Misguided!" "Garrulous!" "Insane!" "Vindictive!" So *ye* write in your easy-chairs, and thus he wounded responds from the floor of the Armory, clear as a cloudless sky, true as the voice of nature is: "No man sent me here; it was my own prompting and that of my Maker. I acknowledge no master in human form."

And in what a sweet and noble strain he proceeds, addressing his captors, who stand over him: "I think, my friends, you are guilty of a great wrong against God and humanity, and it would be perfectly right for any one to interfere with you so far as to free those you willfully and wickedly hold in bondage."

And, referring to his movement: "It is, in my opinion, the greatest service a man can render to God."

"I pity the poor in bondage that have none to help them. That is why I am here; not to gratify any personal animosity, revenge or vindictive spirit. It is my sympathy with the oppressed and the wronged, that are as good as you, and as precious in the sight of God."

You don't know your testament when you see it.

"I want you to understand that I respect the rights of the poorest and weakest of colored people, oppressed by the slave power, just as much as I do those of the most wealthy and powerful."

"I wish to say, furthermore, that you had better, all you people at the South, prepare yourselves for a settlement of that question, that must come up for settlement sooner than you are prepared for it. The sooner you are prepared the better. You may dispose of me very easily. I am nearly disposed of now; but this question is still to be settled,—this negro question, I mean; the end of that is not yet."

I foresee the time when the painter will paint that scene, no longer going to Rome for a subject; the poet will sing it; the historian record it; and, with the Landing of the Pilgrims and the Declaration of Independence, it will be the ornament of some future national gallery, when at least the present form of slavery shall be no more here. We shall then be at liberty to weep for Captain Brown. Then, and not till then, we will take our revenge. *W IV, 409–440*

3. Walt Whitman (1819-1892)

THE EXTRAVAGANCE OF THE UNSAYABLE

Just as Emerson's words provide an interesting introduction to Thoreau, Thoreau's words provide an interesting bridge between him and Whitman. Considering how much common ground there was in their vision of things, it is remarkable how unalike they were; considering that each was a powerful individualist, it is remarkable that they could appreciate each other at all. At the time that they met in 1856, Whitman was practically unknown; those who had heard of him had heard that he wrote obscene and incomprehensible poetry, and those who had actually read him by and large agreed. Thoreau had an advantage over such people, however, for he was himself committed to the task of saying the unsayable. "It is a ridiculous demand which England and America make," he wrote near the end of Walden, *"that you shall speak so that they can understand you. Neither men nor toad-stools grow so. As if that were important, and there were not enough to understand you without them. As if . . .* hush *and* who, *which Bright can understand, were the best English. As if there were safety in stupidity alone. I fear chiefly lest my expression may not be* extravagant *enough, may not wander far enough beyond the narrow limits of my daily experience, so as to be adequate to the truth of which I have been convinced.* Extra vagance! [i.e., wandering beyond] *It depends on how you are yarded." The nineteenth-century American reading public was "yarded" in a very restricted area, and Whitman simply went far beyond anything that they were willing to call poetry. But Whitman waited—through a lifetime of comparative obscurity—and in the end he won. It is interesting to see that Thoreau suspected as much.*

THOREAU ON WHITMAN

Mr. Blake,—

. . . You must excuse me if I write mainly a business letter now, for I am sold for the time,—am merely Thoreau the surveyor here,—and solitude is scarcely obtainable in these parts.

Alcott has been here three times, and, Saturday before last, I went with him and Greeley, by invitation of the last, to G.'s farm, thirty-six miles north of New York. The next day A. and I heard Beecher preach; and what was more, we visited Whitman the next morning (A. had already seen him), and were much interested and provoked. He is apparently the greatest democrat the world has seen. Kings and aristocracy go by the board at once, as they have long deserved to. A remarkably strong though coarse nature, of a sweet disposition, and much prized by his friends. Though peculiar and rough in his exterior, his skin (all over (?)) red, he is essentially a gentleman. I am still somewhat in a quandary about him,—feel that he is essentially strange to me, at any rate; but I am surprised by the sight of him. He is very broad, but, as I have said, not fine. He said that I misapprehended him. I am not quite sure that I do. He told us that he loved to ride up and down Broadway all day on an omnibus, sitting beside the driver, listening to the roar of the carts, and sometimes gesticulating and declaiming Homer at the top of his voice. He has long been an editor and writer for the newspapers,— was editor of the "New Orleans Crescent" once; but now has no employment but to read and write in the forenoon, and walk in the afternoon, like all the rest of the scribbling gentry.

I shall probably be in Concord next week; so you can direct to me there. *Letter to H. G. O. Blake, 11/19/56 Corr 441–442*

Mr. Blake,—

. . . That Walt Whitman, of whom I wrote to you, is the most interesting fact to me at present. I have just read his 2nd edition (which he gave me) and it has done me more good than any reading for a long time. Perhaps I remember best the poem of Walt Whitman an American & the Sun Down Poem ["Song of Myself" and "Crossing Brooklyn Ferry"]. There are 2 or 3 pieces in the book which are disagreeable to say the least, simply sensual. He does not celebrate love at all. It is as if the beasts spoke. I think that men have not been ashamed of themselves without reason. No doubt, there have always been dens where such deeds were unblushingly recited, and it is no merit to compete with their inhabitants. But even on this side, he has spoken more truth than any American or modern that I know. I have found his poem exhilarating encouraging. As for its sensuality,—& it may turn out to be less sensual than it appeared— I do not so much wish that those parts were not written, as that men & women were so pure that they could read them without harm, that is, without understanding them. One woman told me that no woman could read it as if a man could read what a woman could not. Of course Walt Whitman can communicate to us no experience, and if we are shocked, whose experience is it that we are reminded of?

On the whole it sounds to me very brave & American after whatever deductions. I do not believe that all the sermons so called that have been preached in this land put together are equal to it for preaching—

We ought to rejoice greatly in him. He occasionally suggests something a little more than human. You cant confound him with the other inhabitants of Brooklyn or New York. How they must shudder when they read him! He is awfully good.

To be sure I sometimes feel a little imposed on. By his heartiness & broad generalities he puts me into a liberal frame of mind prepared to see wonders—as it were sets me upon a hill or in the midst of a plain—stirs me well up, and then—throws in a thousand of brick. Though rude & sometimes ineffectual, it is a great primitive poem,—an alarum or trumpet-note ringing through the American camp. Wonderfully like the Orientals, too, considering that when I asked him if he had read them, he answered, "No: tell me about them."

I did not get far in conversation with him,—two more being present,—and among the few things which I chanced to say, I remember that one was, in answer to him as representing America, that I did not think much of America or of politics, and so on, which may have been somewhat of a damper to him.

Since I have seen him, I find that I am not disturbed by any brag or egoism in his book. He may turn out the least of a braggart of all, having a better right to be confident.

He is a great fellow.   *Letter to H. G. O. Blake, 12/7/56* Corr *444–445*

LITERATURE AS PERSONAL ENCOUNTER

Aside from Whitman's tendency to refer to sexual topics more casually than previous writers had, the thing that most commonly offended the poet's contemporaries was his apparent egocentricity and his unabashedly self-satisfied tone. Add to these characteristics Whitman's tendency to address the reader with a familiarity usually reserved for intimate friends, and you have a combination that is sometimes quite overwhelming, even to present-day readers—who are considerably more shockproof than Whitman's own contemporaries were.

But, as was suggested in the general introduction to these selections, there is a clear logic behind each of these literary tactics—a logic that adds up to a rationale for a kind of therapeutic poetry, in which the authenticity of the poet's utterance and his ability to create a nonjudgmental presence full of warmth and candor make it possible for the reader to drop his own mask and step forth more honestly as himself. His goal was the central Emersonian one of bringing the person to himself by bringing to full awareness a sense of where he is and what his relation is to his surroundings. Behind the egotism, therefore, is something quite different: the celebration and validation of the reader.

I celebrate myself,
And what I assume you shall assume,
For every atom belonging to me as good belongs to you.
"Song of Myself," 1 (1855, p. 13)

I know perfectly well my own egotism,
And know my omniverous words, and cannot say any less,
And would fetch you whoever you are flush with myself.
"Song of Myself," 42 (1855, p. 47)

After continued personal ambition and effort, as a young fellow, to enter with the rest into competition for the usual rewards, business, political, literary, &c.—to take part in the great *mêlée*, both for victory's prize itself and to do some good—after years of those aims and pursuits, I found myself remaining possess'd, at the age of thirty-one to thirty-three, with a special desire and conviction. Or rather, to be quite exact, a desire that had been flitting through my previous life, or hovering on the flanks, mostly indefinite hitherto, had steadily advanced to the front, defined itself, and finally dominated everything else. This was a feeling or ambition to articulate and faithfully express in literary or poetic form, and uncompromisingly, my own physical, emotional, moral, intellectual, and æsthetic Personality, in the midst of, and tallying, the momentous spirit and facts of its immediate days, and of current America—and to exploit that Personality, identified with place and date, in a far more candid and comprehensive sense than any hitherto poem or book. . . .

Leaves of Grass indeed (I cannot too often reiterate) has mainly been the outcropping of my own emotional and other personal nature—an attempt, from first to last, to put *a Person*, a human being (myself, in the latter half of the nineteenth century, in America,) freely, fully and truly on record. I could not find any similar personal record in current literature that satisfied me. But it is not on *Leaves of Grass* distinctively as *literature*, or a specimen thereof, that I feel to dwell, or advance claims. No one will get at my verses who insists upon viewing them as a literary performance, or attempt at such performance, or as aiming mainly toward art or æstheticism.   *"A Backward Glance O'er Travel'd Roads"*

Behold I do not give lectures or a little charity,
What I give I give out of myself.

You there, impotent, loose in the knees, open your scarfed chops till I blow grit within you,
Spread your palms and lift the flaps of your pockets,
I am not to be denied . . . . I compel . . . . I have stores plenty and to spare,
And any thing I have I bestow.
I do not ask who you are . . . . that is not important to me,
You can do nothing and be nothing but what I will infold you.

To a drudge of the cottonfields or emptier of privies I lean . . . . on his right cheek I put the family kiss,
And in my soul I swear I never will deny him.

On women fit for conception I start bigger and nimbler babes,
This day I am jetting the stuff of far more arrogant republics.

To any one dying . . . . thither I speed and twist the knob of the door,
Turn the bedclothes toward the foot of the bed,
Let the physician and the priest go home.

I seize the descending man . . . . I raise him with resistless will.

O despairer, here is my neck,
By God! you shall not go down! Hang your whole weight upon me.

I dilate you with tremendous breath . . . . I buoy you up;
Every room of the house do I fill with an armed force . . . . lovers of me, bafflers of graves:
Sleep! I and they keep guard all night;
Not doubt, not decease shall dare to lay finger upon you,
I have embraced you, and henceforth possess you to myself,
And when you rise in the morning you will find what I tell you is so.
                    "Song of Myself," 40 (1855, *pp. 40–45*)

Whoever you are, I fear you are walking the walks of dreams,
I fear these supposed realities are to melt from under your feet and hands,
Even now your features, joys, speech, house, trade, manners, troubles, follies, costume, crimes, dissipate away from you,
Your true soul and body appear before me,
They stand forth out of affairs, out of commerce, shops, work, farms, clothes, the house, buying, selling, eating, drinking, suffering, dying.

Whoever you are, now I place my hand upon you, that you be my poem,
I whisper with my lips close to your ear,
I have loved many women and men, but I love none better than you.

O I have been dilatory and dumb,
I should have made my way straight to you long ago,
I should have blabb'd nothing but you, I should have chanted nothing but you.

I will leave all and come and make the hymns of you,
None has understood you, but I understand you,
None has done justice to you, you have not done justice to yourself,
None but has found you imperfect, I only find no imperfection in you,
None but would subordinate you, I only am he who will never consent to subordinate you,
I only am he who places over you no master, owner, better, God, beyond what waits intrinsically in yourself.

Painters have painted their swarming groups and the centre-figure of all,
From the head of the centre-figure spreading a nimbus of gold-color'd light,
But I paint myriads of heads, but paint no head without its nimbus of gold-color'd light,
From my hand from the brain of every man and woman it streams, effulgently flowing forever.

O I could sing such grandeurs and glories about you!
You have not known what you are, you have slumber'd upon yourself all your life,
Your eyelids have been the same as closed most of the time,
What you have done returns already in mockeries,
(Your thrift, knowledge, prayers, if they do not return in mockeries, what is their return?)

The mockeries are not you,
Underneath them and within them I see you lurk,

I pursue you where none else has pursued you,
Silence, the desk, the flippant expression, the night, the accustomed routine, if these conceal you from others or from yourself, they do not conceal you from me,
The shaved face, the unsteady eye, the impure complexion, if these balk others they do not balk me,
The pert apparel, the deform'd attitude, drunkenness, greed, premature death, all these I part aside.

There is no endowment in men or women that is not tallied in you,
There is no virtue, no beauty in man or woman, but as good is in you,
No pluck, no endurance in others, but as good is in you,
No pleasure waiting for others, but an equal pleasure waits for you.

As for me, I give nothing to any one except I give the like carefully to you,
I sing the songs of the glory of none, not God, sooner than I sing the songs of the glory of you.

Whoever you are! claim your own at any hazard!
These shows of the East and West are tame compared to you,
These immense meadows, these interminable rivers, you are immense and interminable as they,
These furies, elements, storms, motions of Nature, throes of apparent dissolution, you are he or she who is master or mistress over them,
Master or mistress in your own right over Nature, elements, pain, passion, dissolution.

The hopples fall from your ankles, you find an unfailing sufficiency,
Old or young, male or female, rude, low, rejected by the rest, whatever you are promulges itself,
Through birth, life, death, burial, the means are provided, nothing is scanted,
Through angers, losses, ambition, ignorance, ennui, what you are picks its way.
"To You"

I speak the password primeval . . . . I give the sign of democracy;
By God! I will accept nothing which all cannot have their counterpart of on the same terms.

Through me many long dumb voices,
Voices of the interminable generations of slaves,
Voices of prostitutes and of deformed persons,
Voices of the diseased and despairing, and of thieves and dwarfs,
Voices of cycles of preparation and accretion,
And of the threads that connect the stars—and of wombs, and of the fatherstuff,

And of the rights of them the others are down upon,
Of the trivial and flat and foolish and despised,
Of fog in the air and beetles rolling balls of dung.

Through me forbidden voices,
Voices of sexes and lusts . . . . voices veiled, and I remove the veil,
Voices indecent by me clarified and transfigured.
                              "*Song of Myself*," 23 (1855, p. 29)

I do not say these things for a dollar, or to fill up the time while I wait for a boat;
It is you talking just as much as myself . . . . I act as the tongue of you,
It was tied in your mouth . . . . in mine it begins to be loosened.
                              "*Song of Myself*," 47 (1855, p. 53)

But I set out with the intention also of indicating or hinting some point-characteristics which I since see (though I did not then, at least not definitely) were bases and object-urgings toward those *Leaves* from the first. The word I myself put primarily for the description of them as they stand at last, is the word Suggestiveness. I round and finish little, if anything; and could not, consistently with my scheme. The reader will always have his or her part to do, just as much as I have had mine. I seek less to state or display any theme or thought, and more to bring you, reader, into the atmosphere of the theme or thought—there to pursue your own flight.   "*A Backward Glance O'er Travel'd Roads*"

He that by me spreads a wider breast than my own proves the width of my own,
He most honors my style who learns under it to destroy the teacher.

The boy I love, the same becomes a man not through derived power but in his own right,
Wicked, rather than virtuous out of conformity or fear, . . .
                              "*Song of Myself*," 47 (1855, p. 53)

All I mark as my own you shall offset it with your own,
Else it were time lost listening to me.   "*Song of Myself*," 19 (1855, p. 25)

Have you reckoned a thousand acres much? Have you reckoned the earth much?
Have you practiced so long to learn to read?
Have you felt so proud to get at the meaning of poems?

Stop this day and night with me and you shall possess the origin of all poems,
You shall possess the good of the earth and sun . . . . there are millions of suns left,

You shall no longer take things at second or third hand . . . . nor look through the eyes of the dead . . . . nor feed on the spectres in books,
You shall not look through my eyes either, nor take things from me,
You shall listen to all sides and filter them from yourself.
"Song of Myself," 2 (1855, p. 14)

I bequeath myself to the dirt to grow from the grass I love,
If you want me again look for me under your bootsoles.

You will hardly know who I am or what I mean,
But I shall be good health to you nevertheless,
And filter and fibre your blood.

Failing to fetch me me at first keep encouraged,
Missing me one place search another,
I stop some where waiting for you.   "Song of Myself," 52 (1855, p. 56)

I teach straying from me, yet who can stray from me?
I follow you whoever you are from the present hour;
My words itch at your ears till you understand them.
"Song of Myself," 47 (1855, p. 53)

STANDING AT THE CENTER, EVERYTHING IN ITS PLACE

Whitman sought, as did Emerson and Thoreau, to put the person back in the center of his experiential world. In this position the person had two different orders of relation to the world. The first was the simple experiential relation, the way things stand vis-à-vis the centered person who sees them for what they are rather than (as most of us do) as helps or threats to our self-system. The second relation was to be measured differently: each object and its degree of realized "itselfness." This second relation was the degree of what Emerson would have called being and the extent to which such an object might serve as a model of being for the person. The first relation was the "original relation" that Emerson said each of us ought to have to the universe—a living sense of what was really out there, as disclosed to us through our own senses and brain.

When he is being his most grandiose and otherworldly, Whitman is simply recording his impression of life as seen in proper relation to a person who is really and fully alive. That is a hard thing to accept, although most of us have had experiences in which everything looked quite wonderful. We tend to write them off, however, as the product of a transitory mood, rather than seeing them, as Whitman does, as the product of an ever-recoverable right relation to things.

Whoever you are! motion and reflection are especially for you,
The divine ship sails the divine sea for you.

Whoever you are! you are he or she for whom the earth is solid and liquid,
You are he or she for whom the sun and moon hang in the sky,
For none more than you are the present and the past,
For none more than you is immortality.

Each man to himself and each woman to herself, is the word of the past and present, and the true word of immortality;
No one can acquire for another—not one,
Not one can grow for another—not one.

The song is to the singer, and comes back most to him,
The teaching is to the teacher, and comes back most to him,
The murder is to the murderer, and comes back most to him,
The theft is to the thief, and comes back most to him,
The love is to the lover, and comes back most to him,
The gift is to the giver, and comes back most to him—it cannot fail,
The oration is to the orator, the acting is to the actor and actress not to the audience,

> And no man understands any greatness or goodness but his own, or the indication of his own. *"A Song of the Rolling Earth,"* 2

> The land and sea, the animals fishes and birds, the sky of heaven and the orbs, the forests mountains and rivers, are not small themes . . . but folks expect of the poet to indicate more than the beauty and dignity which always attach to dumb real objects . . . they expect him to indicate the path between reality and their souls. Men and women perceive the beauty well enough . . . probably as well as he. . . .
>
> Without effort and without exposing in the least how it is done the greatest poet brings the spirit of any or all events and passions and scenes and persons some more and some less to bear on your individual character as you hear or read.
>
> *Preface to first edition of Leaves of Grass* (1855, pp. v–vi)

> Trippers and askers surround me,
> People I meet . . . . . the effect upon me of my early life . . . . of the ward and city I live in . . . . of the nation,
> The latest news . . . . discoveries, inventions, societies . . . . authors old and new,
> My dinner, dress, associates, looks, business, compliments, dues,
> The real or fancied indifference of some man or woman I love,
> The sickness of one of my folks—or of myself . . . . or ill-doing . . . . or loss or lack of money . . . . or depressions or exaltations,
> They come to me days and nights and go from me again,
> But they are not the Me myself.
>
> Apart from the pulling and hauling stands what I am,
> Stands amused, complacent, compassionating, idle, unitary,
> Looks down, is erect, bends an arm on an impalpable certain rest,
> Looks with its sidecurved head curious what will come next,
> Both in and out of the game, and watching and wondering at it.
> *"Song of Myself,"* 4 (1855, p. 15)

> Shall I pray? Shall I venerate and be ceremonious?
>
> I have pried through the strata and analyzed to a hair,
> And counselled with doctors and calculated close and found no sweeter fat than sticks to my own bones.
>
> In all people I see myself, none more and not one a barleycorn less,
> And the good or bad I say of myself I say of them.
>
> And I know I am solid and sound,
> To me the converging objects of the universe perpetually flow,
> All are written to me, and I must get what the writing means.
> And I know I am deathless,

I know this orbit of mine cannot be swept by a carpenter's compass,
I know I shall not pass like a child's carlacue cut with a burnt stick at night.

I know I am august,
I do not trouble my spirit to vindicate itself or be understood,
I see that the elementary laws never apologize,
I reckon I behave no prouder than the level I plant my house by after all.

I exist as I am, that is enough,
If no other in the world be aware I sit content,
And if each and all be aware I sit content.

One world is aware, and by far the largest to me, and that is myself,
And whether I come to my own today or in ten thousand or ten million years,
I can cheerfully take it now, or with equal cheerfulness I can wait.

My foothold is tenoned and mortised in granite,
I laugh at what you call dissolution,
And I know the amplitude of time.
"Song of Myself," 20 (1855, pp. 25–26)

I resist anything better than my own diversity,
And breathe the air and leave plenty after me,
And am not stuck up, and am in my place.

The moth and the fisheggs are in their place,
The suns I see and the suns I cannot see are in their place,
The palpable is in its place and the impalpable is in its place.
"Song of Myself," 16 (1855, p. 24)

I believe a leaf of grass is no less than the journeywork of the stars,
And the pismire is equally perfect, and a grain of sand, and the egg of the wren,
And the tree-toad is a chef-d'ouvre for the highest,
And the running blackberry would adorn the parlors of heaven,
And the narrowest hinge in my hand puts to scorn all machinery,
And the cow crunching with depressed head surpasses any statue,
And a mouse is miracle enough to stagger sextillions of infidels,
And I could come every afternoon of my life to look at the farmer's girl boiling her iron tea-kettle and baking shortcake.
"Song of Myself," 31 (1855, p. 34)

I will take an egg out of the robin's nest in the orchard,
I will take a branch of gooseberries from the old bush in the garden, and go and preach to the world;

You shall see I will not meet a single heretic or scorner,
You shall see how I stump clergymen, and confound them,
You shall see me showing a scarlet tomato, and a white pebble from the beach.   *"Debris"* (1860)

Magnifying and applying come I,
Outbidding at the start the old cautious hucksters,
The most they offer for mankind and eternity less than a spirt of my own seminal wet,
Taking myself the exact dimensions of Jehovah and laying them away,
Lithographing Kronos and Zeus his son, and Hercules his grandson,
Buying drafts of Osiris and Isis and Belus and Brahma and Adonai,
In my portfolio placing Manito loose, and Allah on a leaf, and the crucifix engraved,
With Odin, and the hideous-faced Mexitli, and all idols and images,
Honestly taking them all for what they are worth, and not a cent more,
Admitting they were alive and did the work of their day,
Admitting they bore mites as for unfledged birds who have now to rise and fly and sing for themselves,
Accepting the rough deific sketches to fill out better in myself . . . . bestowing them freely on each man and woman I see,
Discovering as much or more in a framer framing a house,
Putting higher claims for him there with his rolled-up sleeves, driving the mallet and chisel;
Not objecting to special revelations . . . . considering a curl of smoke or a hair on the back of my hand as curious as any revelation;
Those ahold of fire-engines and hook-and-ladder ropes more to me than the gods of the antique wars,
Minding their voices peal through the crash of destruction,
Their brawny limbs passing safe over charred laths . . . . their white foreheads whole and unhurt out of the flames;
By the mechanic's wife with her babe at her nipple interceding for every person born;
Three scythes at harvest whizzing in a row from three lusty angels with shirts bagged out at their waists;
The snag-toothed hostler with red hair redeeming sins past and to come,
Selling all he possesses and traveling on foot to fee lawyers for his brother and sit by him while he is tried for forgery:
What was strewn in the amplest strewing the square rod about me, and not filling the square rod then;
The bull and the bug never worshipped half enough,
Dung and dirt more admirable than was dreamed,
The supernatural of no account . . . . myself waiting my time to be one of the supremes,

The day getting ready for me when I shall do as much good as the best, and be as prodigious,
Guessing when I am it will not tickle me much to receive puffs out of pulpit or print;
By my life-lumps! becoming already a creator!
"Song of Myself," 41 (1855, p. 46)

I have heard what the talkers were talking . . . . the talk of the beginning and the end,
But I do not talk of the beginning or the end.

There was never any more inception than there is now,
Nor any more youth or age than there is now;
And will never be any more perfection than there is now,
Nor any more heaven or hell than there is now. . . .

I am satisfied . . . . I see, dance, laugh, sing;
As God comes a loving bedfellow and sleeps at my side all night and close on the peep of the day,
And leaves for me baskets covered with white towels bulging the house with their plenty,
Shall I postpone my acceptation and realization and scream at my eyes,
That they turn from gazing after and down the road,
And forthwith cipher and show me to a cent,
Exactly the contents of one, and exactly the contents of two, and which is ahead?
"Song of Myself," 3 (1855, pp. 14–15)

I do not call one greater and one smaller,
That which fills its period and place is equal to any.
"Song of Myself," 44 (1855, p. 49)

To be in any form, what is that?
If nothing lay more developed the quahaug and its callous shell were enough.

Mine is no callous shell,
I have instant conductors all over me whether I pass or stop,
They seize every object and lead it harmlessly through me.

I merely stir, press, feel with my fingers, and am happy,
To touch my person to some one else's is about as much as I can stand.
"Song of Myself," 27 (1855, p. 32)

What is commonest and cheapest and nearest and easiest is Me,
Me going in for my chances, spending for vast returns,
Adorning myself to bestow myself on the first that will take me,
Not asking the sky to come down to my goodwill,
Scattering it freely forever. . . .
"Song of Myself," 14 (1855, p. 21)

Standing at the Center

The atmosphere is not a perfume . . . . it has no taste of the distillation
    . . . . it is odorless,
It is for my mouth forever . . . . I am in love with it,
I will go to the bank by the wood and become undisguised and naked.
I am mad for it to be in contact with me.

The smoke of my own breath,
Echos, ripples, and buzzed whispers . . . . loveroot, silkthread, crotch
    and vine,
My respiration and inspiration . . . . the beating of my heart . . . . the
    yearning of blood and air through my lungs,
The sniff of green leaves and dry leaves, and the shore and dark-colored
    sea-rocks, and of hay in the barn,
The sound of the belched words of my voice . . . . words loosed to the
    eddies of the wind,
A few light kisses . . . . a few embraces . . . . a reaching around of
    arms,
The play of shine and shade on the trees as the supple boughs wag,
The delight alone or in the rush of streets, or along the fields and hillsides,
The feeling of health . . . . the full-noon trill . . . . the song of me
    rising from bed and meeting the sun.
"Song of Myself," 2 (1855, p. 13)

I have said that the soul is not more than the body,
And I have said that the body is not more than the soul,
And nothing, not God, is greater to one than one's-self is,
And whoever walks a furlong without sympathy walks to his own funeral,
    dressed in his shroud,
And I or you pocketless of a dime may purchase the pick of the earth,
And to glance with an eye or show a bean in its pod confounds the
    learning of all times,
And there is no trade or employment but the young man following it may
    become a hero,
And there is no object so soft but it makes a hub for the wheeled universe,
And any man or woman shall stand cool and supercilious before a million
    universes.

And I call to mankind, Be not curious about God,
For I who am curious about each am not curious about God,
No array of terms can say how much I am at peace about God and about
    death.

I hear and behold God in every object, yet I understand God not in the
    least,
Nor do I understand who there can be more wonderful than myself.

Why should I wish to see God better than this day?
I see something of God each hour of the twenty-four, and each moment then,
In the faces of men and women I see God, and in my own face in the glass;
I find letters from God dropped in the street, and every one is signed by God's name,
And I leave them where they are, for I know that others will punctually come forever and ever.   "*Song of Myself*," 48 (1855, *p.* 53)

I believe in you my soul . . . . the other I am must not abase itself to you,
And you must not be abased to the other.

Loafe with me on the grass . . . . loose the stop from your throat,
Not words, not music or rhyme I want . . . . not custom or lecture, not even the best,
Only the lull I like, the hum of your valved voice.

I mind how we lay in June, such a transparent summer morning;
You settled your head athwart my hips and gently turned over upon me,
And parted the shirt from my bosom-bone, and plunged your tongue to my barestript heart,
And reached till you felt my beard, and reached till you held my feet.

Swiftly arose and spread around me the peace and joy and knowledge that pass all the art and argument of the earth;
And I know that the hand of God is the elderhand of my own,
And I know that the spirit of God is the eldest brother of my own,
And that all the men ever born are also my brothers . . . . and the women my sisters and lovers,
And that a kelson of the creation is love;
And limitless are leaves stiff or drooping in the fields,
And brown ants in the little wells beneath them,
And mossy scabs of the wormfence, and heaped stones, and elder and mullen and pokeweed.   "*Song of Myself*," 5 (1855, *p.* 16)

I tramp a perpetual journey,
My signs are a rain-proof coat and good shoes and a staff cut from the woods;
No friend of mine takes his ease in my chair,
I have no chair, nor church nor philosophy;
I lead no man to a dinner-table or library or exchange,
But each man and each woman of you I lead upon a knoll,
My left hand hooks you round the waist,

My right hand points to landscapes of continents, and a plain public road.

Not I, not any one else can travel that road for you,
You must travel it for yourself.

It is not far . . . . it is within reach,
Perhaps you have been on it since you were born, and did not know,
Perhaps it is every where on water and on land.
> "Song of Myself," 46 (1855, pp. 51–52)

I am an acme of things accomplished, and I am encloser of things to be.

My feet strike an apex of the apices of the stairs,
On every step bunches of ages, and larger bunches between the steps,
All below duly traveled—and still I mount and mount.

Rise after rise bow the phantoms behind me,
Afar down I see the huge first Nothing, the vapor from the nostrils of death,
I know I was even there . . . . I waited unseen and always,
And slept while God carried me through the lethargic mist,
And took my time . . . . and took no hurt from the fœtid carbon.

Long I was hugged close . . . . long and long.

Immense have been the preparations for me,
Faithful and friendly the arms that have helped me.

Cycles ferried my cradle, rowing and rowing like cheerful boatmen;
For room to me stars kept aside in their own rings,
They sent influences to look after what was to hold me.

Before I was born out of my mother generations guided me,
My embryo has never been torpid . . . . nothing could overlay it;
For it the nebula cohered to an orb . . . . the long slow strata piled to rest it on . . . . vast vegetables gave it sustenance,
Monstrous sauroids transported it in their mouths and deposited it with care.

All forces have been steadily employed to complete and delight me,
Now I stand on this spot with my soul.
> "Song of Myself," 44 (1855, p. 50)

THE STYLE OF BEING

Like anyone who seeks to describe a state of consciousness and a way of relating to experience that is different from the everyday, Whitman faced serious language problems. As he said in "Song of Myself," "My voice goes after what my eyes cannot reach": what he is trying to report is the inner world of response that corresponds to (but is not the same as) the outer world that is experienced.

But in spite of the difficulties, Whitman left an unusually full record of how it would feel to be in that rare state of presence-without-entanglement, detachment-without-withdrawal that he referred to when he spoke of being "both in and out of the game." The characteristics of the state are spontaneity, acceptance of outer and inner phenomena, a noncategorizing awareness, and a distrust of verbal concepts.

Spontaneous me, Nature,
The loving day, the mounting sun, the friend I am happy with,
The arm of my friend hanging idly over my shoulder,
The hillside whiten'd with blossoms of the mountain ash,
The same late in autumn, the hues of red, yellow, drab, purple, and light and dark green,
The rich coverlet of the grass, animals and birds, the private untrimm'd bank, the primitive apples, the pebble-stones,
Beautiful dripping fragments, the negligent list of one after another as I happen to call them to me or think of them,
The real poems, (what we call poems being merely pictures,)
The poems of the privacy of the night, and of men like me,
This poem drooping shy and unseen that I always carry, and that all men carry,
(Know once for all, avow'd on purpose, wherever are men like me, are our lusty lurking masculine poems,)
Love-thoughts, love-juice, love-odor, love-yielding, love-climbers, and the climbing sap,
Arms and hands of love, lips of love, phallic thumb of love, breasts of love, bellies press'd and glued together with love,
Earth of chaste love, life that is only life after love,
The body of my love, the body of the woman I love, the body of the man, the body of the earth,
Soft forenoon airs that blow from the south-west,
The hairy wild-bee that murmurs and hankers up and down, that gripes the full-grown lady-flower, curves upon her with amorous firm legs, takes his will of her, and holds himself tremulous and tight till he is satisfied;
The wet of woods through the early hours,

Two sleepers at night lying close together as they sleep, one with an arm slanting down across and below the waist of the other,
The smell of apples, aromas from crush'd sage-plant, mint, birch-bark,
The boy's longings, the glow and pressure as he confides to me what he was dreaming,
The dead leaf whirling its spiral whirl and falling still and content to the ground,
The no-form'd stings that sights, people, objects, sting me with,
The hubb'd sting of myself, stinging me as much as it ever can any one,
The sensitive, orbic, underlapp'd brothers, that only privileged feelers may be intimate where they are,
The curious roamer the hand roaming all over the body, the bashful withdrawing of flesh where the fingers soothingly pause and edge themselves,
The limpid liquid within the young man,
The vex'd corrosion so pensive and so painful,
The torment, the irritable tide that will not be at rest,
The like of the same I feel, the like of the same in others,
The young man that flushes and flushes, and the young woman that flushes and flushes,
The young man that wakes deep at night, the hot hand seeking to repress what would master him,
The mystic amorous night, the strange half-welcome pangs, visions, sweats,
The pulse pounding through palms and trembling encircling fingers, the young man all color'd, red, ashamed, angry;
The souse upon me of my lover the sea, as I lie willing and naked,
The merriment of the twin babies that crawl over the grass in the sun, the mother never turning her vigilant eyes from them,
The walnut-trunk, the walnut-husks, and the ripening or ripen'd long-round walnuts,
The continence of vegetables, birds, animals,
The consequent meanness of me should I skulk or find myself indecent, while birds and animals never once skulk or find themselves indecent,
The great chastity of paternity, to match the great chastity of maternity,
The oath of procreation I have sworn, my Adamic and fresh daughters,
The greed that eats me day and night with hungry gnaw, till I saturate what shall produce boys to fill my place when I am through,
The wholesome relief, repose, content,
And this bunch pluck'd at random from myself,
It has done its work—I toss it carelessly to fall where it may.
                                                "*Spontaneous Me*"

Showing the best and dividing it from the worst, age vexes age,
Knowing the perfect fitness and equanimity of things, while they discuss I am silent, and go bathe and admire myself.
"Song of Myself," 3 (1855, p. 14)

I think I could turn and live awhile with the animals . . . . they are so placid and self-contained,
I stand and look at them sometimes half the day long.
They do not sweat and whine about their condition,
They do not lie awake in the dark and weep for their sins,
They do not make me sick discussing their duty to God,
Not one is dissatisfied . . . . not one is demented with the mania of owning things,
Not one kneels to another nor to his kind that lived thousands of years ago,
Not one is respectable or industrious over the whole earth.
"Song of Myself," 32 (1855, p. 34)

Me imperturbe, standing at ease in Nature,
Master of all or mistress of all, aplomb in the midst of irrational things,
Imbued as they, passive, receptive, silent as they,
Finding my occupation, poverty, notoriety, foibles, crimes, less important than I thought,
Me toward the Mexican sea, or in the Mannahatta or the Tennessee, or far north or inland,
A river man, or a man of the woods or of any farm-life of these States or of the coast, or the lakes or Kanada,
Me wherever my life is lived, O to be self-balanced for contingencies,
To confront night, storms, hunger, ridicule, accidents, rebuffs, as the trees and animals do.
"Me Imperturbe"

I swear I begin to see little or nothing in audible words,
All merges toward the presentation of the unspoken meanings of the earth,
Toward him who sings the songs of the body and of the truths of the earth,
Toward him who makes the dictionaries of words that print cannot touch.
I swear I see what is better than to tell the best,
It is always to leave the best untold.

When I undertake to tell the best I find I cannot,
My tongue is ineffectual on its pivots,
My breath will not be obedient to its organs,
I become a dumb man.

The best of the earth cannot be told anyhow, all or any is best,
It is not what you anticipated, it is cheaper, easier, nearer,
Things are not dismiss'd from the places they held before,
The earth is just as positive and direct as it was before,
Facts, religions, improvements, politics, trades, are as real as before,
But the soul is also real, it too is positive and direct,
No reasoning, no proof has establish'd it,
Undeniable growth has establish'd it. "*A Song of the Rolling Earth,*" 3

I cannot tell how my ankles bend . . . . nor whence the cause of my faintest wish,
Nor the cause of the friendship I emit . . . . nor the cause of the friendship I take again.

To walk up my stoop is unaccountable . . . . I pause to consider if it really be,
That I eat and drink is spectacle enough for the great authors and schools,
A morning-glory at my window satisfies me more than the metaphysics of books.   "*Song of Myself,*" 24 (1855, p. 30)

Do you guess I have some intricate purpose?
Well I have . . . . for the April rain has, and the mica on the side of a rock has.

Do you take it I would astonish?
Does the daylight astonish? or the early redstart twittering through the woods?
Do I astonish more than they?   "*Song of Myself,*" 19 (1855, p. 25)

If you would understand me go to the heights or water-shore,
The nearest gnat is an explanation and a drop or the motion of waves a key,
The maul the oar and the handsaw second my words.
   "*Song of Myself,*" 47 (1855, p. 53)

Whoever you are holding me now in hand,
Without one thing all will be useless,
I give you fair warning before you attempt me further,
I am not what you supposed, but far different.

Who is he that would become my follower?
Who would sign himself a candidate for my affections?

The way is suspicious, the result uncertain, perhaps destructive,
You would have to give up all else, I alone would expect to be your sole and exclusive standard,

Your novitiate would even then be long and exhausting,
The whole past theory of your life and all conformity to the lives around you would have to be abandon'd,
Therefore release me now before troubling yourself any further, let go your hand from my shoulders,
Put me down and depart on your way.

Or else by stealth in some wood for trial,
Or back of a rock in the open air,
(For in any roof'd room of a house I emerge not, nor in company,
And in libraries I lie as one dumb, a gawk, or unborn, or dead,)
But just possibly with you on a high hill, first watching lest any person for miles around approach unawares,
Or possibly with you sailing at sea, or on the beach of the sea or some quiet island,
Here to put your lips upon mine I permit you,
With the comrade's long-dwelling kiss or the new husband's kiss,
For I am the new husband and I am the comrade.

Or if you will, thrusting me beneath your clothing,
Where I may feel the throbs of your heart or rest upon your hip,
Carry me when you go forth over land or sea;
For thus merely touching you is enough, is best,
And thus touching you would I silently sleep and be carried eternally.

But these leaves conning you con at peril,
For these leaves and me you will not understand,
They will elude you at first and still more afterward, I will certainly elude you,
Even while you should think you had unquestionably caught me, behold!
Already you see I have escaped from you.

For it is not for what I have put into it that I have written this book,
Nor is it by reading it you will acquire it,
Nor do those know me best who admire me and vauntingly praise me,
Nor will the candidates for my love (unless at most a very few) prove victorious,
Nor will my poems do good only, they will do just as much evil, perhaps more,
For all is useless without that which you may guess at many times and not hit, that which I hinted at;
Therefore release me and depart on your way.

"Whoever You Are Holding Me Now in Hand"

THE POEM AS UTTERANCE

Whitman had few preconceptions about what constituted a poem, except that a poem had to be a person's utterance that was so vital and so whole in itself that it formed an organic unit. In this, he both followed and illustrated Emerson's dictum in "The Poet":

For it is not meters, but a meter-making argument that makes a poem,—a thought so passionate and alive that like the spirit of a plant or an animal it has an architecture of its own, and adorns nature with a new thing. . . . The poet has a new thought; he has a whole new experience to unfold; he will tell us how it was with him, and all men will be the richer in his fortune.

This organic impulse lies behind both his very long poems and the brief vignettes with which this section opens.

Except to add that every one of his poems is in some sense a Song of Myself, *it is hard to go beyond the generalization about the organic form of his poems. Each poem is an entity in itself—the record of "how it was with him" at a moment or in a stage of his life. Of the longer poems included below, "Song for Occupations" was chosen because it is a greatly underestimated poem that says important things very well; the second poem (after "Song of Myself") in the original edition of* Leaves of Grass, *it balanced the longer poem by turning outward and speaking to others' conditions. "The Sleepers" is another first-edition poem, one full of haunting and almost surrealistic images. "When Lilacs Last in the Dooryard Bloom'd" was written a decade later, after the pain of the Civil War, and marks the somewhat more somber mood of the later poetry; in the poem he works to come to terms with the death of Abraham Lincoln— and through that, to come to terms with death itself.*

SEVERAL SHORT POEMS

Through the ample open door of the peaceful country barn,
A sunlit pasture field with cattle and horses feeding,
And haze and vista, and the far horizon fading away.   *"A Farm Picture"*

On a flat road runs the well-train'd runner,
He is lean and sinewy with muscular legs,
He is thinly clothed, he leans forward as he runs,
With lightly closed fists and arms partially rais'd.   *"The Runner"*

I see the sleeping babe nestling the breast of its mother,
The sleeping mother and babe—hush'd, I study them long and long.
                                                              "Mother and Babe"

A line in long array where they wind betwixt green islands,
They take a serpentine course, their arms flash in the sun—hark to the musical clank,
Behold the silvery river, in it the splashing horses loitering stop to drink,
Behold the brown-faced men, each group, each person a picture, the negligent rest on the saddles,
Some emerge on the opposite bank, others are just entering the ford—while,
Scarlet and blue and snowy white,
The guidon flags flutter gayly in the wind. *"Cavalry Crossing a Ford"*

On my Northwest coast in the midst of the night a fishermen's group stands watching,
Out on the lake that expands before them, others are spearing salmon,
The canoe, a dim shadowy thing, moves across the black water,
Bearing a torch ablaze at the prow. *"The Torch"*

As Adam early in the morning,
Walking forth from the bower refresh'd with sleep,
Behold me where I pass, hear my voice, approach,
Touch me, touch the palm of your hand to my body as I pass,
Be not afraid of my body. *"As Adam Early in the Morning"*

A noiseless patient spider,
I mark'd where on a little promontory it stood isolated,
Mark'd how to explore the vacant vast surrounding,
It launch'd forth filament, filament, filament, out of itself,
Ever unreeling them, ever tirelessly speeding them.

And you O my soul where you stand,
Surrounded, detached, in measureless oceans of space,
Ceaselessly musing, venturing, throwing, seeking the spheres to connect them,
Till the bridge you will need be form'd, till the ductile anchor hold,
Till the gossamer thread you fling catch somewhere, O my soul.
"A Noiseless Patient Spider"

While the schools and the teachers are teaching after their kind,
Some, obedience to look to the protection of the laws,
Some, to assert a sovereign and God, over all, to rely on,
Some, enjoining to build outside forts and embankments;
Solitary, I here, I to enjoin for you whoever you are you to build inside, invisible forts,
Counseling every man and woman to become the fortress, the lord and sovereign, of himself or herself,
To grow through infinite time finally to be a supreme God himself or herself,

Acknowledging none greater, now or after death, than himself or herself.
                  "*While the Schools and the Teachers Are Teaching*"[1]

What am I after all but a child, pleas'd with the sound of my own name?
    repeating it over and over;
I stand apart to hear—it never tires me.

To you your name also;
Did you think there was nothing but two or three pronunciations in the
    sound of your name?   "*What Am I After All*"

There Was a Child Went Forth

There was a child went forth every day,
And the first object he looked upon and received with wonder or pity or
    love or dread, that object he became,
And that object became part of him for the day or a certain part of the
    day . . . . or for many years or stretching cycles of years.

The early lilacs became part of this child,
And grass, and white and red morningglories, and white and red clover,
    and the song of the phœbe-bird,
And the March-born lambs, and the sow's pink-faint litter, and the mare's
    foal, and the cow's calf, and the noisy brood of the barnyard or by
    the mire of the pondside . . and the fish suspending themselves so
    curiously below there . . and the beautiful curious liquid . . and
    the water-plants with their graceful flat heads . . all became part of
    him.

And the field-sprouts of April and May became part of him . . . .
    wintergrain sprouts, and those of the light-yellow corn, and of the
    esculent roots of the garden,
And the appletrees covered with blossoms, and the fruit afterward . . . .
    and woodberries . . and the commonest weeds by the road;
And the old drunkard staggering home from the outhouse of the tavern
    whence he had lately risen,
And the schoolmistress that passed on her way to the school . . and the
    friendly boys that passed . . and the quarrelsome boys . . and the
    tidy and freshcheeked girls . . and the barefoot negro boy and girl,
And all the changes of city and country wherever he went.

His own parents . . he that had propelled the fatherstuff at night, and
    fathered him . . and she that conceived him in her womb and

---

[1] Reprinted from *Huntington Library Quarterly*, XXII (May, 1959) 259, by permission of the Henry E. Huntington Library and Art Gallery, San Marino, California, the owners of the manuscript.

birthed him . . . . they gave this child more of themselves than that,
They gave him afterward every day . . . . they and of them became part of him.

The mother at home quietly placing the dishes on the suppertable,
The mother with mild words . . . . clean her cap and gown . . . . a wholesome odor falling off her person and clothes as she walks by:
The father, strong, selfsufficient, manly, mean, angered, unjust,
The blow, the quick loud word, the tight bargain, the crafty lure,
The family usages, the language, the company, the furniture . . . . the yearning and swelling heart,
Affection that will not be gainsayed . . . . The sense of what is real . . . . the thought if after all it should prove unreal,
The doubts of daytime and the doubts of nighttime . . . the curious whether and how,
Whether that which appears so is so . . . . Or is it all flashes and specks?
Men and women crowding fast in the streets . . if they are not flashes and specks what are they?
The streets themselves, and the facades of houses . . . . the goods in the windows,
Vehicles . . teams . . the tiered wharves, and the huge crossing at the ferries;
The village on the highland seen from afar at sunset . . . . the river between,
Shadows . . aureola and mist . . light falling on roofs and gables of white or brown, three miles off,
The schooner near by sleepily dropping down the tide . . the little boat slacktowed astern,
The hurrying tumbling waves and quickbroken crests and slapping;
The strata of colored clouds . . . . the long bar of maroontint away solitary by itself . . . . the spread of purity it lies motionless in,
The horizon's edge, the flying seacrow, the fragrance of saltmarsh and shoremud;
These became part of that child who went forth every day, and who now goes and will always go forth every day,
And these become of him or her that peruses them now.

(1855, *pp. 90–91*)

Song for Occupations

Come closer to me,
Push close my lovers and take the best I possess,
Yield closer and closer and give me the best you possess.

Song for Occupations

This is unfinished business with me . . . . how is it with you?
I was chilled with the cold types and cylinder and wet paper between us.

I pass so poorly with paper and types . . . . I must pass with the contact of bodies and souls.

I do not thank you for liking me as I am, and liking the touch of me . . . . I know that it is good for you to do so.

Were all educations practical and ornamental well displayed out of me, what would it amount to?
Were I as the head teacher or charitable proprietor or wise statesman, what would it amount to?
Were I to you as the boss employing and paying you, would that satisfy you?

The learned and virtuous and benevolent, and the usual terms;
A man like me, and never the usual terms.

Neither a servant nor a master am I,
I take no sooner a large price than a small price . . . . I will have my own whoever enjoys me,
I will be even with you, and you shall be even with me.

If you are a workman or workwoman I stand as nigh as the nighest that works in the same shop,
If you bestow gifts on your brother or dearest friend, I demand as good as your brother or dearest friend,
If your lover or husband or wife is welcome by day or night, I must be personally as welcome;
If you have become degraded or ill, then I will become so for your sake;
If you remember your foolish and outlawed deeds, do you think I cannot remember my foolish and outlawed deeds?
If you carouse at the table I say I will carouse at the opposite side of the table;
If you meet some stranger in the street and love him or her, do I not often meet strangers in the street and love them?
If you see a good deal remarkable in me I see just as much remarkable in you.

Why what have you thought of yourself?
Is it you then that thought yourself less?
Is it you that thought the President greater than you? or the rich better off than you? or the educated wiser than you?

Because you are greasy or pimpled—or that you was once drunk, or a thief, or diseased, or rheumatic, or a prostitute—or are so now—or from frivolity or impotence—or that you are no scholar, and never saw your name in print . . . . do you give in that you are any less immortal?

Souls of men and women! it is not you I call unseen, unheard, untouchable and untouching;
It is not you I go argue pro and con about, and to settle whether you are alive or no;
I own publicly who you are, if nobody else owns . . . . and see and hear you, and what you give and take;
What is there you cannot give and take?
I see not merely that you are polite or whitefaced . . . . married or single . . . . citizens of old states or citizens of new states . . . . eminent in some profession . . . . a lady or gentleman in a parlor . . . . or dressed in the jail uniform . . . . or pulpit uniform,
Not only the free Utahan, Kansian, or Arkansian . . . . not only the free Cuban . . . not merely the slave . . . . not Mexican native, or Flatfoot, or negro from Africa,
Iroquois eating the warflesh—fishtearer in his lair of rocks and sand . . . . Esquimaux in the dark cold snowhouse . . . . Chinese with his transverse eyes . . . . Bedowee—or wandering nomad—or tabounschik at the head of his droves,
Grown, half-grown, and babe—of this country and every country, indoors and outdoors I see . . . . and all else is behind or through them.

The wife—and she is not one jot less than the husband,
The daughter—and she is just as good as the son,
The mother—and she is every bit as much as the father.

Offspring of those not rich—boys apprenticed to trades,
Young fellows working on farms and old fellows working on farms;
The naive . . . . the simple and hardy . . . . he going to the polls to vote . . . . he who has a good time, and he who has a bad time;
Mechanics, southerners, new arrivals, sailors, mano'warsmen, merchantmen, coasters,
All these I see . . . . but nigher and farther the same I see;
None shall escape me, and none shall wish to escape me.

I bring what you much need, yet always have,
I bring not money or amours or dress or eating . . . . but I bring as good;
And send no agent or medium . . . . and offer no representative of value—but offer the value itself.

Song for Occupations

There is something that comes home to one now and perpetually,
It is not what is printed or preached or discussed . . . . it eludes discussion and print,
It is not to be put in a book . . . . it is not in this book,
It is for you whoever you are . . . . it is no farther from you than your hearing and sight are from you,
It is hinted by nearest and commonest and readiest . . . . it is not them, though it is endlessly provoked by them . . . . What is there ready and near you now?

You may read in many languages and read nothing about it;
You may read the President's message and read nothing about it there,
Nothing in the reports from the state department or treasury department . . . . or in the daily papers, or the weekly papers,
Or in the census returns or assessors' returns or prices current or any accounts of stock.

The sun and stars that float in the open air . . . . the appleshaped earth and we upon it . . . . surely the drift of them is something grand;
I do not know what it is except that it is grand, and that it is happiness,
And that the enclosing purport of us here is not a speculation, or bon-mot or reconnoissance,
And that it is not something which by luck may turn out well for us, and without luck must be a failure for us,
And not something which may yet be retracted in a certain contingency.

The light and shade—the curious sense of body and identity—the greed that with perfect complaisance devours all things—the endless pride and outstretching of man—unspeakable joys and sorrows,
The wonder every one sees in every one else he sees . . . . and the wonders that fill each minute of time forever and each acre of surface and space forever,
Have you reckoned them as mainly for a trade or farmwork? or for the profits of a store? or to achieve yourself a position? or to fill a gentleman's leisure or a lady's leisure?

Have you reckoned the landscape took substance and form that it might be painted in a picture?
Or men and women that they might be written of, and songs sung?
Or the attraction of gravity and the great laws and harmonious combinations and the fluids of the air as subjects for the savans?
Or the brown land and the blue sea for maps and charts?
Or the stars to be put in constellations and named fancy names?
Or that the growth of seeds is for agricultural tables or agriculture itself?

Old institutions . . . . these arts libraries legends collections—and the practice handed along in manufactures . . . . will we rate them so high?
Will we rate our prudence and business so high? . . . . I have no objection,
I rate them as high as the highest . . . . but a child born of a woman and man I rate beyond all rate.

We thought our Union grand and our Constitution grand;
I do not say they are not grand and good—for they are,
I am this day just as much in love with them as you,
But I am eternally in love with you and with all my fellows upon the earth.

We consider the bibles and religions divine . . . . I do not say they are not divine,
I say they have all grown out of you and may grow out of you still,
It is not they who give the life . . . . it is you who give the life;
Leaves are not more shed from the trees or trees from the earth than they are shed out of you.

The sum of all known value and respect I add up in you whoever you are;
The President is up there in the White House for you . . . . it is not you who are here for him,
The Secretaries act in their bureaus for you . . . . not you here for them,
The Congress convenes every December for you,
Laws, courts, the forming of states, the charters of cities, the going and coming of commerce and mails are all for you.

All doctrines, all politics and civilization exurge from you,
All sculpture and monuments and anything inscribed anywhere are tallied in you,
The gist of histories and statistics as far back as the records reach is in you this hour—and myths and tales the same;
If you were not breathing and walking here where would they all be?
The most renowned poems would be ashes . . . . orations and plays would be vacuums.

All architecture is what you do to it when you look upon it;
Did you think it was in the white or gray stone? or the lines of the arches and cornices?

All music is what awakens from you when you are reminded by the instruments,
It is not the violins and the cornets . . . . it is not the oboe nor the beating drums—nor the notes of the baritone singer singing his

Song for Occupations

sweet romanza . . . . nor those of the men's chorus, nor those of the women's chorus,
It is nearer and farther than they.

Will the whole come back then?
Can each see the signs of the best by a look in the lookingglass? Is there nothing greater or more?
Does all sit there with you and here with me?

The old forever new things . . . . you foolish child! . . . . the closest simplest things—this moment with you,
Your person and every particle that relates to your person,
The pulses of your brain waiting their chance and encouragement at every deed or sight;
Anything you do in public by day, and anything you do in secret betweendays,
What is called right and what is called wrong . . . . what you behold or touch . . . . what causes your anger or wonder,
The anklechain of the slave, the bed of the bedhouse, the cards of the gambler, the plates of the forger;
What is seen or learned in the street, or intuitively learned,
What is learned in the public school—spelling, reading, writing and ciphering . . . . the blackboard and the teacher's diagrams:
The panes of the windows and all that appears through them . . . . the going forth in the morning and the aimless spending of the day;
(What is it that you made money? what is it that you got what you wanted?)
The usual routine . . . . the workshop, factory, yard, office, store, or desk;
The jaunt of hunting or fishing, or the life of hunting or fishing,
Pasturelife, foddering, milking and herding, and all the personnel and usages;
The plum-orchard and apple-orchard . . . . gardening . . seedlings, cuttings, flowers and vines,
Grains and manures . . marl, clay, loam . . the subsoil plough . . the shovel and pick and rake and hoe . . irrigation and draining;
The currycomb . . the horse-cloth . . the halter and bridle and bits . . the very wisps of straw,
The barn and barn-yard . . the bins and mangers . . the mows and racks:
Manufactures . . commerce . . engineering . . the building of cities, and every trade carried on there . . and the implements of every trade,
The anvil and tongs and hammer . . the axe and wedge . . the square and mitre and jointer and smoothingplane;

The plumbbob and trowel and level . . the wall-scaffold, and the work of walls and ceilings . . or any mason-work:
The ship's compass . . the sailor's tarpaulin . . the stays and lanyards, and the ground-tackle for anchoring or mooring,
The sloop's tiller . . the pilot's wheel and bell . . the yacht or fish-smack . . the great gay-pennanted three-hundred-foot steamboat under full headway, with her proud fat breasts and her delicate swift-flashing paddles;
The trail and line and hooks and sinkers . . the seine, and hauling the seine;
Smallarms and rifles . . . . the powder and shot and caps and wadding . . . . the ordnance for war . . . . the carriages;
Everyday objects . . . . the housechairs, the carpet, the bed and the counterpane of the bed, and him or her sleeping at night, and the wind blowing, and the indefinite noises:
The snowstorm or rainstorm . . . . the tow-trowsers . . . . the lodge-hut in the woods, and the still-hunt:
City and country . . fireplace and candle . . gaslight and heater and aqueduct;
The message of the governor, mayor, or chief of police . . . . the dishes of breakfast or dinner or supper;
The bunkroom, the fire-engine, the string-team, and the car or truck behind;
The paper I write on or you write on . . and every word we write . . and every cross and twirl of the pen . . and the curious way we write what we think . . . . yet very faintly;
The directory, the detector, the ledger . . . . the books in ranks or the bookshelves . . . . the clock attached to the wall,
The ring on your finger . . the lady's wristlet . . the hammers of stone-breakers or coppersmiths . . the druggist's vials and jars;
The etui of surgical instruments, and the etui of oculist's or aurist's instruments, or dentist's instruments;
Glassblowing, grinding of wheat and corn . . casting, and what is cast . . tinroofing, shingledressing,
Shipcarpentering, flagging of sidewalks by flaggers . . dockbuilding, fishcuring, ferrying;
The pump, the piledriver, the great derrick . . the coalkiln and brickkiln,
Ironworks or whiteleadworks . . the sugarhouse . . steam-saws, and the great mills and factories;
The cottonbale . . the stevedore's hook . . the saw and buck of the sawyer . . the screen of the coalscreener . . the mould of the moulder . . the workingknife of the butcher;
The cylinder press . . the handpress . . the frisket and tympan . . the compositor's stick and rule,

The implements for daguerreotyping . . . . the tools of the rigger or grappler or sailmaker or blockmaker,
Goods of guttapercha or papiermache . . . . colors and brushes . . . . glaziers' implements,
The veneer and gluepot . . the confectioner's ornaments . . the decanter and glasses . . the shears and flatiron;
The awl and kneestrap . . the pint measure and quart measure . . the counter and stool . . the writingpen of quill or metal;
Billiards and tenpins . . . . the ladders and hanging ropes of the gymnasium, and the manly exercises;
The designs for wallpapers or oilcloths or carpets . . . . the fancies for goods for women . . . . the bookbinder's stamps;
Leatherdressing, coachmaking, boilermaking, ropetwisting, distilling, signpainting, limeburning, coopering, cottonpicking,
The walkingbeam of the steam-engine . . the throttle and governors, and the up and down rods,
Stavemachines and plainingmachines . . . . the cart of the carman . . the omnibus . . the ponderous dray;
The snowplough and two engines pushing it . . . . the ride in the express train of only one car . . . . the swift go through a howling storm:
The bearhunt or coonhunt . . . . the bonfire of shavings in the open lot in the city . . the crowd of children watching;
The blows of the fighting-man . . the upper cut and one-two-three;
The shopwindows . . . . the coffins in the sexton's wareroom . . . . the fruit on the fruitstand . . . . the beef on the butcher's stall,
The bread and cakes in the bakery . . . . the white and red pork in the pork-store;
The milliner's ribbons . . the dressmaker's patterns . . . . the tea-table . . the homemade sweetmeats:
The column of wants in the one-cent paper . . the news by telegraph . . . . the amusements and operas and shows:
The cotton and woolen and linen you wear . . . . the money you make and spend;
Your room and bedroom . . . . your piano-forte . . . . the stove and cookpans,
The house you live in . . . . the rent . . . . the other tenants . . . . the deposite in the savings-bank . . . . the trade at the grocery,
The pay on Saturday night . . . . the going home, and the purchases;
In them the heft of the heaviest . . . . in them far more than you estimated, and far less also,
In them, not yourself . . . . you and your soul enclose all things, regardless of estimation,

In them your themes and hints and provokers . . if not, the whole earth
    has no themes or hints or provokers, and never had.

I do not affirm what you see beyond is futile . . . . I do not advise you
    to stop,
I do not say leadings you thought great are not great,
But I say that none lead to greater or sadder or happier than those lead
    to.

Will you seek afar off? You surely come back at last,
In things best known to you finding the best or as good as the best,
In folks nearest to you finding also the sweetest and strongest and
    lovingest,
Happiness not in another place, but this place . . not for another hour,
    but this hour,
Man in the first you see or touch . . . . always in your friend or brother
    or nighest neighbor . . . . Woman in your mother or lover or wife,
And all else thus far known giving place to men and women.

When the psalm sings instead of the singer,
When the script preaches instead of the preacher,
When the pulpit descends and goes instead of the carver that carved the
    supporting desk,
When the sacred vessels or the bits of the eucharist, or the lath and plast,
    procreate as effectually as the young silversmiths or bakers, or the
    masons in their overalls,
When a university course convinces like a slumbering woman and child
    convince,
When the minted gold in the vault smiles like the nightwatchman's
    daughter,
When warrantee deeds loafe in chairs opposite and are my friendly
    companions,
I intend to reach them my hand and make as much of them as I do of
    men and women.   (1855, *pp. 57–64*)

The Sleepers

I wander all night in my vision,
Stepping with light feet . . . . swiftly and noiselessly stepping and
    stopping,
Bending with open eyes over the shut eyes of sleepers;
Wandering and confused . . . . lost to myself . . . . ill-assorted . . . .
    . . . . contradictory,
Pausing and gazing and bending and stopping.

How solemn they look there, stretched and still;
How quiet they breathe, the little children in their cradles.

The wretched features of ennuyees, the white features of corpses, the livid faces of drunkards, the sick-gray faces of onanists,
The gashed bodies on battlefields, the insane in their strong-doored rooms, the sacred idiots,
The newborn emerging from gates and the dying emerging from gates,
The night pervades them and enfolds them.

The married couple sleep calmly in their bed, he with his palm on the hip of the wife, and she with her palm on the hip of the husband,
The sisters sleep lovingly side by side in their bed,
The men sleep lovingly side by side in theirs,
And the mother sleeps with her little child carefully wrapped.

The blind sleep, and the deaf and dumb sleep,
The prisoner sleeps well in the prison . . . . the runaway son sleeps,
The murderer that is to be hung next day . . . . how does he sleep?
And the murdered person . . . . how does he sleep?

The female that loves unrequited sleeps,
And the male that loves unrequited sleeps;
The head of the moneymaker that plotted all day sleeps,
And the enraged and treacherous dispositions sleep.

I stand with drooping eyes by the worstsuffering and restless,
I pass my hands soothingly to and fro a few inches from them;
The restless sink in their beds . . . . they fitfully sleep.

The earth recedes from me into the night,
I saw that it was beautiful . . . . and I see that what is not the earth is beautiful.

I go from bedside to bedside . . . . I sleep close with the other sleepers, each in turn;
I dream in my dream all the dreams of the other dreamers,
And I become the other dreamers.

I am a dance . . . . Play up there! the fit is whirling me fast.

I am the everlaughing . . . . it is new moon and twilight,
I see the hiding of douceurs . . . . I see nimble ghosts whichever way I look,
Cache and cache again deep in the ground and sea, and where it is neither ground or sea.

Well do they do their jobs, those journeymen divine,
Only from me can they hide nothing and would not if they could;

I reckon I am their boss, and they make me a pet besides,
And surround me, and lead me and run ahead when I walk,
And lift their cunning covers and signify me with stretched arms, and resume the way;
Onward we move, a gay gang of blackguards with mirthshouting music and wildflapping pennants of joy.

I am the actor and the actress . . . . the voter . . the politician,
The emigrant and the exile . . the criminal that stood in the box,
He who has been famous, and he who shall be famous after today,
The stammerer . . . . the wellformed person . . the wasted or feeble person.

I am she who adorned herself and folded her hair expectantly,
My truant lover has come and it is dark.

Double yourself and receive me darkness,
Receive me and my lover too . . . . he will not let me go without him.

I roll myself upon you as upon a bed . . . . I resign myself to the dusk.

He whom I call answers me and takes the place of my lover,
He rises with me silently from the bed.

Darkness you are gentler than my lover . . . . his flesh was sweaty and panting,
I feel the hot moisture yet that he left me.

My hands are spread forth . . I pass them in all directions,
I would sound up the shadowy shore to which you are journeying.

Be careful, darkness . . . . already, what was it touched me?
I thought my lover had gone . . . . else darkness and he are one,
I hear the heart-beat . . . . I follow . . I fade away.

O hotcheeked and blushing! O foolish hectic!
O for pity's sake, no one must see me now! . . . . my clothes were stolen while I was abed,
Now I am thrust forth, where shall I run?

Pier that I saw dimly last night when I looked from the windows,
Pier out from the main, let me catch myself with you and stay . . . . I will not chafe you;
I feel ashamed to go naked about the world,
And am curious to know where my feet stand . . . . and what is this flooding me, childhood or manhood . . . . and the hunger that crosses the bridge between.

The cloth laps a first sweet eating and drinking,
Laps life-swelling yolks . . . . laps ear of rose-corn, milky and just ripened:
The white teeth stay, and the boss-tooth advances in darkness,
And liquor is spilled on lips and bosoms by touching glasses, and the best liquor afterward.

I descend my western course . . . . my sinews are flaccid,
Perfume and youth course through me, and I am their wake.

It is my face yellow and wrinkled instead of the old woman's,
I sit low in a strawbottom chair and carefully darn my grandson's stockings.

It is I too . . . . the sleepless widow looking out on the winter midnight,
I see the sparkles of starshine on the icy and pallid earth.
A shroud I see—and I am the shroud . . . . I wrap a body and lie in the coffin;
It is dark here underground . . . . it is not evil or pain here . . . . it is blank here, for reasons.

It seems to me that everything in the light and air ought to be happy;
Whoever is not in his coffin and the dark grave, let him know he has enough.

I see a beautiful gigantic swimmer swimming naked through the eddies of the sea,
His brown hair lies close and even to his head . . . . he strikes out with courageous arms . . . . he urges himself with his legs.
I see his white body . . . . I see his undaunted eyes;
I hate the swift-running eddies that would dash him headforemost on the rocks.

What are you doing you ruffianly red-trickled waves?
Will you kill the courageous giant? Will you kill him in the prime of his middle age?

Steady and long he struggles;
He is baffled and banged and bruised . . . . he holds out while his strength holds out,
The slapping eddies are spotted with his blood . . . . they bear him away . . . . they roll him and swing him and turn him:
His beautiful body is borne in the circling eddies . . . . it is continually bruised on rocks,
Swiftly and out of sight is borne the brave corpse.

I turn but do not extricate myself;
Confused . . . . a pastreading . . . . another, but with darkness yet.

The beach is cut by the razory ice-wind . . . . the wreck-guns sound,
The tempest lulls and the moon comes floundering through the drifts.

I look where the ship helplessly heads end on . . . . I hear the burst as she strikes . . I hear the howls of dismay . . . . they grow fainter and fainter.

I cannot aid with my wringing fingers;
I can but rush to the surf and let it drench me and freeze upon me.

I search with the crowd . . . . not one of the company is washed to us alive;
In the morning I help pick up the dead and lay them in rows in a barn.

Now of the old war-days . . the defeat at Brooklyn;
Washington stands inside the lines . . he stands on the entrenched hills amid a crowd of officers,
His face is cold and damp . . . . he cannot repress the weeping drops . . . . he lifts the glass perpetually to his eyes . . . . the color is blanched from his cheeks,
He sees the slaughter of the southern braves confided to him by their parents.

The same at last and at last when peace is declared,
He stands in the room of the old tavern . . . . the wellbeloved soldiers all pass through,
The officers speechless and slow draw near in their turns,
The chief encircles their necks with his arm and kisses them on the cheek,
He kisses lightly the wet cheeks one after another . . . . he shakes hands and bids goodbye to the army.

Now I tell what my mother told me today as we sat at dinner together,
Of when she was a nearly grown girl living home with her parents on the old homestead.

A red squaw came one breakfasttime to the old homestead,
On her back she carried a bundle of rushes for rushbottoming chairs;
Her hair straight shiny coarse black and profuse halfenveloped her face,
Her step was free and elastic . . . . her voice sounded exquisitely as she spoke.

My mother looked in delight and amazement at the stranger,
She looked at the beauty of her tallborne face and full and pliant limbs,

The more she looked upon her she loved her,
Never before had she seen such wonderful beauty and purity;
She made her sit on a bench by the jamb of the fireplace . . . . she cooked food for her,
She had no work to give her but she gave her remembrance and fondness.

The red squaw staid all the forenoon, and toward the middle of the afternoon she went away;
O my mother was loth to have her go away,
All the week she thought of her . . . . she watched for her many a month,
She remembered her many a winter and many a summer,
But the red squaw never came nor was heard of there again.

Now Lucifer was not dead . . . . or if he was I am his sorrowful terrible heir;
I have been wronged . . . . I am oppressed . . . . I hate him that oppresses me,
I will either destroy him, or he shall release me.

Damn him! how he does defile me,
How he informs against my brother and sister and takes pay for their blood,
How he laughs when I look down the bend after the steamboat that carries away my woman.

Now the vast dusk bulk that is the whale's bulk . . . . it seems mine,
Warily, sportsman! though I lie so sleepy and sluggish, my tap is death.

A show of the summer softness . . . . a contact of something unseen . . . . an amour of the light and air;
I am jealous and overwhelmed with friendliness,
And will go gallivant with the light and the air myself,
And have an unseen something to be in contact with them also.

O love and summer! you are in the dreams and in me,
Autumn and winter are in the dreams . . . . the farmer goes with his thrift,
The droves and crops increase . . . . the barns are wellfilled.

Elements merge in the night . . . . ships make tacks in the dreams . . . . the sailor sails . . . . the exile returns home,
The fugitive returns unharmed . . . . the immigrant is back beyond months and years;
The poor Irishman lives in the simple house of his childhood, with the wellknown neighbors and faces,

They warmly welcome him . . . . he is barefoot again . . . . he forgets he is welloff;
The Dutchman voyages home, and the Scotchman and Welchman voyage home . . and the native of the Mediterranean voyages home;
To every port of England and France and Spain enter wellfilled ships;
The Swiss foots it toward his hills . . . . the Prussian goes his way, and the Hungarian his way, and the Pole goes his way,
The Swede returns, and the Dane and Norwegian return.

The homeward bound and the outward bound,
The beautiful lost swimmer, the ennuyee, the onanist, the female that loves unrequited, the moneymaker,
The actor and actress . . those through with their parts and those waiting to commence,
The affectionate boy, the husband and wife, the voter, the nominee that is chosen and the nominee that has failed,
The great already known, and the great anytime after to day,
The stammerer, the sick, the perfectformed, the homely,
The criminal that stood in the box, the judge that sat and sentenced him, the fluent lawyers, the jury, the audience,
The laugher and weeper, the dancer, the midnight widow, the red squaw,
The consumptive, the erysipalite, the idiot, he that is wronged,
The antipodes, and every one between this and them in the dark,
I swear they are averaged now . . . . one is no better than the other,
The night and sleep have likened them and restored them.
I swear they are all beautiful,
Every one that sleeps is beautiful . . . . every thing in the dim night is beautiful,
The wildest and bloodiest is over and all is peace.

Peace is always beautiful,
The myth of heaven indicates peace and night.

The myth of heaven indicates the soul;
The soul is always beautiful . . . . it appears more or it appears less . . . . it comes or lags behind,
It comes from its embowered garden and looks pleasantly on itself and encloses the world;
Perfect and clean the genitals previously jetting, and perfect and clean the womb cohering,
The head wellgrown and proportioned and plumb, and the bowels and joints proportioned and plumb.

The soul is always beautiful,
The universe is duly in order . . . . every thing is in its place,
What is arrived is in its place, and what waits is in its place;

The twisted skull waits . . . . the watery or rotten blood waits,
The child of the glutton or venerealee waits long, and the child of the drunkard waits long, and the drunkard himself waits long,
The sleepers that lived and died wait . . . . the far advanced are to go on in their turns, and the far behind are to go on in their turns,
The diverse shall be no less diverse, but they shall flow and unite . . . . they unite now.

The sleepers are very beautiful as they lie unclothed,
They flow hand in hand over the whole earth from east to west as they lie unclothed;
The Asiatic and African are hand in hand . . . . the European and American are hand in hand,
Learned and unlearned are hand in hand . . and male and female are hand in hand;
The bare arm of the girl crosses the bare breast of her lover . . . . they press close without lust . . . . his lips press her neck,
The father holds his grown or ungrown son in his arms with measureless love . . . . and the son holds the father in his arms with measureless love,
The white hair of the mother shines on the white wrist of the daughter,
The breath of the boy goes with the breath of the man . . . . friend is inarmed by friend,
The scholar kisses the teacher and the teacher kisses the scholar . . . . the wronged is made right,
The call of the slave is one with the master's call . . and the master salutes the slave,
The felon steps forth from the prison . . . . the insane becomes sane . . . . the suffering of sick persons is relieved,
The sweatings and fevers stop . . the throat that was unsound is sound . . the lungs of the consumptive are resumed . . the poor distressed head is free,
The joints of the rheumatic move as smoothly as ever, and smoother than ever,
Stiflings and passages open . . . . the paralysed become supple,
The swelled and convulsed and congested awake to themselves in condition,
They pass the invigoration of the night and the chemistry of the night and awake.

I too pass from the night;
I stay awhile away O night, but I return to you again and love you;
Why should I be afraid to trust myself to you?
I am not afraid . . . . I have been well brought forward by you;

I love the rich running day, but I do not desert her in whom I lay so
    long:
I know not how I came of you, and I know not where I go with you
    . . . . but I know I came well and shall go well.
I will stop only a time with the night . . . . and rise betimes.
I will duly pass the day O my mother and duly return to you;
Not you will yield forth the dawn again more surely than you will yield
    forth me again,
Not the womb yields the babe in its time more surely than I shall be
    yielded from you in my time. (1855, *pp. 70–77*)

Scented Herbage of My Breast

Scented herbage of my breast,
Leaves from you I glean, I write, to be perused best afterwards,
Tomb-leaves, body-leaves growing up above me above death,
Perennial roots, tall leaves, O the winter shall not freeze you delicate
    leaves,
Every year shall you bloom again, out from where you retired you shall
    emerge again;
O I do not know whether many passing by will discover you or inhale
    your faint odor, but I believe a few will;
O slender leaves! O blossoms of my blood! I permit you to tell in your
    own way of the heart that is under you,
O I do not know what you mean there underneath yourselves, you are
    not happiness,
You are often more bitter than I can bear, you burn and sting me,
Yet you are beautiful to me you faint-tinged roots, you make me think of
    death,
Death is beautiful from you, (what indeed is finally beautiful except
    death and love?)
O I think it is not for life I am chanting here my chant of lovers, I think it
    must be for death,
For how calm, how solemn it grows to ascend to the atmosphere of
    lovers,
Death or life I am then indifferent, my soul declines to prefer,
(I am not sure but the high soul of lovers welcomes death most,)
Indeed O death, I think now these leaves mean precisely the same as you
    mean,
Grow up taller sweet leaves that I may see! grow up out of my breast!
Spring away from the conceal'd heart there!
Do not fold yourself so in your pink-tinged roots timid leaves!

Do not remain down there so ashamed, herbage of my breast!
Come I am determin'd to unbare this broad breast of mine, I have long enough stifled and choked;
Emblematic and capricious blades I leave you, now you serve me not,
I will say what I have to say by itself,
I will sound myself and comrades only, I will never again utter a call only their call,
I will raise with it immortal reverberations through the States,
I will give an example to lovers to take permanent shape and will through the States,
Through me shall the words be said to make death exhilarating.
Give me your tone therefore O death, that I may accord with it,
Give me yourself, for I see that you belong to me now above all, and are folded inseparably together, you love and death are,
Nor will I allow you to balk me any more with what I was calling life,
For now it is convey'd to me that you are the purports essential,
That you hide in these shifting forms of life, for reasons, and that they are mainly for you,
That you beyond them come forth to remain, the real reality,
That behind the mask of materials you patiently wait, no matter how long,
That you will one day perhaps take control of all,
That you will perhaps dissipate this entire show of appearance,
That may-be you are what it is all for, but it does not last so very long,
But you will last very long.

Of the Terrible Doubt of Appearances

Of the terrible doubt of appearances,
Of the uncertainty after all, that we may be deluded,
That may-be reliance and hope are but speculations after all,
That may-be identity beyond the grave is a beautiful fable only,
May-be the things I perceive, the animals, plants, men, hills, shining and flowing waters,
The skies of day and night, colors, densities, forms, may-be these are (as doubtless they are) only apparitions, and the real something has yet to be known,
(How often they dart out of themselves as if to confound me and mock me!
How often I think neither I know, nor any man knows, aught of them,)
May-be seeming to me what they are (as doubtless they indeed but seem) as from my present point of view, and might prove (as of course they would) nought of what they appear, or nought anyhow, from entirely changed points of view;

To me these and the like of these are curiously answer'd by my lovers, my
    dear friends,
When he whom I love travels with me or sits a long while holding me by
    the hand,
When the subtle air, the impalpable, the sense that words and reason
    hold not, surround us and pervade us,
Then I am charged with untold and untellable wisdom, I am silent, I
    require nothing further,
I cannot answer the question of appearances or that of identity beyond
    the grave,
But I walk or sit indifferent, I am satisfied,
He ahold of my hand has completely satisfied me.

The Base of All Metaphysics

And now gentlemen,
A word I give to remain in your memories and minds,
As base and finalè too for all metaphysics.

(So to the students the old professor,
At the close of his crowded course.)

Having studied the new and antique, the Greek and Germanic systems,
Kant having studied and stated, Fichte and Schelling and Hegel,
Stated the lore of Plato, and Socrates greater than Plato,
And greater than Socrates sought and stated, Christ divine having
    studied long,
I see reminiscent to-day those Greek and Germanic systems,
See the philosophies all, Christian churches and tenets see
Yet underneath Socrates clearly see, and underneath Christ the divine I
    see,
The dear love of man for his comrade, the attraction of friend to friend,
Of the well-married husband and wife, of children and parents,
Of city for city and land for land.

The Wound-Dresser

1

An old man bending I come among new faces,
Years looking backward resuming in answer to children,
Come tell us old man, as from young men and maidens that love me,
    (Arous'd and angry, I'd thought to beat the alarum, and urge relentless
    war,
But soon my fingers fail'd me, my face droop'd and I resign'd myself,

To sit by the wounded and soothe them, or silently watch the dead;)
Years hence of these scenes, of these furious passions, these chances,
Of unsurpass'd heroes, (was one side so brave? the other was equally brave;)
Now be witness again, paint the mightiest armies of earth,
Of those armies so rapid so wondrous what saw you to tell us?
What stays with you latest and deepest? of curious panics,
Of hard-fought engagements or sieges tremendous what deepest remains?

2

O maidens and young men I love and that love me,
What you ask of my days those the strangest and sudden your talking recalls,
Soldier alert I arrive after a long march cover'd with sweat and dust,
In the nick of time I come, plunge in the fight, loudly shout in the rush of successful charge,
Enter the captur'd works—yet lo, like a swift-running river they fade,
Pass and are gone they fade—I dwell not on soldiers' perils or soldiers' joys,
(Both I remember well—many the hardships, few the joys, yet I was content.)

But in silence, in dreams' projections,
While the world of gain and appearance and mirth goes on,
So soon what is over forgotten, and waves wash the imprints off the sand,
With hinged knees returning I enter the doors, (while for you up there,
Whoever you are, follow without noise and be of strong heart.)

Bearing the bandages, water and sponge,
Straight and swift to my wounded I go,
Where they lie on the ground after the battle brought in,
Where their priceless blood reddens the grass the ground,
Or to the rows of the hospital tent, or under the roof'd hospital,
To the long rows of cots up and down each side I return,
To each and all one after another I draw near, not one do I miss,
An attendant follows holding a tray, he carries a refuse pail,
Soon to be fill'd with clotted rags and blood, emptied, and fill'd again.

I onward go, I stop,
With hinged knees and steady hand to dress wounds,
I am firm with each, the pangs are sharp yet unavoidable,

One turns to me his appealing eyes—poor boy! I never knew you,
Yet I think I could not refuse this moment to die for you, if that would save you.

3

On, on I go, (open doors of time! open hospital doors!)
The crush'd head I dress, (poor crazed hand tear not the bandage away,)
The neck of the cavalry-man with the bullet through and through I examine,
Hard the breathing rattles, quite glazed already the eye, yet life struggles hard,
(Come sweet death! be persuaded O beautiful death!
In mercy come quickly.)

From the stump of the arm, the amputated hand,
I undo the clotted lint, remove the slough, wash off the matter and blood,
Back on his pillow the soldier bends with curv'd neck and side-falling head,
His eyes are closed, his face is pale, he dares not look on the bloody stump,
And has not yet look'd on it.

I dress a wound in the side, deep, deep,
But a day or two more, for see the frame all wasted and sinking,
And the yellow-blue countenance see.

I dress the perforated shoulder, the foot with the bullet-wound,
Cleanse the one with a gnawing and putrid gangrene, so sickening, so offensive,
While the attendant stands behind aside me holding the tray and pail.

I am faithful, I do not give out,
The fractur'd thigh, the knee, the wound in the abdomen,
These and more I dress with impassive hand, yet deep in my breast a fire, a burning flame.)

4

Thus in silence in dreams' projections,
Returning, resuming, I thread my way through the hospitals,
The hurt and wounded I pacify with soothing hand,
I sit by the restless all the dark night, some are so young,
Some suffer so much, I recall the experience sweet and sad,
(Many a soldier's loving arms about this neck have cross'd and rested,
Many a soldier's kiss dwells on these bearded lips.)

When Lilacs Last in the Dooryard Bloom'd

1

When lilacs last in the dooryard bloom'd,
And the great star early droop'd in the western sky in the night,
I mourn'd, and yet shall mourn with ever-returning spring.

Ever-returning spring, trinity sure to me you bring,
Lilac blooming perennial and drooping star in the west,
And thought of him I love.

2

O powerful western fallen star!
O shades of night—O moody, tearful night!
O great star disappear'd—O the black murk that hides the star!
O cruel hands that hold me powerless—O helpless soul of me!
O harsh surrounding cloud that will not free my soul.

3

In the dooryard fronting an old farm-house near the white-wash'd palings,
Stands the lilac-bush tall-growing with heart-shaped leaves of rich green,
With many a pointed blossom rising delicate, with the perfume strong I love,
With every leaf a miracle—and from this bush in the dooryard,
With delicate-color'd blossoms and heart-shaped leaves of rich green,
A sprig with its flower I break.

4

In the swamp in secluded recesses,
A shy and hidden bird is warbling a song.

Solitary the thrush,
The hermit withdrawn to himself, avoiding the settlements,
Sings by himself a song.

Song of the bleeding throat,
Death's outlet song of life, (for well dear brother I know,
If thou wast not granted to sing thou would'st surely die.)

5

Over the breast of the spring, the land, amid cities,
Amid lanes and through old woods, where lately the violets peep'd from the ground, spotting the gray debris,

Amid the grass in the fields each side of the lanes, passing the endless grass,
Passing the yellow-spear'd wheat, every grain from its shroud in the dark-brown fields uprisen,
Passing the apple-tree blows of white and pink in the orchards,
Carrying a corpse to where it shall rest in the grave,
Night and day journeys a coffin.

6

Coffin that passes through lanes and streets,
Through day and night with the great cloud darkening the land,
With the pomp of the inloop'd flags with the cities draped in black,
With the show of the States themselves as of crape-veil'd women standing,
With processions long and winding and the flambeaus of the night,
With the countless torches lit, with the silent sea of faces and the unbared heads,
With the waiting depot, the arriving coffin, and the sombre faces,
With dirges through the night, with the thousand voices rising strong and solemn,
With all the mournful voices of the dirges pour'd around the coffin,
The dim-lit churches and the shuddering organs—where amid these you journey,
With the tolling tolling bells' perpetual clang,
Here, coffin that slowly passes,
I give you my sprig of lilac.

7

(Nor for you, for one alone,
Blossoms and branches green to coffins all I bring,
For fresh as the morning, thus would I chant a song for you O sane and sacred death.

All over bouquets of roses,
O death, I cover you over with roses and early lilies,
But mostly and now the lilac that blooms the first,
Copious I break, I break the sprigs from the bushes,
With loaded arms I come, pouring for you,
For you and the coffins all of you O death.)

8

O western orb sailing the heaven,
Now I know what you must have meant as a month since I walk'd,
As I walk'd in silence the transparent shadowy night,
As I saw you had something to tell as you bent to me night after night,

As you droop'd from the sky low down as if to my side, (while the other stars all look'd on,)
As we wander'd together the solemn night, (for something I know not what kept me from sleep,)
As the night advanced, and I saw on the rim of the west how full you were of woe,
As I stood on the rising ground in the breeze in the cool transparent night,
As I watch'd where you pass'd and was lost in the netherward black of the night,
As my soul in its trouble dissatisfied sank, as where you sad orb,
Concluded, dropt in the night, and was gone.

9

Sing on there in the swamp,
O singer bashful and tender, I hear your notes, I hear your call,
I hear, I come presently, I understand you,
But a moment I linger, for the lustrous star has detain'd me,
The star my departing comrade holds and detains me.

10

O how shall I warble myself for the dead one there I loved?
And how shall I deck my song for the large sweet soul that has gone?
And what shall my perfume be for the grave of him I love?

Sea-winds blown from east and west,
Blown from the Eastern sea and blown from the Western sea, till there on the prairies meeting,
These and with these and the breath of my chant,
I'll perfume the grave of him I love.

11

O what shall I hang on the chamber walls?
And what shall the pictures be that I hang on the walls,
To adorn the burial-house of him I love?

Pictures of growing spring and farms and homes,
With the Fourth-month eve at sundown, and the gray smoke lucid and bright,
With floods of the yellow gold of the gorgeous, indolent, sinking sun, burning, expanding the air,
With the fresh sweet herbage under foot, and the pale green leaves of the trees prolific,
In the distance the flowing glaze, the breast of the river, with a wind-dapple here and there,

With ranging hills on the banks, with many a line against the sky, and shadows,
And the city at hand with dwellings so dense, and stacks of chimneys,
And all the scenes of life and the workshops, and the workmen homeward returning.

12

Lo, body and soul—this land,
My own Manhattan with spires, and the sparkling and hurrying tides, and the ships,
The varied and ample land, the South and the North in the light, Ohio's shores and flashing Missouri,
And ever the far-spreading prairies cover'd with grass and corn.

Lo, the most excellent sun so calm and haughty,
The violet and purple morn with just-felt breezes,
The gentle soft-born measureless light,
The miracle spreading bathing all, the fulfill'd noon,
The coming eve delicious, the welcome night and the stars,
Over my cities shining all, enveloping man and land.

13

Sing on, sing on you gray-brown bird,
Sing from the swamps, the recesses, pour your chant from the bushes,
Limitless out of the dusk, out of the cedars and pines.

Sing on dearest brother, warble your reedy song,
Loud human song, with voice of uttermost woe.

O liquid and free and tender!
O wild and loose to my soul—O wondrous singer!
You only I hear—yet the star holds me, (but will soon depart,)
Yet the lilac with mastering odor holds me.

14

Now while I sat in the day and look'd forth,
In the close of the day with its light and the fields of spring, and the farmers preparing their crops,
In the large unconscious scenery of my land with its lakes and forests,
In the heavenly aerial beauty, (after the perturb'd winds and the storms,)
Under the arching heavens of the afternoon swift passing, and the voices of children and women,
The many-moving sea-tides, and I saw the ships how they sail'd,

And the summer approaching with richness, and the fields all busy with labor,
And the infinite separate houses, how they all went on, each with its meals and minutia of daily usages,
And the streets how their throbbings throbb'd, and the cities pent—lo, then and there,
Falling upon them all and among them all, enveloping me with the rest,
Appear'd the cloud, appear'd the long black trail,
And I knew death, its thought, and the sacred knowledge of death.

Then with the knowledge of death as walking one side of me,
And the thought of death close-walking the other side of me,
And I in the middle as with companions, and as holding the hands of companions,
I fled forth to the hiding receiving night that talks not,
Down to the shores of the water, the path by the swamp in the dimness,
To the solemn shadowy cedars and ghostly pines so still.

And the singer so shy to the rest receiv'd me,
The gray-brown bird I know receiv'd us comrades three,
And he sang the carol of death, and a verse for him I love.

From deep secluded recesses,
From the fragrant cedars and the ghostly pines so still,
Came the carol of the bird.

And the charm of the carol rapt me,
As I held as if by their hands my comrades in the night,
And the voice of my spirit tallied the song of the bird.

Come lovely and soothing death,
Undulate round the world, serenely arriving, arriving,
In the day, in the night, to all, to each,
Sooner or later delicate death.

Prais'd be the fathomless universe,
For life and joy, and for objects and knowledge curious,
And for love, sweet love—but praise! praise! praise!
For the sure-enwinding arms of cool-enfolding death.

Dark mother always gliding near with soft feet,
Have none chanted for thee a chant of fullest welcome?
Then I chant it for thee, I glorify thee above all,
I bring thee a song that when thou must indeed come, come unfalteringly.

Approach strong deliveress,
When it is so, when thou hast taken them I joyously sing the dead,

Lost in the loving floating ocean of thee,
Laved in the flood of thy bliss O death.

From me to thee glad serenades,
Dances for thee I propose saluting thee, adornments and feastings for thee,
And the sights of the open landscape and the high-spread sky are fitting,
And life and the fields, and the huge and thoughtful night.

The night in silence under many a star,
The ocean shore and the husky whispering wave whose voice I know,
And the soul turning to thee O vast and well-veil'd death,
And the body gratefully nestling close to thee.

Over the tree-tops I float thee a song,
Over the rising and sinking waves, over the myriad fields and the prairies wide,
Over the dense-pack'd cities all and the teeming wharves and ways,
I float this carol with joy, with joy to thee O death.

15

To the tally of my soul,
Loud and strong kept up the gray-brown bird,
With pure deliberate notes spreading filling the night.

Loud in the pines and cedars dim,
Clear in the freshness moist and the swamp-perfume,
And I with my comrades there in the night.

While my sight that was bound in my eyes unclosed,
As to long panoramas of visions.

And I saw askant the armies,
I saw as in noiseless dreams hundreds of battle-flags,
Borne through the smoke of the battles and pierc'd with missiles I saw them,
And carried hither and yon through the smoke, and torn and bloody,
And at last but a few shreds left on the staffs, (and all in silence,)
And the staffs all splinter'd and broken.

I saw battle-corpses, myriads of them,
And the white skeletons of young men, I saw them,
I saw the debris and debris of all the slain soldiers of the war,
But I saw they were not as was thought,
They themselves were fully at rest, they suffer'd not,
The living remain'd and suffer'd, the mother suffer'd,

And the wife and the child and the musing comrade suffer'd,
And the armies that remain'd suffer'd.

16

Passing the visions, passing the night,
Passing, unloosing the hold of my comrades' hands,
Passing the song of the hermit bird and the tallying song of my soul,
Victorious song, death's outlet song, yet varying ever-altering song,
As low and wailing, yet clear the notes, rising and falling, flooding the night,
Sadly sinking and fainting, as warning and warning, and yet again bursting with joy,
Covering the earth and filling the spread of the heaven,
As that powerful psalm in the night I heard from recesses,
Passing, I leave thee lilac with heart-shaped leaves,
I leave thee there in the dooryard, blooming, returning with spring.

I cease from my song for thee,
From my gaze on thee in the west, fronting the west, communing with thee,
O comrade lustrous with silver face in the night.

Yet each to keep and all, retrievements out of the night,
The song, the wondrous chant of the gray-brown bird,
And the tallying chant, the echo arous'd in my soul,
With the lustrous and drooping star with the countenance full of woe,
With the holders holding my hand nearing the call of the bird,
Comrades mine and I in the midst, and their memory ever to keep, for the dead I loved so well,
For the sweetest, wisest soul of all my days and lands—and this for his dear sake,
Lilac and star and bird twined with the chant of my soul,
There in the fragrant pines and the cedars dusk and dim.

I Saw in Louisiana a Live-Oak Growing

I saw in Louisiana a live-oak growing,
All alone stood it and the moss hung down from the branches,
Without any companion it grew there uttering joyous leaves of dark green,
And its look, rude, unbending, lusty, made me think of myself,
But I wonder'd how it could utter joyous leaves standing alone there without its friend near, for I knew I could not,
And I broke off a twig with a certain number of leaves upon it, and twined around it a little moss,

And brought it away, and I have placed it in sight in my room,
It is not needed to remind me as of my own dear friends,
(For I believe lately I think of little else than of them,)
Yet it remains to me a curious token, it makes me think of manly love;
For all that, and though the live-oak glistens there in Louisiana solitary in a wide flat space,
Uttering joyous leaves all its life without a friend or lover near,
I know very well I could not.

When I Heard the Learn'd Astronomer

When I heard the learn'd astronomer,
When the proofs, the figures, were ranged in columns before me,
When I was shown the charts and diagrams, to add, divide, and measure them,
When I sitting heard the astronomer where he lectured with much applause in the lecture-room,
How soon unaccountable I became tired and sick,
Till rising and gliding out I wander'd off by myself,
In the mystical moist night-air, and from time to time,
Look'd up in perfect silence at the stars.

Chanting the Square Deific

1

Chanting the square deific, out of the One advancing, out of the sides,
Out of the old and new, out of the square entirely divine,
Solid, four-sided, (all the sides needed,) from this side Jehovah am I,
Old Brahm I, and I Saturnius am;
Not Time affects me—I am Time, old, modern as any,
Unpersuadable, relentless, executing righteous judgments,
As the Earth, the Father, the brown old Kronos, with laws,
Aged beyond computation, yet ever new, ever with those mighty laws rolling,
Relentless I forgive no man—whoever sins dies—I will have that man's life;
Therefore let none expect mercy—have the seasons, gravitation, the appointed days, mercy? no more have I,
But as the seasons and gravitation, and as all the appointed days that forgive not,
I dispense from this side judgments inexorable without the least remorse.

2

Consolator most mild, the promis'd one advancing,
With gentle hand extended, the mightier God am I,
Foretold by prophets and poets in their most rapt prophecies and poems,
From this side, lo! the Lord Christ gazes—lo! Hermes I—lo! mine is Hercules' face,
All sorrow, labor, suffering, I, tallying it, absorb in myself,
Many times have I been rejected, taunted, put in prison, and crucified, and many times shall be again,
All the world have I given up for my dear brothers' and sisters' sake, for the soul's sake,
Wending my way through the homes of men, rich or poor, with the kiss of affection,
For I am affection, I am the cheer-bringing God, with hope and all-enclosing charity,
With indulgent words as to children, with fresh and sane words, mine only,
Young and strong I pass knowing well I am destin'd myself to an early death;
But my charity has no death—my wisdom dies not, neither early nor late,
And my sweet love bequeath'd here and elsewhere never dies.

3

Aloof, dissatisfied, plotting revolt,
Comrade of criminals, brother of slaves,
Crafty, despised, a drudge, ignorant,
With sudra face and worn brow, black, but in the depths of my heart, proud as any,
Lifted now and always against whoever scorning assumes to rule me,
Morose, full of guile, full of reminiscences, brooding, with many wiles,
(Though it was thought I was baffled and dispel'd, and my wiles done, but that will never be,)
Defiant, I, Satan, still live, still utter words, in new lands duly appearing, (and old ones also,)
Permanent here from my side, warlike, equal with any, real as any,
Nor time nor change shall ever change me or my words.

4

Santa Spirita, breather, life,
Beyond the light, lighter than light,
Beyond the flames of hell, joyous, leaping easily above hell,
Beyond Paradise, perfumed solely with mine own perfume,

Including all life on earth, touching, including God, including Saviour and Satan,
Ethereal, pervading all, (for without me what were all? what were God?)
Essence of forms, life of the real identities, permanent, positive, (namely the unseen,)
Life of the great round world, the sun and stars, and of man, I, the general soul,
Here the square finishing, the solid, I the most solid,
Breathe my breath also through these songs.

So Long

To conclude, I announce what comes after me.

I remember I said before my leaves sprang at all,
I would raise my voice jocund and strong with reference to consummations.

When America does what was promis'd,
When through these States walk a hundred millions of superb persons,
When the rest part away for superb persons and contribute to them,
When breeds of the most perfect mothers denote America,
Then to me and mine our due fruition.

I have press'd through in my own right,
I have sung the body and the soul, war and peace have I sung, and the songs of life and death,
And the songs of birth, and shown that there are many births.

I have offer'd my style to every one, I have journey'd with confident step;
While my pleasure is yet at the full I whisper *So long!*
And take the young woman's hand and the young man's hand for the last time.

I announce natural persons to arise,
I announce justice triumphant,
I announce uncompromising liberty and equality,
I announce the justification of candor and the justification of pride.

I announce that the identity of these States is a single identity only,
I announce the Union more and more compact, indissoluble,
I announce splendors and majesties to make all the previous politics of the earth insignificant.

I announce adhesiveness, I say it shall be limitless, unloosen'd,
I say you shall yet find the friend you were looking for.

So Long

I announce a man or woman coming, perhaps you are the one, (*So long!*)
I announce the great individual, fluid as Nature, chaste, affectionate, compassionate, fully arm'd.
I announce a life that shall be copious, vehement, spiritual, bold,
I announce an end that shall lightly and joyfully meet its translation.
I announce myriads of youths, beautiful, gigantic, sweet-blooded,
I announce a race of splendid and savage old men.

O thicker and faster—(*So long!*)
O crowding too close upon me,
I foresee too much, it means more than I thought,
It appears to me I am dying.

Hasten throat and sound your last,
Salute me—salute the days once more. Peal the old cry once more.

Screaming electric, the atmosphere using,
At random glancing, each as I notice absorbing,
Swiftly on, but a little while alighting,
Curious envelop'd messages delivering,
Sparkles hot, seed ethereal down in the dirt dropping,
Myself unknowing, my commission obeying, to question it never daring,
To ages and ages yet the growth of the seed leaving,
To troops out of the war arising, they the tasks I have set promulging,
To women certain whispers of myself bequeathing, their affection me more clearly explaining,
To young men my problems offering—no dallier I—I the muscle of their brains trying,
So I pass, a little time vocal, visible, contrary,
Afterward a melodious echo, passionately bent for, (death making me really undying,)
The best of me then when no longer visible, for toward that I have been incessantly preparing.

What is there more, that I lag and pause and crouch extended with unshut mouth?
Is there a single final farewell?

My songs cease, I abandon them,
From behind the screen where I hid I advance personally solely to you.

Camerado, this is no book,
Who touches this touches a man,
(Is it night? are we here together alone?)
It is I you hold and who holds you,
I spring from the pages into your arms—decease calls me forth.

O how your fingers drowse me,
Your breath falls around me like dew, your pulse lulls the tympans of my
  ears,
I feel immerged from head to foot,
Delicious, enough.
Enough O deed impromptu and secret,
Enough O gliding present—enough O summ'd-up past.

Dear friend whoever you are take this kiss,
I give it especially to you, do not forget me,
I feel like one who has done work for the day to retire awhile,
I receive now again of my many translations, from my avataras ascend-
  ing, while others doubtless await me,
An unknown sphere more real than I dream'd, more direct, darts awaken-
  ing rays about me, *So long!*
Remember my words, I may again return,
I love you, I depart from materials,
I am as one disembodied, triumphant, dead.

AFTERWORD

Knowing and Knowing About

In 1859 Emerson recorded in his journal his awareness of one of the most problematic aspects of his career:

> I have been writing and speaking what were once called novelties, for twenty-five or thirty years, and have not now one disciple. Why? Not that what I said was not true; not that it has not found intelligent receivers; but because it did not go from any wish in me to bring men to me, but to themselves. . . . I should account it a measure of the impurity of insight, if it did not create independence.[1]

As noted in the introduction to this anthology, this tendency to "bring men . . . to themselves" not only was shared by Thoreau and Whitman but was their central purpose.

For the general reader, the modern editor can do little more than to identify this purpose and remind the reader that the rest is up to him—the awareness, development, and reverence of whatever is closest to the center of his own nature. But for anyone using this book in an academic setting (students and teachers alike), the situation is not so simple. To put the problem bluntly, the question is whether one can really study, write papers on, and take tests concerning somebody who says, "I hate quotations. Tell me what you know" (Emerson). What shall we do with this material in the classroom?

Well, one answer is steadfastly to overlook the point being made by these writers: converting their utterances into a dubious system of philosophy, the reader can discuss what they say about "man" and "one's self" and "the person" and never permit what is being said to penetrate those levels of awareness where his own life is being lived. And, given the bias of the Western intellectual style—for knowing *about* things and away from any approach that would blur the subject-object dichotomy—it is difficult to do anything else in an educational context. When the model on which an undertaking is based is that of information collection, storage, and retrieval, everything will be converted into information to be manipulated in that way.

[1] *Journal*, IX, 188–199.

This is not to say that there is nothing worth saying *about* these writers—no researches that a student could profitably undertake or papers he could profitably write. Quite the contrary, for anything that helps him to understand just what these writers are saying to him is valuable indeed. In the introduction I noted that for me the work of modern psychologists has been useful in suggesting in more modern terms what these writers are saying. Another modern parallel that many students find helpful is the work of the more spiritually oriented existentialists, and a third is to be found in modern studies of Eastern thought. Here are eleven titles that offer leads along one or another of these modern parallels:

> Martin Buber, *The Knowledge of Man* (New York: Harper, 1965)
> Victor Frankl, *Man's Search for Meaning* (New York: Washington Square Press, 1963)
> Erich Fromm, *The Sane Society* (New York: Fawcett, 1955)
> Aldous Huxley, *The Perennial Philosophy* (New York: Meridian/World Publishing Co., 1944)
> Gabriel Marcel, *Being and Having* (New York: Harper, 1965)
> Abraham Maslow, *Towards a Psychology of Being* (Princeton: Van Nostrand-Reinhold, 1962)
> Rollo May, ed., *Existential Psychology* (New York: Random House, 1961)
> Frederick Perls, *Gestalt Therapy Verbatim* (Walnut Creek, Calif.: Real People Press, 1969)
> Carl Rogers, *On Becoming a Person* (Boston: Houghton Mifflin, 1961)
> Paul Tillich, *The Courage to Be* (New Haven: Yale University Press, 1961)
> Alan Watts, *Psychotherapy East and West* (New York: Ballantine Books, 1961)

Any one of these books can open up a line of inquiry into the work of these nineteenth-century American writers, and in so doing illuminate the reader's own experience.

The advantage of beginning with such books or others in the fields of humanistic psychology, existentialism, or Eastern thought is that the investigator can chart out the parallels for himself and make his own discoveries concerning what Emerson, Thoreau, and Whitman have to say. But it would be unrealistic to forget that an immense amount has already been written about the three writers, including some along the lines that are herein being suggested. Anyone who wants to find such material had better begin with one of the several comprehensive bibliographies of writing by and about these men. One of the best is a paperback called *Eight American Authors*, edited by Floyd Stovall (New York: Norton, 1963), which has a fifty-page section on each man in which what has been written on him is not only listed but described and sometimes evaluated. Another extensive bibliography will be found in the *Literary History of the United States*, edited by Robert E. Spiller and others (New York: Macmillan, 1948 and 1959). Neither book covers very recent scholarship, so that must be pursued separately. Annual bibliographies appear in *American Literature* and *PMLA*, two scholarly journals that can be found in all college libraries.

The student who wants to go into the lives of the three writers will find innumerable titles offered in the bibliographies cited above, but if he simply wants to find out some particular thing about the man, he may want simply to go to a basic and sound biography. In the case of Emerson, this would take him to Ralph Rusk's *Life* (New York: Columbia University Press, 1949); for Thoreau he could use Joseph Wood Krutch's biography (New York: Sloane, 1948) or Walter Harding's *The Days of Henry Thoreau* (New York: Knopf, 1965); for Whitman, the standard biography is Gay Wilson Allen's *The Solitary Singer* (New York University Press, 1955).

As pathways toward a more substantial understanding of what Emerson, Thoreau, and Whitman had to say, such books as these are very useful. But Emerson's dictum remains to plague the investigator with the sense that it is into his own life rather than theirs that he is meant to be carried. Thoreau counseled him to "Direct your eye right inward" and to become "Expert in home-cosmography," and no amount of studying Thoreau's mind will suffice to reach that goal.

There is no best way to reach that goal, although there are a number of possibilities that would be more or less appropriate, depending on the context. All of the writers agreed that there was nowhere to begin but with the person's own experience—not just with the outward events of his days and hours but with the inward responses to those events. It is no accident that Emerson and Thoreau kept diaries and that Whitman filled notebooks and stray scraps of paper with jottings of ideas and impressions and feelings. Whatever use they were finally put to, these were the raw materials of these writers' art. One thing to consider, then, is the possibility of keeping a record that is not intended to be like theirs, except insofar as anything uniquely one's own is like theirs in being a product of a deeply personal experience.

For many people a journal is its own end, particularly as it begins to illuminate the life that is being recorded. But for others there will be a dissatisfaction with the fragmentariness of the journal and a desire to work it up into something with more form to it. Each of the three writers suggests a different way of accomplishing this: Emerson's essays, Thoreau's narrative, and Whitman's poems all suggest formats for self-discovery through writing. At first it may be useful to keep the model in mind (and to experiment with all three), but the goal is to move beyond models into whatever manner of vital utterance seems right for the speaker and the occasion. It may be useful to recall from time to time what Emerson says about the poet, as the one who can tell us how it was with him and say it so directly that nature can accept the utterance as part of her order.

This sort of writing may sound more appropriate for a creative writing course than for a freshman course in literature or an upper-class survey of American literature—and it may sound quite irrelevant to any reading done outside a formal classroom situation. But let us not be trapped by our traditional preconceptions on these matters. To Emerson, for instance, the problem of self-expression was not literary but developmental or therapeutic. In "The Poet" he writes that the two great human needs are for truth and expression, that men express themselves unwittingly in all that they do, and that "the man is only half himself, the other half is his expression." Writing, thus, is not something that is academic in intent but rather deeply personal—the person's disclosure of himself that is the first step in knowing himself.

Near the beginning of this afterword we noted the irony inherent in Emerson's being the object of study, when his basic demand was that we study ourselves ("I hate quotations. Tell me what you know"). But that is only half of the story, for Emerson, the master of paradoxes, also wrote "Next to the originator of a good sentence is the first quoter of it."[2] In the first quotation he is attacking those who have abandoned their own powers of thinking and knowing to others and now exercise these powers only at second hand. In the second quotation he is not contradicting himself. He is simply praising those whose awareness is developed to the point where they know when something is meaningful in terms of their own lives. Such persons, who can sense when something resonates within their consciousness, are discovering meaning for themselves quite as much as are those who first string together the words in a phrase.

It is in that spirit that Emerson, Thoreau, and Whitman are worth studying—as seekers after selfhood whose task parallels our own. The records they left illuminate the process, but only to those who have undertaken it on their own terms. Whitman said it best when he wrote of his intent in these words:

I will not be a great philosopher, and found any school, and build it with iron pillars, and gather the young men around me, and make them my disciples, that new superior churches and politics shall come. But I will take each man and woman of you to the window and open the shutters and the sash, and my left arm shall hook you round the waist, and my right shall point you to the endless and beginningless road along whose sides are crowded the rich cities of all living philosophy, and oval gates that pass you in to fields of clover and landscapes clumped with sassafras, and orchards of good apples, and every breath through your mouth shall be of a new perfumed and elastic air, which

[2] Emerson, "Quotation and Originality," *Works,* VIII, 191.

is love.—Not I—not God—can travel this road for you.—It is not far, it is within the stretch of your thumb; perhaps you shall find you are on it already and did not know.--Perhaps you shall find it every where over the ocean and over the land, when you once have the vision to behold it.[3]

Here Whitman uses one of his favorite metaphors, the age-old image of the road—the path or way from which things can be seen in their proper relation to the person. The discovering of this road is the image for awakening to a new dimension of experience as a result of repossessing the natural human capacity to experience life fully and directly and to find it, thereby, deeply meaningful.

Each reader must come to such writing as this in his own way, and that will be the way that grows out of his own experience. And these writers knew that, and that is why they are ultimately so elusive; for just as one expects to pin them down for *the answer,* they slip away and leave the reader alone to answer his own questions. But they do bring him to the source of all answers—himself.

[3] *The Uncollected Poetry and Prose of Walt Whitman,* ed. Emory Holloway (Garden City, New York, 1921), pp. 66–67.

OHIO UNIVERSITY LIBRARY

Please return this book as soon as you have finished with it. In order to avoid a fine it must be returned by the latest date stamped below. All books are subject to recall after two weeks or immediately if needed for reserve.

JUN 1 6 2005

MAR 0 7 2005

CF